LaVell's Leadership Playbook:

The strategy that changed NCAA Football

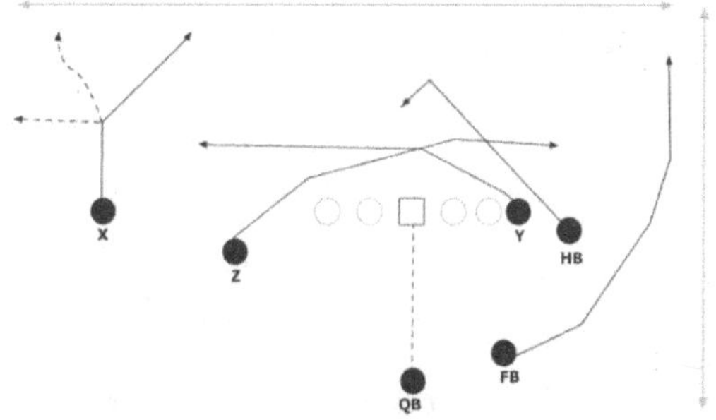

David P. Hanna

Cover photo: Salt Lake Tribune

ISBN: 979-8-9997390-1-8

ACKNOWLEDGMENTS

Writing a book about a great coach and his great teams requires a lot of teamwork itself. I am most grateful for the contributions and cooperation from many wonderful people and organizations.

Thank you to BYU Sports Information and the BYU Photo Studio for permitting the use of player photos and football action photos to bring to life much of LaVell's "magic."

Thank you to Hema Heimuli, a fellow graduate of the BYU Organizational Behavior Masters Program and a BYU football alum who has provided helpful comments that led to the inclusion of corporate examples that aligned LaVell's leadership.

Thank you to Rae Allen Everett for designing the cover pages. Thank you to Ritchey Marbury for the technical layout improvements. Thank you to Charlee Hanna for being a much-needed sounding board for the entire process.

Thank you to Gary Sheide, Brad Oates, Lance Reynolds, Vai Sikahema, and Malik Hamilton for your "insider" perspectives on LaVell and his effect on BYU football development.

Thank you to Lee Benson, Dick Harmon, Dave McCann and Doug Robinson, four veteran Deseret News writers I have long admired and who shared their own writings and recommended the self-publishing route to me… and they were right.

Contents

Introduction

How many of you would want to sign up for this college football coaching job?

Wanted: Football Coach to Produce a Nationally Ranked Program

- Your school does not have much of a football tradition. The combined winning percentage for the last 47 years is only .424.
- You must compete in the Mountain West – where publicity is limited, and competition is viewed to be weaker than most other areas. The pollsters do not take you very seriously.
- Your school has very strict standards for dress and moral conduct that are out of step with trends at other universities.
- You will have few, if any, real blue-chip players. Most prefer to go where the "fringe benefits" are better.
- Generally speaking, your players will be no better than average in terms of size, speed and strength when compared to other teams.
- Nearly half of your players will interrupt their playing career for two years to do missionary work all over the world. Some may never return to play football.
- Your predecessor tried to build "the Notre Dame of the West." His record in eight years was 39-42-1 for a winning percentage of .482.

Now go out and win a national championship!

This book is a narrative history about coach LaVell Edwards, the man who signed up for this job. It describes some of the fundamental principles he practiced on his path to success. It documents the impact he made the on the entire NCAA football industry. It illustrates how his example guided many of his players to make tremendous contributions to this world – far beyond the football field.

Look for meaningful ways you might apply LaVell's fundamentals to benefit yourself – and those around you!

Best wishes for your success!

David Hamm

May 2026
Mapleton, Utah

PLAYBOOK FUNDAMENTAL ONE:

Compete using your unique strengths.

Prologue: LaVell and BYU Football before 1972

"To tell a true story truly,

one must always begin in the middle."

– Sir Michael York

LaVell Edwards' tenure as head football coach at BYU was the middle of a bigger story. Let's appreciate the coach's playbook by first examining where BYU football stood in college football **BLE** (**B**efore **L**aVell **E**dwards became head coach).

Brigham Young University's beginning was a veritable whisper in the annals of college football – something not surprising for a small private, church-sponsored institution competing against larger, more sophisticated state-sponsored universities. BYU's early years were anything but sensational.

Alvin Twitchell was the head coach of the

inaugural program in 1922 with a 1-5 record. In the 38 years that followed, BYU only had 12 winning seasons. G. Ott Romney, in nine of those seasons from 1928-1936, had the best coaching record of 42 wins, 31 losses and five ties.

BYU was a perennial cellar dweller in its conferences with only a few exceptions. Then came the formation of the Western Athletic Conference (WAC) 1n 1962 with the BYU Cougars as charter members along with Arizona, Arizona State, New Mexico, Utah, and Wyoming.

In those days I rooted for my hometown New Mexico Lobos. They won or tied for the football title in the WAC's first three years (1962, '63 and '64). BYU, on the other hand, finished next to last in 1962 and winless (dead last) in '63 and ' However, one bright spot for BYU in 1962 was Eldon ("The Phantom") Fortie. In those days BYU ran the single wing formation with the tailback in shotgun formation taking the direct snap from the center and then running or passing the ball. Fortie, like most tailbacks of the day, ran more

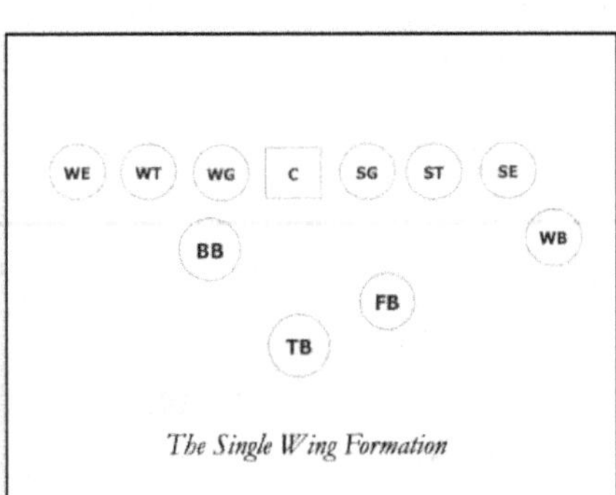

The Single Wing Formation

than he passed. The formation gave him many blockers to provide an open field for run-pass-options64.

"Eldon was tailor-made made for the single wing," recalled former coach Glen Tuckett. "He was not a power runner, he was a dipsy-do runner who was very good in the open field and could feint inside-outside."

"The Phantom" in action. (BYU photo)

Defenders would try to converge on the 5'11" 169 lb. Fortie, but his multiple moves would leave them grasping only air. Hence, his nickname "The Phantom."

My brother Terry attended BYU in those days and told me when the Cougars broke their offensive huddle, Fortie often would survey the defensive alignment, then motion some of his teammates to change their position in the formation to set up their play.

Author's Note: *Fortie and BYU provided both the valley and the peak for this Lobo fan in 1962.*

The Valley: *New Mexico, playing in BYU's homecoming game in Provo, fell victim to the Cougars and Fortie, 27-0. Eldon carried the ball 31 times for 162 yards and one touchdown and passed for 70 yards and two touchdowns. Listening to the game on the radio, I couldn't imagine how such a "little guy" could wreak so much havoc on my Lobos!*

The Peak: *two weeks after beating New Mexico, Fortie and the Cougars knocked off mighty league-leading Wyoming in Laramie. I was attending the UNM game in Albuquerque when the PA announced the final score:* ***BYU 14, Wyoming 7.*** *You've never heard so many people in Albuquerque cheer a BYU victory! Wyoming's loss meant New Mexico was the WAC champion! After the game UNM coach Bill Weeks sent a telegram to BYU coach Hal Mitchell. The message was simple, but heartfelt: "All is forgiven."*

Eldon Fortie (BYU photo)

In 1962 Eldon Fortie was BYU's first player to be named to an All-America team. He finished second in the nation in total offense and rushing that year. He might have been the leader in both categories if he had not suffered a separated clavicle. He played only a few downs in that upset of Wyoming in the season finale, just enough to score the first BYU touchdown and position his team for the win. In his three-year career in Provo, Fortie ran for 1,532 yards and 17 touchdowns. As a signal-caller, he also threw for 1,367 yards, 12 touchdowns, and 24 interceptions.

Tommy Hudspeth
BYU photo

Tommy Hudspeth and the first WAC title

Tommy Hudspeth was hired as BYU's head coach starting in 1964 and he was given a rude awakening to WAC football, losing all four conference games and posting a 3-6-1 overall record.

In the following months, Coach Hudspeth spread his recruiting net wider than ever before and landed seven Marine veterans, including wide receiver Phil Odle. They joined the team that returned quarterback Virgil Carter and the running back brothers John and Steve Ogden

Nevertheless, BYU was picked to finish in the conference cellar again in 1965.

1965: A Season of Breakthroughs

BYU's football fortunes had four huge

breakthroughs in 1965:

1) The Cougars defeated powerhouse Arizona State (in Tempe no less) in the season opener.
2) They notched their third victory in the overall series of 41 games with archrival Utah.
3) They defeated Utah for the first time in Provo!
4) They won their first WAC championship by trouncing New Mexico in the season finale.

Breakthrough #1: Beating Arizona State in the season opener in Tempe

Arizona State, because of schedule commitments previously made with other schools, did not play enough conference games in the early years to be eligible for the conference football championship. It was, however, at or near the top of the league in overall wins each year. This was the Sun Devil team that hosted BYU in the 1965 season opener.

The Date: September 18, 1965 – evening game
The Place: Sun Devil Stadium @ Tempe
Weather: Hot and dry; temperature in the 90s
Attendance: 35,354

No one expected the Cougars to go down to Tempe and win. HOWEVER – paced by junior quarterback Virgil Carter and a smothering defensive unit, the Cougars pounded the Sun Devils into submission, 24-6, and ended their home-game winning streak at 12 games.

In the first quarter BYU moved through ASU's defense on an 85-yard scoring drive. Carter provided the major plays on the drive – 18 and 16-yard passes to end Phil Odle. Phil's second reception was followed by a pass interference charged to ASU cornerback Travis Williams that moved the Cougars to the ASU one-yard line. On the next play Carter dove into the end zone with 3:03 left in the first period. **BYU 7, ASU 0**

Both teams struggled a bit in the second quarter. Finally, the Cougars scored as Dave Duran, kicked a field goal with eight seconds showing in the second period. His kick gave the Cougars a **10-0 halftime lead**. Duran was given his 28-yard field goal opportunity on a great catch by Odle, who gained a step on ASU's Chuck Kolb to gather in Carter's 45-yard bomb.

The second half was more of the same as BYU scored twice in the third quarter in a six-minute span. John Ogden scored on a two-yard run and Phil Odle caught a five-yard touchdown pass from Carter.

The Sun Devils, meanwhile, saw their two most productive drives – those of 65 and 47 yards – end in frustration when middle guard Grant Wilson kept barging into ASU's backfield. First, Wilson threw the ASU quarterback John Goodman for a six-yard loss to the Cougar 23 and the hosts never recovered. ASU's Rick Davis's 27-yard field goal was deflected and fell short.

When ASU threatened later, moving on Goodman's arm to the 17, Wilson came to the rescue again. He trapped Goodman for an eight-yard loss on second down, then collaborated with two other Cougars to turn a fourth-down pass attempt into an 11-yard loss. (**Note:** who coached the defensive line that rose to the occasion? None other than LaVell Edwards.)

The Sun Devils averted their first shutout since 1956 in the fourth period when quarterback Goodman fired a 48-yard scoring pass to flanker Ben Hawkins. Carter finished, completing 10 of 18 passes for 134 yards with one touchdown and one interception, and rushing 10 times for 83 and one touchdown. Odle had five receptions for 92 yards and one touchdown.

It was ASU's first defeat in Tempe since the 1963 opener when Wichita scored a 33-13 decision.

	1st	2nd	3rd	4th	Final
BYU	7	3	14	0	24
ASU	0	0	0	6	6

Team Statistics	BYU	ASU
First Downs	14	22
Total Offense Yards	234	304
Rushing Yards	96	266
Passing Yards	146	134
Passes (Att-Comp-Int)	18-10-1	11-4-1
TDs Passing	1	0
Fumbles Lost	0	7
Penalties/Yards	9-93	8-79

Any fans from either ASU or BYU, who did not attend the game, had to double check the final score when they heard it. It was truly unbelievable!

From there the Cougars won contests with Kansas State and San Jose State and lost games at Oregon, Wyoming, and Utah State. Next on the schedule was a homecoming game with archrival Utah.

Breakthroughs #2 and #3: Beating the perennial Utah hex – finally!!

The Date: November 6, 1965
The Place: Cougar Stadium
Weather: High cloudiness; temperatures in the 30s
Attendance: 29,842

Coming into the game, Utah led the series with 34 wins, 2 losses and 4 ties, including 17 wins in the last 18 games. It was by far BYU's biggest series deficit with any opponent.

A near-capacity crowd of 29,842 had high expectations for this game given the Cougars' success in previous weeks. And it was a homecoming game. Could this be the year Provo fans actually witnessed the first win in Provo over the dominant Utes?

First Half

The Cougars took the opening kickoff and moved swiftly down the field for 71 yards in only four minutes for their first touchdown. Carter's passing and running sparked the drive along with John Ogden's plunges. With the ball on the Utah 31, Carter found Tim Russell open in the end zone and fired a strike to him. Dave Duran's boot for the extra point was no good. **BYU 6, Utah 0.**

The Cougars' lead didn't hold up long, as Utah marched 63 yards for a touchdown in seven plays with 5:47 to play in the quarter. The big play was a pitch out to Marv Lowery, who ran 54 yards to the BYU four. Two plays later Ben Woodson dove in from the Cougar one for the TD. Lane Walsh kicked the extra point for the lead. **Utah 7, BYU 6.**

Utah's second touchdown came after Gonzelo Cureton intercepted a Carter pass on the Utah 43 and returned to the BYU 33. Woodson went around right end for 14 and, after Lowery was thrown for a five-yard loss, quarterback Rich Groth threw a perfect 24-yard pass to Mike Butera in the end zone for a touchdown. Walsh once again booted the conversion and, with 2:06 to play in the first quarter, it was: **Utah 14, BYU 6.**

The Cougars then went on a rampage, scoring three touchdowns before halftime.

First, the Cougars took the next kickoff and moved 80 yards in 13 plays for a touchdown. Carter's passing again sparked the drive. The touchdown came on a four-yard toss from Carter to Russell. Carter tried to pass to Odle for the two-point conversion, but Utah's Al White deflected the pass to spoil the attempt. **Utah 14, BYU 12.**

Less than six minutes later BYU took the lead as the Cougars drove 65 yards in six plays. The drive started when BYU's John Greene recovered Lowery's fumble on the BYU 35. Four plays later a 14-yard Carter-to-Odle pass put the ball on the Utah 36 and then Carter hit Dennis Palmer with an over-the-middle pass on the 15 and the Cougar wingman raced the rest of the way for the touchdown.

Carter tried a two-point conversion pass to Odle, but again it was no good. With 5:15 to play in the half, it was **BYU 18, Utah 14.**

But the Cougars weren't finished yet.

With 1:06 to play in the half, Bob Ashdown, intercepted a Groth pass and ran the ball back 34 yards to the Utah 43 to set up the drive. Carter's 11-yard pass to Russell and a 22-yarder to Odle for the touchdown were the big blows for the Cougars. Duran booted the extra point.

Halftime Score: BYU 25, Utah 14

Second Half

But the game was not over. Utah made its final touchdown in the first four minutes following the second half kickoff.

The running of Woodson and Lowery, along with a 15-yard Groth-to-Frank Mazzotta pass moved the Utes to their TD. They went 67 yards in eight plays for the score, with Woodson going the final 25 yards around left end to paydirt. **BYU 25, Utah 20**

The Cougars took the ensuing kickoff and moved from their own 23 to the Utah 21 with the passing of Carter and running of John Ogden leading the attack. But after the Cats reached the Utes' 21, Pat McKissick intercepted Carter's pass on the Utah one to stop the drive.

After a Utah punt midway through the third quarter, BYU started moving again and reached the Utah 16, when the drive faltered, and Duran tried a field goal from the 23. But the kick failed.

Utah came right back and surged from its own 30 to the BYU 19 with Woodson carrying the brunt of the attack. But then Steve Peterson and Moses Kim led a BYU defensive charge that stopped Woodson cold on a fourth-and-one situation early in the fourth period.

Later in the fourth, BYU's Ben Laverty punted, and the ball bounced just inside the sideline and then rolled all the way down to the Utah one where Kent Oborn downed it.

That put Utah in a hole, but the Utes dug out quickly as a 34-yard pass from Groth to Gary Heard put the ball on the Utah 47. But then the BYU defensive unit held, and the Cats took over on the BYU 49.

However, three plays later, Carter nearly gave the Cougar fans heart failure when he fumbled, and Utah's Bill Morley recovered on the BYU 47.

Groth found Butera behind the BYU defenders on the first play after the fumble recovery but overshot his target. Groth still refused to give up as he ran for 12 yards on the next play.

Ashdown then came up with his second big interception with less than a minute to go and the Cougars held onto the ball during the final seconds.

Final score: BYU 25, Utah 20

	1st	2nd	3rd	4th	Final
UTAH	**14**	**0**	**6**	**0**	**20**
BYU	**6**	**19**	**0**	**0**	**25**

Team Statistics	**BYU**	**UTAH**
First Downs	**24**	**20**
Total Offense Yards	**436**	**453**
Rushing Yards	**183**	**292**
Passing Yards	**253**	**161**
Passes (Att-Comp-Int)	**29-16-3**	**18-9-3**
TDs Passing	**4**	**1**
Fumbles Lost	**1**	**1**
Penalties/Yards	**8-85**	**8-74**

Virgil Carter: the first prototype of "Quarterback U."

The second and third hexes had been broken as the Cougars won their third game ever against the Utes and earned their first series win in Provo!

Cougar Offense Leaders

- **Virgil Carter** was 16 of 29 passes for 253 yards with three interceptions and four TDs. He also ran 19 times for 111 yards (only 83 yards after sacks).
- **Phil Odle** had four catches for 79 yards and one TD.
- **John Ogden** carried 22 times for 67 yards.
- **Steve Ogden** had three catches for 31 yards and also carried eight times for 33 yards.
- **Tim Russell** had four catches for 60 yards and two TDs.

Cougar Defense Leaders

- **Sid Frazier** had 14 tackles (three solo).
- **Bob Ashdown** had 12 tackles (seven solo) and two pass interceptions.
- **Curg Belcher** had 10 tackles (seven solo) and one pass break up.
- **Moses Kim** had eight tackles (three solo) and two pass break ups.
- **Kent Oborn** had one pass interception and returned it 20 yards.

Breakthrough #4: Winning the WAC championship

The Date: November 27, 1965
The Place: University Stadium @ Albuquerque
Weather: Temperature in the 40s; dry with a light wind
Attendance: 14,289

These two teams were moving in very different directions:

> (1) New Mexico, after three consecutive WAC titles, would finish the season 3-7 overall and in fourth place in the WAC.

(2) BYU, after going winless in the previous two WAC seasons, would win the first conference championship in its history. Once again those who would only read the results of this last game, had to rub their eyes and then reread it before they could believe what they saw.

(3)

Author's Note: *There were 14,289 fans in attendance in Albuquerque, and I was one of them. Until that day I had still rooted for my hometown Lobos even though I had my eye on going to BYU eventually. My brother got me a ticket in the middle of the BYU fans. I nervously scanned the home crowd to make sure none of my friends saw me as I was about to enter the BYU section. Attending that game that day was a personal breakthrough for me. Witnessing a real passing attack in person for the first time was an exhilarating experience! The excitement the Cougars generated persuaded this Lobo fan to become a die-hard BYU fan.*

First Half

BYU ran onto the field to the music of the Marine Hymn:

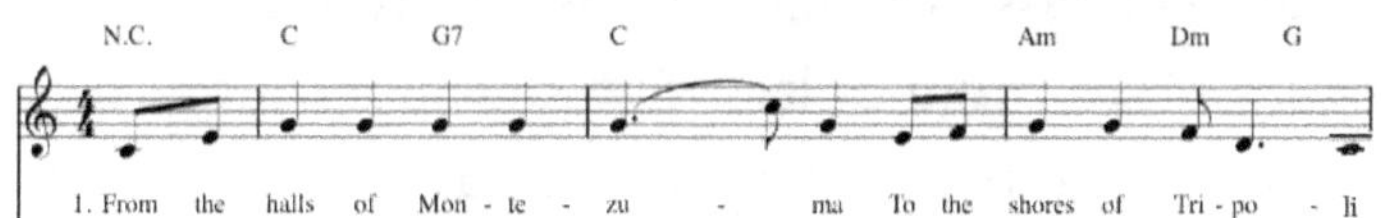

The Marine Hymn was played in recognition of seven former Marines who were in their first year at BYU. Every time one of the Marines made a good play, the Cougar band would strike up the Marine Hymn. It was repeated many times during the game, mostly due to wide receiver Phil Odle, who caught 10 passes for 137 yards and two touchdowns.

The first quarter ended in a scoreless tie. BYU began throwing the ball right away. Quarterback Virgil Carter, sixth in the nation in total offense before the game, passed for 139 first period yards. But the Cougars failed to score as a penalty, and a Lobo pass interception stopped them twice.

Thereafter the Cougars were unstoppable, eventually amassing 534 yards total offense in the game. They scored two touchdowns in each of the second, third, and fourth quarters. New Mexico scored its only TD in the fourth quarter.

The Cougars moved 68-yards in only eight plays for the first Cougar score early in the second period. The touchdown drive started when the Lobos were forced to punt to the BYU 32. Carter mixed passing and running to move to the Lobo 26. A Carter pass to Dennis Palmer moved the ball to the 11 and fullback John Ogden carried it to the seven to set up another pass to Palmer for the touchdown.

A few minutes later Steve Ogden ended an 80-yard drive by slanting over right tackle from two yards out for the second Cougar score. The TD was set up by a Carter look-in pass to Steve Ogden late in the drive for 13 yards.

Halftime Score: BYU 14, UNM 0

The Cougars completely dominated the first half of play as Carter passed for 212 yards, completing 16 of 21 attempts. And they also moved the ball at will on the ground as the brother combination of Steve and John Ogden carried for 69 first-half yards.

The Cougars picked up where they left off in the third period, scoring the first time they got the ball. Carter again unleashed his aerial attack by hitting Steve Ogden on a 22-yard scoring strike. Ogden caught the ball on the Lobo five and shrugged off three Lobo tacklers before crossing the goal line.

With the score **21-0** and Carter looking unstoppable, the Cougars turned to a running game to score again with four minutes left in the third quarter. Carter dropped back to pass at the Lobo 35, but handed off to John Ogden on a draw and Ogden went through the middle of the Lobo defense for the score. LaVern Swanson's fourth PAT made it, 28-0.

The only Lobo touchdown came early in the fourth quarter when fullback Carl Jackson ran it in from one yard out. Quarterback Stan Quintana ran for the two-point conversion. **BYU 28, UNM 8.**

But the Cougars weren't finished yet. They scored again with 8:49 remaining in the game when Carter hit Odle with a 14-yard scoring toss.

Then, a few minutes later Odle caught another TD toss. This time it was from reserve quarterback Stewart Simpson.

Final Score BYU 42, UNM 8

The victory, BYU's sixth against four losses, was especially sweet for the Cougars who were dropped 26-14 the previous year by the Lobos during a dismal 3-6-1 season. The Lobos tied for the 1964 WAC crown. This time around the Lobos finished the season with a 3-7 record, their worst since 1955.

	1st	2nd	3rd	4th	Final
BYU	0	14	14	14	42
UNM	0	0	0	8	8

Team Statistics	BYU	UNM
First Downs	31	11
Total Offense Yards	534	252
Rushing Yards	187	160
Passing Yards	347	92
Passes (Att-Comp-Int)	38-26-2	15-7-4
TDs Passing	4	0

Fumbles Lost	**0**	**1**
Penalties/Yards	**2-20**	**5-35**

After 43 tough, long years, BYU had its first conference football championship!

In the words of Dave Schulthess, BYU sports information director at the time and my boss during my BYU days, "*November 27, 1965, was a special date, which might be called a historical turning point. BYU came on to win the championship the hard way — by winning three of four conference games on the road.*"

Dave Schulthess
(BYU photo)

Cougar Offense Leaders

- **Virgil Carter** was 23 of 32 passes for 309 yards with two interceptions and three TDs. He also ran 11 times for 38 yards (net of only 14 yards after sacks).
- **Phil Odle** caught 10 passes for 137 yards and two TDs.
- **Steve Ogden** carried 14 times for 53 yards and one TD and also had six catches for 93 yards and one TD.
- **John Ogden** carried 12 times for 106 yards and one TD.

- **Dennis Palmer** had six catches for 68 yards and one TD.

Special Note: Phil Odle's two TD receptions in the game gave him a total of 11 for the year. This was a new WAC record for most *career* TD receptions.

Cougar Defense Leaders

- **Sid Frazier** had 14 tackles.
- **Grant Wilson** had nine tackles.
- **Ben Laverty** had six tackles (four solo).
- **Bob Ashdown** had six tackles (two solo) and one interception.
- **Terry Colson, Craig Belcher, and Bobby Roberts** each had one interception for a total of 59 return yards.

Author's personal postscript:

In 1996 in Provo, I met Phil Odle for the first time. He was a car salesman, and he sold me a car. Here is one short excerpt from our conversation:

Dave: "Phil, where were you on the Saturday after Thanksgiving in 1965?"

Phil: "I don't know."

Dave: "Well, I know because I was there with you in the stadium in Albuquerque when you guys won BYU's first WAC football title."

A big grin spread across his face. We then rehearsed our memories of that glorious day.

Later...we got around to finishing the car transaction.

A Tragic Framing to the Breakthroughs

Early in the morning of the New Mexico game day, a DC-3 passenger plane flew very low in conditions of snow and poor visibility and crashed into a hillside near what is now the rifle range at Camp Williams at the Point of the Mountain. All thirteen people aboard were killed, including these prominent BYU boosters bound for Albuquerque to cheer on their football team:

- Dr. J. Bernard Critchfield, 42, Taylorsville
- Dr. Antoine Dalton, 35, Holladay
- T.R. Gledhill, 43, Salt Lake City
- Dr. Gordon Lewis, 39, Salt Lake City
- Dr. Roger Parkinson, 37, Holladay
- Jim Peterson, 40, Holladay
- Dr. Marion Probert, 32, Murray
- Richard Wilkins, 38, Salt Lake City

Salt Lake City Crew members:

- Diane Edde, 18, Grantsville
- Garth Edde, 45, Grantsville
- Calvin Higgs, 41, Salt Lake City
- Norma Jenkins, 23, Salt Lake City
- Kenneth Myers, 43, Bountiful

The plane intended to make a stop in Provo before continuing to Albuquerque. Among the 20 would-be Provo passengers were Susie Odle (Phil's wife), BYU President Ernest L. Wilkinson, and Ron Hyde, executive director of the newly formed Cougar Club.

Author's Note: *some people around me in the stands during the New Mexico game made vague references to "a plane crash," but nobody had any details.*

The team first learned of the crash and loss of lives at breakfast before the game. Beverley Probert, wife of flight victim and former BYU star Marion Probert, sent a telegram message that coach Tommy Hudspeth read to the team at breakfast. Beverley cited her husband's hopes that BYU someday would win a championship and inspired the Cougars to "do your best to see his wish fulfilled."

"We are deeply saddened by this news," a teary-eyed Coach Hudspeth told the press that day. *"We dedicated this game to them."*

In the Provo area flags flew at half-mast until the

final funeral had been held.

The Cougars' 42-8 victory over New Mexico forever will be framed by these tragic circumstances.

Seven Marines at that "Religious School?"

Odle Impresses Cougar Faithful

September 19, 1965 By Ray Schwartz, Provo Daily Herald Sports Editor

A group of the Cougar "faithful" watched as Phil Odle, BYU's first-string split end, made a difficult catch of a forward pass look remarkably easy.

"That Odle's got all the moves and a great pair of hands," one of the sideline observers remarked. "I believe he'll provide a great show for the fans around these parts this season."

Odle, who hails from Elgin, Ill., and is among the Marine Corps transfers who enrolled at BYU last winter, stands an even six feet and weights 181, not too big as college ends go. But he's as elusive as a halfback in a broken field.

A sideline observer who had seen him play for the San Diego Marines said he was one of the most exciting players he had seen all season.

"In one particular game," the fan said, "Odle was headed for the goal line with only one defender to beat. Odle pointed his finger at an imaginary blocker and yelled, 'take him.' The defensive player turned his head

for just a second to look for the blocker who wasn't there.

"That second was all Odle needed as he cut away from the defender and raced for a touchdown."

One of the Marine Corps transfers was telling some of the fans about how the Leatherneck gridders happened to enroll at BYU.

"Most of the guys probably have a hard time realizing they're attending a religious school like BYU," he said. "In fact, if somebody had told these guys a year ago that they would be playing for BYU, most of them probably would have said, you're nuts."

"I know personally that there was a time when I never would have even considered attending a religious school. But a couple of guys visited the BYU campus. They returned and started raving about the great facilities at BYU. They also talked about all the beautiful girls there were on the campus. Pretty soon a couple of them said they were going to BYU and that started the thing snowballing. The next thing we knew we were here."

Cougar Football Moved Into the '70s

Paced by the final year for Virgil Carter in 1966, the Cougars went 8-2 and finished second behind WAC champion Wyoming.

The next few years saw a drop in wins: 1968: 2-8, 1970: 3-8, 1971: 5-6. Not by coincidence, these years also saw a decline in the passing attack. BYU went back to its roots of *"run first, pass when we must."*

A New Head Coach Searches for Unique Strengths

Coach LaVell (BYU photo)

After '71's losing season, head coach Tommy Hudspeth was replaced by his defensive coordinator, 41-year-old R. LaVell Edwards ("R" for Reuben). LaVell's appointment came as no surprise to anyone. He had a strong reputation as a player at Utah State and as a coach for military teams and Granite High School in Salt Lake City. LaVell remained close with Tommy Hudspeth and consistently credited him for raising the level of the program. Hudspeth compiled a 39-42-1 record at BYU from 1964-71. The Cougars had four winning seasons during his eight-year tenure after recording just 12 winning seasons in their first 39.

Now LaVell was the head guy for the 1972 season. He had been all about defense up to this point in his career, both as a player at Utah State and as an assistant coach since he first came to BYU in 1962. His Utah State teams had been successful. But BYU was a very different story.

The string of losing seasons from '68-'71 made a deep impression on LaVell. Way down deep, these results and his own experiences told him that BYU could only become a consistent winner if it could develop a dominant passing attack. In those days the Cougars were not able to attract the talented athletes that could compete with the teams in the Big 10, the Big Eight, the Southeast Conference, the Southwest Conference, or the Pacific Eight. Because the passing attack had helped the Cougars reach parity with many competitors, LaVell felt BYU needed to perfect the passing game. But this went against the grain of the latest innovative thinking in college football.

The Wishbone "Y" Triple Option

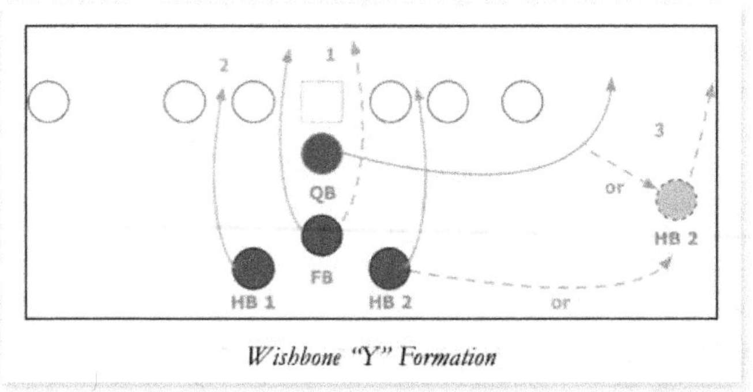

Wishbone "Y" Formation

In the '70s, ***the*** innovative offensive plan was the Wishbone "Y" triple option that rolled out three running options within seconds of each other:

1. Fullback dives either left or right, or

2. Halfback slashes to the left or right, or
3. Quarterback keeps to the right or left and/or option
   pitches to the trailing halfback.

Defenses were frequently overwhelmed by trying to anticipate and defend against these three options all at once.

LaVell wanted to provide such a game-changer for his Cougars. But he didn't know what that might be or how to get it. He needed some help!

Revolutionizing the Passing Plan: *Compete using your unique strengths.*

As LaVell reached out to his many coaching acquaintances, he connected with Lon Herzbrun, a former assistant at Tennessee who knew another coach whose time had come. Lon recommended former Vol quarterback Dewey Warren to assist LaVell. At that time Dewey was a quarterback for Paul Brown's Cincinnati Bengals. Lon knew that Dewey was discussing ways to innovate the passing plan with Bengals offensive coordinator Bill Walsh.

Dewey Warren (BYU photo)

Marvin West, a Tennessee writer who knows Dewey very well, described his offensive plan this way: *"He turned every running play into a possible pass. He overwhelmed defenses with five receivers. But it was simple to learn the basics. Players knew the offense by the second day of practice.*

"Edwards gave Warren full credit for what he did in the early 1970s. What he did is now regarded as a precursor of the West Coast offense made famous by coach Bill Walsh and the San Francisco 49ers."

Adjustments: Dewey Warren to BYU and vice versa

West described this classic encounter welcoming Dewey to the Cougar lair:

"I must say this delicately. The Swamp Rat was not a perfect fit for the Mormon school. He had to trim his sideburns and learn at least a little something about church discipline.

"Warren beat the boss to work on his first day in Provo. Coach Edwards came in and caught the smell of fresh-brewed coffee.

"You want some?" asked Dewey.

"Coffee is not permitted on the BYU campus," said Edwards in a gentle, but firm coaching tip.

"Dewey poured out some really good coffee."

But LaVell and the other coaches appreciated the spirit of Dewey's brewing. Their new colleague was anxious to get off to a fast start, and he contributed what he could (and what he was accustomed to) in the process.

Then Dewey unveiled his terrific passing plan to the coaches.

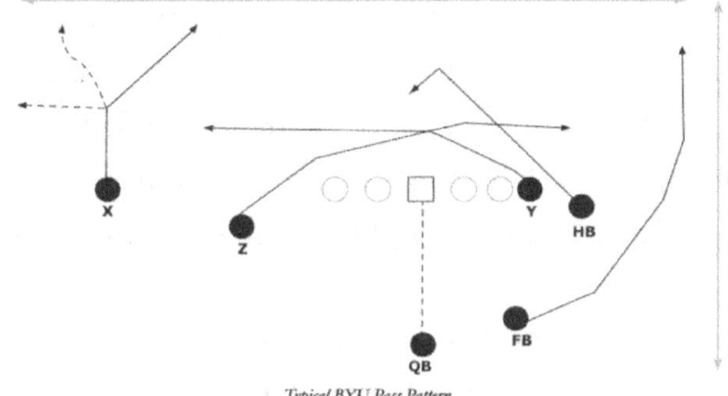

Typical BYU Pass Pattern

West continued, "Warren remembers the week Walsh came to Provo to see what the Swamp Rat was doing – keys, routes, reads, the idea of short passes that opened up lanes for bigger gains. The offense was designed to stretch the field vertically and horizontally. It involved clear-out routes to create seams for the tight end and flare vacancies for running backs.

The 1972 Season

"Dewey has fond memories of his two seasons at BYU. LaVell Edwards let Dewey do his thing. 'The head coach called one play in two years,' said Dewey.

'It lost 15 yards. LaVell said if he ever tried to butt in again, to 'just tell him no.'"

Many of us in the press box in 1972 could hear Dewey at times loudly complaining on the phone from his upper-level box to his coaching colleagues on the sidelines about what was not going according to "the plan" on the field. He was a perfectionist who insisted that things be done right. But making such changes to an established offense took some time.

As the 15th century diplomat Niccoló Machiavelli said, "There is nothing more... uncertain in its success than to take the lead in the introduction of a new order of things, because the innovator has for enemies all those who have done well under the old conditions, and lukewarm defenders in those who may do well under the new."

LaVell and Dewey were making changes to the habits and game strategies for winning and not everyone was able to "march in formation" right away.

But 1972 was a good leap forward for the Cougars. First of all, they had a *winning* season (7-4), they also finished second in the WAC. They beat Kansas State and Long Beach State decisively in addition to beating WAC rivals Texas-El Paso, Colorado State, Wyoming, Utah, and New Mexico.

However, all the key resources were not yet fully on board. Paradoxically, in this first year of the new passing era, BYU's halfback Pete Van Valkenburg was the nation's leading *rusher*, gaining 1,386 yards. The BYU team gained 2,312 yards rushing with 19 TDs and only 1,665 yards passing with eight TDs for the season.

The 1973 Season

With a year of practices and skull sessions starting to pay off, the 1973 numbers were: 1,881 yards rushing with 17 TDs and 2,930 yards passing with 24 TDs.

This season was actually two seasons in one:

(1) a 1-5 record to start off: (Can't you just hear Dewey Warren's screaming from the press box in Provo, Logan, Tempe, and Laramie?)

(2) a 4-1 finish with four blowouts:

- 56-21 over New Mexico in Provo
- 45-14 over Weber State in Provo
- 46-22 over Utah in a Salt Lake City snowstorm
- 63-0 over Texas-El Paso in El Paso

After these four wins, the secret of BYU's new offense was no longer a secret. The Cougars were now a force to be reckoned with. Even Dewey Warren was speechless!

Two players emerged as the new passing game leaders:

Quarterback Gary Sheide

Gary Sheide hunts for receivers.

He was All-League in three sports at Antioch High in Concord, CA (He hit .436 as a shortstop in baseball, averaged 22 points a game in basketball, and completed 60% of his passes in football).

He quarterbacked two years at Diablo Junior College but battled some injuries both years.

LaVell and Dewey were able to sign him for BYU. But injuries continued to plague Gary in his first season in Provo. He missed the first game with a thigh bruise and only got in for one play in the second game against Oregon State – a 68-yard touchdown bomb to wide receiver Sam Lobue. As fate would have it, that pass completion was the reason Gary did *not* win the NCAA passing crown in 1973. In those days passing leaders were measured by the number of completions per game. One game with only one completion put him in a big hole statistically. But not so on the field!

Sheide made his first start two weeks later in Provo against Iowa State. A last-second penalty took away what would have been BYU's game-winning touchdown pass in a 26-24 defeat.

"We had them. It was something college football hadn't seen before," Sheide said. "We threw the ball 41 times for 439 yards. That set the tone for what LaVell wanted to do — which was throw the football."

Gary finished second nationally in passing and ended up completing 177 of 294 passes for 2,350 yards (beating Virgil Carter's 1966 BYU best mark of 2,182) with 22 TDs and 12 interceptions. Gary's six touchdown passes against New Mexico were the most in an NCAA game in 1973. BYU was second nationally in per game passing yards with 266.4 and eighth in total offense with 437.4. yards per game.

Wide Receiver Jay Miller: Someone had to be catching those Sheide passes and the leader for BYU and the NCAA was Jay Miller. Jay came out of San Jose, California, who, like Gary Sheide, was a multi-sport athlete in baseball (.427 batting average), football,

Jay Miller clutches one of his 100 receptions in 1973 *(BYU photo)*

and basketball.

Jay led the NCAA in 1973 with 9.1 catches per game. But, that average, like Sheide's passing average, was not the most impressive number Jay recorded. His per-game average was generated by the 100 receptions he had in 1973 (an NCAA record for a season at the time)! His 1,181 receiving yards also led the NCAA that year.

Against New Mexico he set another NCAA record with 22 receptions in the game. He totaled 263 yards for the game. For his effort he was named WAC Offensive Player of the Week and lineman of the week by the Associated Press and Sports Illustrated. He also was a unanimous selection on the All-WAC team.

A Most Satisfying Win Over Utah:

Everything came together for the Cougars in their game against Utah in Salt Lake City.

The Date: November 24, 1973
The Place: Rice Stadium @ Salt Lake City
Weather: Temperature 34° with a lot of snow
Attendance: 18,243

Conventional wisdom says stormy weather does not favor a passing attack. That being so, this win over rival Utah was anything but conventional!

The Cougars piled up 599 yards of total offense

(357 passing, 242 rushing) compared to Utah's 334 yards (248 passing and 86 rushing).

Gary Sheide had four touchdown passes (three in the second quarter). Fullback Steve Stratton (120 yards) and halfback Jeff Blanc (87 yards and two TDs) were the leading rushers. Utah's defense threw everybody but their mascot at Jay Miller (only four catches on this day), so tight end Mike Pistorius led the way with eight catches and a touchdown.

Wide receiver John Betham had two 30+ yard touchdown catches.

The Cougars led, **30-3**, at halftime.

Keith Rivera pressuures Utah's Don Van Galder. (BYU photo)

Defensive End Keith Rivera led the defensive charge with eight tackles including a safety.

Four players each had seven tackles: linebackers Larry Carr and Doug Adams, and defensive backs Dave Atkinson and Mike Russell. Atkinson and Carr also each had one interception.

The Cougars won, **46-22**, scoring more points against Utah than in any of their previous 54 games of the rivalry.

"I remember coming to the sideline and getting pelted by snowballs from their fans," Gary said. "We just crushed them."

For BYU, it was easy to ignore the cold, wet weather.

Final Score: BYU 46,Utah 22

	1st	2nd	3rd	4th	Final
BYU	3	27	16	0	46
UTAH	0	3	6	13	22

Team Statistics	BYU	UTAH
First Downs	28	18
Total Offense Yards	599	334
Rushing Yards	242	66
Passing Yards	357	248
Passes (Att-Comp-Int)	37-24-0	41-14-2
TDs Passing	4	3
Fumbles Lost	5-3	2-2
Penalties/Yards	14-125	5-65

How well did BYU's new passing plan rate as a unique strength in 1973?

NATIONAL RECOGNITION: INDIVIDUALS

- Sheide #2 in passing, #3 in total offense
- Sheide also set a new WAC record with a .602 completion percentage.
- Miller #1 in receiving – 100 receptions.

NATIONAL RECOGNITION: TEAM

- No. 2 in passing – 266.4 yards/game
- No. 8 in total offense – 437.4 yards/game

It looked like the new passing plan was unique – and beginning to pay off!

But this team only had a 5-6 record to show for all the progress it had made. Skeptics were not convinced. The team and its fans were eager for the 1974 season to begin.

PLAYBOOK FUNDAMENTAL TWO:

Instinctively follow the game plan

Yes, optimism was high that 1974 was a year the Cougars could go all the way to the WAC title and a berth in the Fiesta Bowl. But nobody was smiling after the first four games of the season:

- Hawaii beat the Cougars, **15-13**, in its island paradise playground.
- Utah State beat them, **9-6**, in Provo. The Cougars were on USU's four-yard line as the game clock ran out.
- Iowa State totally dismantled them, **34-7**, in Ames.
- Then in Fort Collins: the ultimate embarrassment. Holding a 33-27 lead over the Rams, the BYU defense stopped the Rams cold at the BYU 15-yard line. The Cougars took possession of the ball with six seconds to play in the game. Then…

The Cougars fumbled the ball on the snap and the Rams recovered with three seconds left.…

CSU quarterback Mark Driscoll found receiver Willie Miller all alone in the end zone for a touchdown that tied the game, 33-33. Hysterical teammates and fans swarmed Miller in the end zone.

BUT the bedlam drew a yellow flag, and the Rams were penalized 15 yards for unsportsmanlike conduct. Then…Ram kicker Clark Kemble lined up for the potential game-winning extra point. But he was kicking from the 25-yard line instead of the 10 because of the penalty. The kick hooked sharply to the left and was no good. Then the final gun sounded, and the game ended in a **33-33** tie.

That added up to a record of 0-3-1 in the year

BYU was supposed to go all the way!

But these were just the headlines. Below the surface some thorns were letting out the air of BYU's balloon.

Thorn #1: No Jay Miller to catch all those passes.

Jay broke a scapula (shoulder blade) in a pre-season practice. He would miss the first three games in 1974. Then in week five against Wyoming in Provo, Jay returned and caught two passes for 33 yards before tearing some knee ligaments on a non-contact play.

Thorn #2: Too few Gary Sheide passes to catch.

Here are Gary's passing statistics (Attempts-Completions-Interceptions) for the first four games:

- 24-13-4 for 154 yards
- 28-18-4 for 170 yards
- 17-6-2 for 56 yards
- 14-11-0 for 123 yards

This was an average of 125 yards per game with 10 pass interceptions! What is wrong with this picture? Miller was gone. But what's with Sheide?

Thorn #3: A new, improved (?) passing game plan (in other words, no Dewey Warren).

Despite his energy for the BYU program, Dewey Warren received a coaching opportunity ("too good to pass up") from a Tennessee alum at Kansas State in the Big Eight (now Big 12) Conference. As you can see, Dewey disappeared and so did the passing magic at BYU.

Dwain Painter, the new quarterbacks coach had installed a different offense he was comfortable with.

What to do?

First, team captains Gary Sheide, Keith Rivera and Brad Oates spearheaded a players-only meeting. What was the agenda of this meeting? A gripe session? Finger pointing? A rebellion? None of these.

"We needed to focus on the team instead of ourselves," Sheide said. *"It was a very emotional meeting. There were tears in that room. We pushed the reset button."*

Keith Rivera was the chief reset button pusher, according to Brad Oates. *"Keith was a dear, close friend. We were competitors on the field and close friends off. Keith's passion and love for the game and his teammates was felt by everyone in the room that day...from a depth of emotion that was authentically who Keith Rivera was. It was a rare balance of deep love for his teammates with an intense personal distaste of losing because we weren't playing up to the standard that we were capable of as a team."*

The players were frustrated that the 1973 offense playbook, the one that had turned them around the year before, was not being used any longer.

Somehow LaVell was unaware that the playbook

had been shelved. *"Those guys got together and met, and the three captains told me that we needed to return to last year's playbook."*

LaVell said, *"I told them to go back to that playbook and use it only. And if anybody, including me, told them to do anything else – ignore them."*

At the heart of this turnaround is the main point of **Fundamental Number Two: *Instinctively* follow the game plan**. The players had gone through the pains to learn a revolutionary new passing plan. They had practiced it again and again. And they had seen what a competitive advantage it delivered. They knew *instinctively* they could win the WAC title by following that same game plan. That is what brought the three captains to meet with their coach.

Then it was *instinctively clear* to LaVell why his team had been struggling in this new season. BYU practices and game preparation made a swift return to the 1973 game plan.

"The players went out and beat Wyoming and won our last seven games," LaVell said. *"I've often thought that that week changed the direction of my whole career because without those guys doing that and coming together, I don't think any of this would have happened, at least with me."*

(LaVell once told one of the three captains he didn't expect to be the head coach at BYU more than four years. That was close to the average tenure for the

10 coaches who had preceded him.)

GAME #5:
BYU 38, Wyoming 7
Date: October 12, 1974
Location: Cougar Stadium
Weather: Temperature in the 60s and clear
Attendance: 29,555

Into Cougar Stadium came Wyoming, a team picked preseason to finish ahead of BYU in the WAC.

Gary Sheide erased any doubts about whether he and his teammates were up for this game. At one point against the Cowboys, he completed 16 of 19 passes. John Betham filled Miller's shoes, catching four passes for 69 yards and two touchdowns. He also had two punt returns of 48 and 40 yards to set up two short yardage touchdown runs by Jeff Blanc.

Sheide finished the day completing 20 of 28 passes with two TDs before giving way to Mark Giles with 13 minutes left in the fourth quarter. Giles continued the air assault, completing four of five passes for 35 yards and one more touchdown.

But this was far from an offensive show only. BYU's defense was strong in the first half and totally suffocated the visitors in the second half. In the final 30 minutes the Cowboys managed a minus two yards rushing and only three yards of total offense.

First Half

BYU scored first on Dev Duke's 42-yard field goal in the first quarter. Wyoming countered early in the second quarter with freshman quarterback Rick Costello finishing a 55-yard drive with a five-yard touchdown pass to Walter Howard. **Wyoming 7, BYU 3.**

But the Cougars struck back quickly with Betham's 48-yard punt return starting the next drive. Ten plays later Jeff Blanc scored from one yard out to make the score **10-7 for BYU**, with 2:52 remaining in the half.

And the Cougars weren't through yet. With 1:17 to play, they got the ball back on their own 44-yard line. This time Sheide marched the team down the field in six plays. His 21-yard TD pass to Betham came with 14 seconds to play.

Halftime Score: BYU 17, Wyoming 7

Second Half

Then began the second half and the Cougars' terrific defensive stand. The Cougars took the opening kickoff, but Duke missed a 32-yard field goal. Two plays later defensive lineman Stan Varner recovered a Wyoming fumble. After a Cowboy penalty put them on their own eight-yard line, Jeff Blanc rushed on four straight downs to score from the one-foot line. That made it, **24-7, for BYU**.

Early in the fourth quarter the Cougars increased their lead to **31-7** on a 63-yard drive in eight plays. Two third-down conversions kept the drive alive. On third and 13 Sheide hit Jeff Nilsson for a first down on the Wyoming 44. On third and 16, Sheide hit Sam Lobue for 26 yards and another first down on the Wyoming 24-yard line. Then it was Sheide to Betham again for 23 yards and a touchdown.

The Cougars' last score came early in the fourth quarter. Wyoming's Joe Marion, averaging 47 yards/punt for the game, got off another strong kick, but John Betham had a long return before being forced out of bounds at the Wyoming eight-yard line.

With 13 minutes to go in the game, Sheide turned over quarterback duties to Mark Giles. Giles hit fullback Tim Mahoney for a three-yard TD to close out the win, **38-7**.

	1st	**2nd**	**3rd**	**4th**	**Final**
Wyoming	**0**	**7**	**0**	**0**	**7**
BYU	**3**	**14**	**7**	**14**	**38**

Team Statistics	**BYU**	**Wyoming**
First Downs	**23**	**7**
Total Offense Yards	**418**	**131**
Rushing Yards	**120**	**46**

Passing Yards	**298**	**85**
Passes (Att-Comp-Int)	**33-24-0**	**19-8-2**
TDs Passing	**3**	**1**
Fumbles Lost	**3-2**	**2-1**
Penalties/Yards	**11-81**	**5-43**

Wyoming coach Fritz Shurmur said, "I can't think of anything (we did well). BYU really put it all together. We thought we were ready for BYU's passing, but Sheide did a super job of picking us apart. And the BYU defense is tough. Every time I looked up that defensive line was all over us. We just couldn't sustain a drive."

A relieved LaVell Edwards said, "It really felt good to win this one. It was a long time in coming. We came out in the second half and really played football."

BYU Offense Leaders

- **Gary Sheide** was 20-28 passing for 263 yards and two TDs.
- **Jeff Blanc** carried 24 times for 74 yards and two TDs.
- **John Betham** caught four passes for 69 yards and two TDs.
- **Kirk Tanner** caught four passes for 48 yards.

- **Mark Giles** was four for five passing for 35 yards and one TD and also carried six times for 48 yards
- **Tim Mahoney** caught three passes for 28 yards and one TD and also carried three times for 22 yards.

BYU Defense Leaders

- **Larry Carr** nine tackles (four solo, one for loss).
- **Phil Jensen** had seven tackles (three solo).
- **Wayne Baker** had seven tackles (two solo, two for loss).
- **Frank Linford** had five tackles (one solo, one for loss).
- **Gary Shaw** had four tackles (two solo) and one interception.
- **Mike Russell** had three solo tackles and one interception.

GAME #7:

BYU 37, (No. 16) Arizona 13
Date: October 26, 1974
Location: Arizona Stadium @ Tucson
Weather: Temperature in the 80s and clear
Attendance: 34,116

Arizona was the favorite to win the WAC title

that year and was ranked No. 16 heading into this game. The Wildcats were an undefeated, 5-0, and were ranked No. 9 until losing to Texas Tech the week before playing BYU.

Tom Foust, sports editor of the Tucson Daily Star, wrote this lead to his post-game report:

> *The University of Arizona's bubble burst yesterday, punctured by bullets from the hottest gun in the west.*
>
> *Brigham Young quarterback Gary Sheide riddled the Arizona defense with 20 pass completions for 267 yards and five touchdowns to lead the inspired Cougars to a* ***37-13*** *victory that knocked the favored Wildcats out of the driver's seat in the Western Athletic Conference.*

First Half

Arizona won the opening toss and moved the ball in a few plays up to midfield. Then quarterback Bruce Hill connected with wide receiver Scott Piper breaking over the middle, who then went the distance to the end zone. Arizona led **7-0** with only 1:17 gone in the game.

This only made Sheide & Co. even more eager to get going! They immediately went 79 yards in 13 plays to tie the score. Jeff Blanc carried the ball five times for 20 yards and Sheide completed four of six passes for 55 yards, including the 13-yard scoring strike to John Betham. **Arizona 7, BYU 7.**

Arizona fumbled the ball on the first play after the next kickoff and Keith Rivera recovered for the Cougars on the Wildcat 21. But the Arizona defense held at the 17-yard line.

Then the Cougars struck twice for two touchdowns within 40 seconds after Mike Russell and Gary Shaw each intercepted a Hill pass.

Sheide took over both times with TD passes of 17 and 27 yards to Blanc to boost the **BYU lead to 21-7**.

Arizona then drove from its own 24 to the BYU 14 only to yield Shaw's second interception after Hill's pass bounced off receiver T. Bell's shoulder pad into Shaw's hands in the end zone.

In the second quarter the score was unchanged until the Cougars moved 80 yards in 13 plays. Sheide again was four for six passing for 42 yards. Charlie Ah You, subbing for the injured Blanc, ran for 24 yards in five carries. The drive was capped by John Betham's 16-yard TD reception from Sheide with 3:36 to play in the half.

The Cougar lead was, 28-7, at halftime over the team picked to win the WAC.

The only score in the third quarter was Hill's screen pass to Willie Hamilton, who waited for a key block, and then raced 70 yards for Arizona's second score. BYU's Paul Linford blocked the PAT, making the score, **28-13**.

In the fourth quarter, defensive end Stan Varner intercepted Hill's pass and returned it four yards to the Arizona 30-yard line. On third and four, Sheide found Betham, who made a circus catch, juggling the ball with one hand, then securing possession and carrying it into the end zone. The PAT sailed wide, making the score, **34-13** with 12:09 left to play.

Middle linebacker Larry Carr made the Cougars' fifth interception off Hill and returned the ball from his 35 to the Arizona 45. Eight plays later Dev Duke kicked a 31-yard field goal to finish the scoring, **BYU 37, Arizona 13.**

The win evened BYU's season record at 3-3-1 and upped its leading conference record to 3-0-1.

	1st	2nd	3rd	4th	Final
BYU	**21**	**7**	**0**	**9**	**37**
Arizona	**7**	**0**	**6**	**0**	**13**

Team Statistics	**BYU**	**Arizona**
First Downs	**17**	**22**
Total Offense Yards	**434**	**328**
Rushing Yards	**131**	**123**
Passing Yards	**303**	**205**
Passes (Att-Comp-Int)	**37-21-0**	**35-10-5**
TDs Passing	**5**	**2**

Fumbles Lost	**2-0**	**3-1**
Penalties/Yards	**12-104**	**5-54**

Arizona coach Jim Young, (as you can appreciate, was dejected). **His short and painful comments were,** "Brigham Young completely outplayed us, and I don't think there is any doubt that they deserved to win…We were not ready to play, we did not play up to our potential and as head coach I take responsibility for that. There was no turning point. We just didn't play."

LaVell Edwards was excited to say the least. "I just can't say enough about our game plan and the members of the coaching staff who put it together. Primarily, our plan was to take away their running game and force them into a passing game. Our pressure was good, and we managed to maintain our poise throughout. We were really ready for this afternoon and fortunately, we were able to make our adjustments quickly when necessary. We also figured that we needed to establish a running attack of our own. We didn't get a lot of yards, but we got good yards that helped our passing game."

BYU Offense Leaders

- **Gary Sheide** was 20-35 passing for 267 yards and five TDs.

- **John Betham** caught 10 passes for 144 yards and three TDs.
- **Jeff Blanc** carried nine times for 34 yards and also caught four passes for 61 yards and two TDs.
- **Charlie Ah You** carried 22 times for 60 yards.
- **Todd Christensen** carried seven times for 27 yards and also caught two passes for 10 yards.
- **Craig Van Leeuwen** caught one pass for 36 yards.

BYU Defense Leaders

- **Keith Rivera** had eight tackles (four solo, two for loss) and one fumble recovery.
- **Dana Wilgar** had seven tackles (five solo) and one pass break up.
- **Wayne Baker** had seven tackles (three solo, one for loss) and two forced fumbles.
- **Gary Shaw** had seven tackles (two solo) and two interceptions.
- **Larry Carr** had seven tackles (two solo, one for loss) and one interception.
- **Stan Varner** had four tackles (one solo, one for loss), one pass break up, and one interception.
- **Mike Russell** had one forced fumble, two pass break ups, and one interception.

GAME #9:
BYU 21, (No. 16) **Arizona State 18**
Date: November 9, 1974
Location: Cougar Stadium
Weather: 42° partly cloudy
Attendance: 29, 422

Let's set the stage for this most important game for BYU:

- For the second time in three weeks BYU had the good fortune of playing a team from Arizona ranked No. 16.
- Despite what the folks at *Sports Illustrated* would have you believe *(BYU "the most hated team in college football"),* the Sun Devils loved BYU!
- Up to that point ASU had won 15 of the 18 contests with its Provo neighbors, including routs of 49-17 and 52-12 in their last two meetings. Now the Sun Devils were back and ready to feast again upon the upstart Cougars.
- But this year's four-game winning streak had the Provo fans thinking WAC title and a Fiesta Bowl berth. The winner on November 9 would have the inside track to all the

hardware and honors. *Would this be the year ASU didn't win the WAC?* A regional television audience and a crowd of 29,422 at Cougar Stadium were anxious to find out.

- It appeared that the winner of this game would be the WAC champion.

First Quarter

The Cougars won the coin toss and chose to receive the ball to start the game. John Betham caught the ball in the end zone and returned it out to the BYU 20. Two short plays by Jeff Blanc and Gary Sheide's incomplete long pass forced a punt. Then Mark Giles' punt from the 26-yard line traveled exactly 17 yards, giving the Sun Devils the ball on the BYU 43.

ASU mirrored BYU's opening drive play selection with two short runs for five yards. Then on third and five quarterback Ray Alexander hit flanker Morris Owens for a 38-yard touchdown. And just like that, with less than three minutes off the clock, **the Sun Devils had the lead, 6-0**.

What were we loyal BYU fans supposed to think? *Did ASU lead a charmed life when playing our guys?*

The Cougars retaliated by going 60 yards in nine plays. Sheide completed four of six passes for 55 yards before Lobue's catch and fumble turned the ball over to ASU at their 17 yard-line.

But the Sun Devils couldn't do anything and had to punt back to the Cougars.

- Sheide started things off with a pass to fullback Tim Mahoney for 13 yards and a first down.
- Then Blanc's three-yard run, an incompletion, and a five-yard completion to tight end Kirk Tanner brought up a fourth and two at the ASU 30-yard line.
- Sheide then hit tight end Tom Toolson for seven yards and a first down at the ASU 23.
- Tim Mahoney ran off the left side for three yards and then caught Sheide's pass at the nine for a first-and-goal.
- Then, just as we were all getting excited about the imminent score, ASU defensive back Mike Haynes intercepted Sheide's pass at the two-yard line.

Author's Note: *(BYU people in the press box were not allowed to voice any noisy emotions in front of our guests. But our desktops got pounded aplenty on this interception!)*

Not to worry. On the first play the Sun Devils' Freddie Williams was trapped in the end zone by linebacker Larry Carr for a safety. It wasn't exactly the score BYU fans were hoping for, but at least the Cougars were on the board, **6-2,** with 3:57 to play in the first quarter.

The battle of possession changes continued after John Betham's kick return of 23 yards to the BYU 48. Blanc fumbled the ball away on the first play from scrimmage.

Again, the visitors couldn't do anything and punted the ball away.

Blanc gained 10 yards on three carries to give the Cougars a first down on their own 30-yard line as the first quarter ended.

If you are feeling a bit weary at this point in your reading, you can relate to what the fans and BYU players were feeling like after just one quarter.

Second Quarter

ASU's Owens ended BYU's opening second quarter drive by intercepting Sheide's pass at ASU's 16. Moments later ASU's long pass was picked off by Cougar Mark McCluskey.

Next BYU faked a punt on fourth-and-two and came up one yard short at the ASU 43.

Another ASU three-and-out and BYU had the ball again.

After two plays, ASU's Ed Vaughn intercepted a Sheide pass and took it all the way to the end zone. The extra point again was no good, leaving the score at **12-2 for the Sun Devils** with 8:35 to play in the half.

On the ensuing possession BYU converted a three-and-out into six points. Mark Giles punted to Haynes who fumbled into BYU linebacker Larry Tucker's hands at ASU's 24.

- Sheide started the drive with a seven-yard completion to Blanc.
- The next play call was a tricky one. Sheide pitched the ball to Mahoney (a former quarterback) who then returned the favor to Sheide, who caught the 11-yard pass for a first-and-goal at the six-yard line.
- There was one run for no gain and then an incomplete pass in the end zone.
- Then on third down, Sheide found Mahoney in the end zone for a touchdown with 5:01 left in the half.

Score: ASU 12, BYU 8.

But the excitement wasn't over yet! BYU cornerback Mike Russell intercepted an ASU pass and returned it to the ASU 33-yard line. Two pass completions later and Jeff Blanc's over-the-ASU-line jump put the Cougars at first-and-goal at the ASU five. On the next play Blanc fumbled the ball into the end zone and ASU recovered. *(More fist pounding on the press box desktops!)*

Both teams fizzled on their final possessions.

Halftime Score: ASU 12, BYU 8.

There was a total of 10 first-half turnovers between the two teams and there was still another half to go!

Third Quarter

The Sun Devils received the second half kickoff. They had a three-and-out possession and punted to Betham, who made a fair catch at his own 38-yard line.

The Cougars drove 62 yards in 10 plays for the touchdown. Sheide was four-for-four passing, and ASU interfered on his fifth pass putting the Cats on the ASU one-yard line. Jeff Blanc scored on the next play clutching the ball in the "hug of life" to ensure the TD. The PAT failed. No matter. The headline here was: **BYU had its first lead, 14-12,** with 8:28 to play in the third quarter.

ASU moved the ball 42 yards in 10 plays before (you guessed it!) running back Garland Evans fumbled at the BYU 35-yard line and defensive end Keith Rivera recovered for BYU. The Cougar elation was very short, however.

Five plays later Mike Haynes intercepted Sheide for the second time in the game and ran 55 yards for a touchdown. The PAT failed (again), leaving the score **ASU 18, BYU 14** with 2:23 to play in the third quarter.

John Betham returned the ensuing kickoff from

his 10-yard line to the 25 before he fumbled. Luckily, a BYU teammate fell on this loose ball. The Cougars ran five plays before punting to the ASU 18.

A short two-yard run by Fred Williams ended the third quarter.

Fourth Quarter: All or Nothing

So, the showdown came down to the final quarter. BYU still trailed the Sun Devils despite having a huge 307-160 total yardage lead for three quarters.

ASU ran six plays, but the only big gainer was a 20-yard pass interference penalty on the Cougars. The 'Devils ended up punting back to BYU.

Taking over on the BYU 10, three Sheide passes yielded no yards gained.

The ball went back to ASU. Three plays netted three yards. ASU's Kory Schuhknecht punted the ball into the BYU end zone.

It would appear both teams were running out of gas with 10 minutes to play, but the Cougars were willing to go again.

"Everyone in the huddle knew this was it," said Sheide. *"We had come too far to fold now."*

Starting on their 20, this was the Cougars' big drive:

- A pitchout to Blanc gained four yards.

- Sheide passed complete to Jeff Nilsson for eight yards and a first down.
- Sheide was sacked for a loss of five.
- No problem! Sheide passed to Blanc at the BYU 47 for a gain of 20.

Gary Sheide leads the charge. (Mark Philbrick BYU photo)

- Tim Mahoney ran up the middle, fumbled, but recovered the ball for a gain of nine.
- Blanc ran left for two yards and a big first down at ASU's 42.
- Blanc on the same play gained four more to the ASU 38.
- A penalty was called on the Sun Devils for pass interference, moving the ball to the ASU 22.
- Mahoney ran to the left for 13 yards.

- Sheide passed nine yards to Mahoney for the score! Mark Uselman's PAT was good! (The only successful PAT for either team that day.)

That was 80 yards in nine plays and with 6:11 to go; BYU led again, 21-18.

The Sun Devils' comeback was stopped after five plays when Larry Carr intercepted Ray Alexander's pass and returned it seven yards to the ASU 49.

BYU moved the ball for five plays before punting into the Sun Devils' end zone.

Alexander slipped trying to pass at the 10. Gary Shaw then intercepted Alexander with one minute to play.

Sheide then fell on the ball to end the game.

FINAL SCORE: BYU 21, ASU 18

	1st	2nd	3rd	4th	Final
ASU	6	6	6	0	18
BYU	2	6	6	7	21

Team Statistics	BYU	ASU
First Downs	25	11
Total Offense Yards	363	186
Rushing Yards	129	78

Passing Yards	**234**	**108**
Passes (Att-Comp-Int)	**42-25-5**	**21-8-4**
TDs Passing	**2**	**1**
Fumbles Lost	**5-3**	**2-2**
Penalties/Yards	**7-50**	**5=68**

ASU coach Frank Kush said, "We received a very poor offensive effort… We never got anything going. We were ahead late in the game, but it was only a matter of time until BYU went ahead…Our defense did everything we could ask of it…they scored two of our touchdowns…but they were on the field way too long.

Give Brigham Young a world of credit…Sheide was on and off, but he never quit. We gave him some good shots, but he'd just get up and come back throwing. The Cougars are now in the driver's seat, and they'll make an excellent Fiesta Bowl representative…On films we've watched them improve game by game."

LaVell Edwards said, "It was a team effort all the way. I'd have to say this is the biggest win I've had at BYU. We gave up the ball a lot in the first half, but we kept coming back. The offense drove 80 yards late in the game when we had to have it. "The defense today was the best we've ever had. I think the turning point of the game was the way we were able to control the line of scrimmage both on offense and defense. The way we were playing, I just knew we were going to come back and win it some way.

"There were a lot of turnovers in the game today and I attribute that to the fierce hitting by both defenses plus the high tension that both teams felt for this game.

"I know our team was really keyed up for the Fiesta Bowl. I've been to the Fiesta Bowl by myself the last two years and it will be certainly nice to be able to take the whole team with me this year."

BYU Offense Leaders

- **Gary Sheide** was 24-41 passing for 223 yards with five interceptions and two TDs.
- **Jeff Blanc** carried 28 times for 68 yards and one TD and also caught six passes for 61 yards.
- **Tim Mahoney** carried 11 times for 54 yards and also caught six passes for 51 yards and two TDs.
- **John Betham** caught four passes for 48 yards and also had four kick returns for 81 yards.

BYU Defense Leaders

- **Gary Shaw** had nine tackles (three solo), one pass break up, and one interception.
- **Larry Carr** had nine tackles (two solo) one interception and one safety.

- **Phil Jensen** had nine tackles (four solo), and one pass break up.
- **Keith Rivera** seven tackles (two solo) and one fumble recovery.
- **Stan Varner** had five tackles (two solo).
- **Mike Russell** had five tackles (four solo) and one interception.
- **Mark McCluskey** had one tackle and one interception.

Author's Report:

BYU-ASU Post-Game Locker Room Vibes

As soon as the Cougars scored the go-ahead touchdown, Sports Information Director Dave Schulthess asked me to make my way down to the locker room, jot down some of the coach's comments and phone them up to the press box so the writers could include them in their stories. (This was in the Pre-Jurassic Period when Cougar Stadium had only 30,000 seats...Paul James' voice wasn't transmitted throughout the stadium...There weren't even such things as fax machines or cellular phones.)

I moved through the stadium as the heavyweights punched on. A Larry Carr interception ended one ASU drive, but the Cougars couldn't move the ball and had to punt. At field level now, I watched Gary Shaw's interception drive the final nail in the visitors' coffin with only one minute to play. People were dancing throughout Cougar Stadium as I left the field area.

My press pass granted me entrance into the inner sanctum of the team dressing room. I took a place in the corner to enjoy the festivities. In a matter of moments, the players started filing in.

In no time the dressing room was a madhouse! The ecstatic players hugged each other, shouted, and pounded the steel lockers with their helmets. Pandemonium doesn't even begin to describe what was going on in there!

In the din of celebration, one scene caught my eye. Two of the most battered Cougars that day, Gary Sheide and Keith Rivera, found each other and embraced in a big bear hug. Both had given all they had out on the playing field. Sheide had been booed for his early miscues, but had hung tough and redeemed himself on that final, make-or-break touchdown drive.

Rivera, playing on a bad ankle that would require surgery after the season's end, was in on seven tackles, including two for losses, and recovered a fumble. He symbolized a gutsy defense that had shut down the vaunted Sun Devils after their initial touchdown bomb in the first quarter.

One by one the assistant coaches trickled in and finally LaVell himself entered. He moved to the center of the room and though no one gave any kind of signal, everyone was instantly silent. Coach had something to say.

LaVell's face *was...well, you know...without emotion. He spoke slowly in quiet, understated tones:*

Mark Philbrick (BYU photo)

"We played a very good team out there today. We made some mistakes and gave them every opportunity to win. But we never gave up. The defense shut them down...and then when we had to have it, the offense..."

Right there in midsentence, the unthinkable happened. LaVell's voice suddenly faltered and ran out of words. And then, as the enormity of what had just happened really hit home, the Great Stone Face first cracked, then shattered.

LaVell Edwards stood in front of BYU's biggest and toughest and wept unashamedly.

He tried to say something more, but the words just weren't there. All that was left was pure emotion. The supportive vibes from two hundred eyes weren't enough to help the coach find his voice. Finally, after what seemed to be a full minute, all he could muster was a "thumbs up" sign.

Larry Carr stops ASU's Freddie Williams. (BYU photo)

LaVell's gesture was answered by the loudest ovation I have ever heard in my life. The capacity crowds in Cougar Stadium have been mute in comparison to the noise generated by the 100 players and coaches while their leader stood before them with tears rolling down his cheeks. The lockers became kettle drums again. The cheering, it seemed to me, was going to lift the roof right off the locker room. In a way, I wish it had so that all the other Cougar fans could have joined in the moment. The shouts came from deep down inside — expelling years of frustration by those who had struggled for a little respect.

"You play football where? Do they actually play football at BYU?"

Wayne Baker, first discovered playing eight-man football in Montana, was one of the loudest. Almost lost in the emotion of the game was the performance that he, Rivera, Paul Linford, and Stan Varner had turned in on the defensive line. The Sun Devils' speedsters had gained only 78 yards rushing in 34 tries—a measly 2.3 yards a crack. And the Cougar defense had forced six turnovers of its own. This was Arizona State, not UTEP.

Yes, we play football at BYU!

Tim Mahoney, a converted quarterback, led the shouting in another corner. A relative unknown prior to this game, he had run for 54 yards in 11 carries on a day when two yards per crack was par for both teams. He was also on the receiving end of both Sheide touchdown passes, including, of course, the game winner.

Yes, we play football at BYU!

Larry Carr and Gary Shaw were hysterical in another part of the room. Each had made big stops all day long. The final statistics showed the defense had held Kush's troops to 186 yards of total offense. That was for the whole game...186 yards...Arizona State.

Yes, we play football at BYU!

Standing quietly in the corner, chills ricocheted up

and down my spine!

Paradoxically, LaVell's silent tears and his players' deafening shouts both announced that BYU football had arrived in the big time. I thought to myself, "This year the Sun Devils can watch **us** *play in the Fiesta Bowl!"*

***Y**es, we play football at BYU!*

The final scene in that wild locker room was a discussion between LaVell and a member of the Fiesta Bowl selection committee. The Fiesta representative told LaVell the committee was pleased to offer a conditional invitation to BYU — conditional on beating New Mexico and Utah the next two weekends.

The official concluded, "We know it's time for the sake of the bowl that someone other than ASU represents the WAC. We're so glad it's you!"

Little did we know the torch was not being passed not only for one game, but also for nearly three decades of dominance.

The rest, as they say, is history. And we have all been beneficiaries of the Edwards legacy. No more avoiding your friends from the U of U. No more listening politely — silently — while your cousins tell stories about the great teams at Utah State. No more living in fear of playing Arizona State's speed merchants, or anyone else for that matter.

So, there it is, Cougar fans! My technicolor replay of the game that lifted BYU out of football obscurity.

Though it happened many years ago, time hasn't dimmed its impact on me. I've replayed it dozens of times—complete with tingling spine.

I play the "tape" to remind myself how precious even one conference championship is. How special it is to go to any bowl game. And to remind myself when I get too worked up about a football game, that we who wear Cougar blue and white really have become a bit spoiled by LaVell's incredible success.

As boys, my friends and I would dream about becoming All-America players at Texas, or Notre Dame or UCLA. During the LaVell Edwards era, BYU has defeated each of those schools as well as Miami, Penn State, Oklahoma, Michigan, Wisconsin, Colorado, Pittsburgh, Texas A&M, Oregon, Kansas State, California and Washington. Today kids in many parts of the country dream of playing football in Provo.

Yes, we play football at BYU!

The red-hot Cougars next attended to their most urgent business – finishing the last two games to qualify for the Fiesta Bowl.

First, they faced the New Mexico Lobos in Albuquerque. The Lobos would suffer their sixth loss to the Cougars against three wins. Gary Sheide (244 yards passing for one TD and two short TD runs), Jeff Blanc (74 yards rushing and 94 yards receiving –

including a 51-yard TD bomb from Sheide), and Mark Uselman's three field goals were the big guns on offense.

Larry Carr (eight tackles – three solo), Frank Linford (one 24-yard pick six), and Dana Wilgar (six tackles – three solo– and one interception) were the heavy hitters on defense.

GAME #11:
BYU 48, Utah 20
Date: November 23, 1974
Location: Cougar Stadium
Weather: 40s° clear
Attendance: 30,978

So, that left only Utah, the team at the bottom of the WAC standings with a 1-8 record, as the Cougars' last obstacle to the Fiesta Bowl. The large home crowd anticipated a wonderful win that would clinch the WAC title and send their heroes to the school's first bowl game.

The fireworks started early in this one as John Betham ran back the opening kickoff 103 yards for a touchdown. The Provo Herald's Joe Watts called Betham's gem *"handwriting on the wall and when the writing was finally completed it showed BYU with its third straight win over the Utes, a 7-3-1 season's record, and an undefeated mark of 6-0-1 in conference play."*

After Betham's opening strike, Gary Sheide and Jeff Blanc took over to increase the Cougars' lead. Sheide threw a 12-yard scoring pass to fullback Tim Mahoney. Then Sheide scored on fourth-and-inches from the goal line on a quarterback sneak. Blanc dominated the first quarter with 94 yards gained on only 11 carries. Then he scored two TDs to open the third quarter, making the score 35-6. He finished the game with 122 yards on 20 carries and the two touchdowns. At that point, Sheide sat down and Mark Giles took his place at quarterback.

The Cougars' final tallies came in the fourth quarter. (Sheide was re-inserted into the game when LaVell learned that Gary needed only one more touchdown pass to tie ASU's Danny White for the most touchdown passes in a WAC season with 23). In short order Sheide got after the record. He hit fullback Todd Christensen with a five-yarder for the score. Later in the fourth BYU linebacker Frank Linford intercepted a Utah pass and ran it back 55 yards into the end zone.

The final score, **48-20,** was the largest victory margin ever by the Cougars over the Utes and was their third win in a row in the rivalry.

	1st	2nd	3rd	4th	Final
UTAH	0	6	0	14	20
BYU	14	7	14	13	48

Team Statistics	BYU	UTAH
First Downs	16	19
Total Offense Yards	298	224
Rushing Yards	173	37
Passing Yards	125	187
Passes (Att-Comp-Int)	25-13-2	30-14-3
TDs Passing	2	1
Fumbles Lost	3-1	5-2
Penalties/Yards	11-116	8-74

WAC commissioner Stan Bates presented the championship trophy to BYU and **Carl Eller, president of the Fiesta Bowl**, officially invited BYU to play in its first ever bowl game.

LaVell Edwards said, "Looking back, that tie with Colorado State might have been the best thing that happened to us. Because of that tie, the pressure was on us all the way and we couldn't afford to lose. I really think that was what kept us going, otherwise we might have had a letdown someplace."

(About sending Sheide back in the fourth quarter

to try for the WAC season TD passes record): "I hesitate to do anything like that because it looks like we're pouring it on. But Gary has done so much for us in the last two years we felt we owed him one last chance for the record."

In the locker room, LaVell said to the players simply, "You guys know how I feel about winning today!"

Cougar Offense Leaders

- **Gary Sheide** was 11 of 22 passes for 104 yards with one interception and two TDs. He also ran for one TD.
- **Jeff Blanc** carried 20 times for 122 yards and two TDs and also had two catches for 33 yards.
- **John Betham** caught two passes for 40 yards and had two kick returns for 118 yards and one TD.
- **Tim Mahoney** caught two passes for 12 yards and one TD.
- **Todd Christensen** caught two passes for eight yards and one TD.

Cougar Defense Leaders

- **Paul Linford** had 11 tackles (four solo).
- **Gary Shaw** had 10 tackles (five solo, two for loss).

- **Wayne Baker** had 10 tackles (one solo, three for loss).
- **Stan Varner** had seven tackles (two solo, two for loss) and one interception.
- **Craig Jensen** had five solo tackles and one pass break up.
- **Frank Linford, Dana Wilgar, and Larry Carr** each had one interception. Linford returned his 55 yarder into a "Pick Six."

The Cougars had a total of 21 tackles for loss in this game! Also contributing to this amazing feat were Marcus Kanahele (four), Phil Jensen (two), Gary Peterson (two), Keith Rivera (two), Clark Carlson (1), Larry Carr (1), Blake Murdock (1), and Steve Dewey (

As WAC champions, BYU received an automatic berth in the fourth annual Fiesta Bowl in Tempe, AZ. The Cougars were ranked No. 17 coming into the game.

Oklahoma State 16, BYU 6
Date: December 28, 1974
Location: Sun Devil Stadium, Tempe
Weather: 60s° cloudy, light rain
Attendance: 50,878

The Cougars at 7-3-1 were well matched with Oklahoma State, whose season record of 6-5 was a bit deceptive. The Cowboys had beaten No. 10 Arkansas on the road and lost two squeakers on the road to No. 10 Texas Tech and No. 9 Nebraska. They finished fourth in the Big 8 Conference, just one win short of finishing in a three-way tie for second in the conference.

The Cougars started off as if they would make quick work of beating the Cowboys as they had done with their WAC rivals. Gary Sheide guided the Cougars' first possession within range for Mark Uselman to boot a 30-yard field goal to give a **3-0** lead. Everything seemed to be warming up for another big BYU win.

Then, disaster struck on the Cougars' second field goal drive. Sheide was blindsided by OSU tackle Phillip Dokes after he released his pass and was driven into the ground.

Gary got up but his right throwing arm was hanging limply at his side. He was done for the day, and the Cougars' hopes were sidelined with him.

Phillip Dokes makes a late hit on Gary Sheide
(BYU photo)

Uselman did come in and kick his second field goal to make the score, **6-0**.

But the Cougars' bowl game dream turned into a nightmare. Junior quarterback Mark Giles replaced Sheide but couldn't lead any further scoring drives.

The Cowboys, obviously, gathered themselves together with the dramatic turn of events. They squeezed out three scores against the stingy Cougar defense:

Running back Kenny Walker ran 12 yards for a tying touchdown. Abby Daigle's PAT made the score, **7-6**.

And that single point turned out to be all OSU

needed to claim the victory. They managed to add two more scores in the second half:

Daigle added a 42-yard field goal in the third period to boost the lead to 10-6.

Then the Cowboys "swiped" a page out of the BYU playbook, faking a run into the middle of the Cougar defense and completing a 40-yard touchdown pass to a wide- open Gerald Bain. The PAT failed.

Final Score: OSU 16, BYU 6

A Painful P.S.

Oklahoma State coach Jim Stanley said after the game, "Gary Sheide's injury had to have a great deal of influence on the outcome of the game. My heart goes out to them. I know how they feel."

Gary Sheide leaves the field after the Fiesta Bowl (BYU photo)

The coach's kind words lost their meaning years later. Sheide contended Oklahoma State placed a bounty on him to get him knocked out of the game and a former Cowboys player confirmed that was true a few years later.

The forgotten quarterback of BYU will finally be enshrined in Hall of Fame

By Doug Robinson

Deseret News

Sept 21, 2011

BYU announced this week that it will induct Gary Sheide into the school's Hall of Fame.

That's nice. Just one question: What took them so long?

Sheide's career ended in 1974 — and they're just getting around to putting him in the Hall?

Was there a filing problem? A clerical error?

Does Sheide deserve to be in the Hall? Duh. Was there ever even a debate, yet alone one that took 37 years?

Sheide will be introduced as an inductee during halftime of Friday's BYU-Central Florida game. He will be officially inducted at a ceremony the following day, thus correcting a ridiculous oversight.

"One of the guys from the Cougar Club called and asked me to send in some stuff and they'd consider me," says Sheide.

Are they kidding? Gary Sheide had to submit his credentials? Memo to Cougar Club: Try reading a newspaper. Here are Sheide's credentials:

- *Winner of the 1974 Sammy Baugh Trophy, awarded annually to the nation's best passer.*
- *Eighth in the 1974 Heisman Trophy balloting (with 12 first-place votes), the highest finish of any BYU player to that point and two places better than Cal's Steve Bartkowski, the first-team All-America quarterback that year.*
- *MVP of the Western Athletic Conference.*
- *Led BYU to the conference championship and a No. 15 national ranking.*
- *Led BYU to its first bowl invitation ever.*
- *Ranked No. 2 in the nation in passing in both 1973 and 1974, losing by one pass completion as a senior to Bartkowski, the No. 1 pick in the NFL draft (Sheide was the second quarterback drafted).*
- *Passed for 4,524 yards and 45 touchdowns in two seasons on just 594 attempts (his successors would throw more than 400 passes in just one season), completing 60 percent of his attempts.*

Sheide is The Forgotten Quarterback at BYU. He is to BYU quarterbacks what Ringo Starr was to the Beatles. Everyone remembers Nielsen, Wilson, McMahon, Young, Bosco, etc., but without Sheide none of those guys becomes a star and maybe the LaVell Edwards Era never happens.

It all started with Sheide, although someone forgot

to tell BYU. When I wrote about this subject in 2000, I called Edwards, who was just ending his career as BYU's coach. Apparently, he wasn't convinced that Sheide was forgotten because when I asked him about it, Edwards replied that Sheide had been included in a painting of BYU's great quarterbacks, which was hanging on the back wall of his office. As Edwards was saying this, he turned in his chair to give the painting a closer inspection.

"Wait, he's not in the picture," he said. "There's McMahon, Young, Detmer, Wilson, Bosco, Nielsen, ... but he's not in there."

The painting had been unveiled at a ceremony a couple years earlier, and all the old greats were invited to be honored. But not Sheide.

Now jump ahead to 2010. BYU hosted the so-called "Y. Quarterback Weekend" to honor BYU's great quarterbacks as part of a fund-raising event. It included, among other things, a golf tournament, a banquet and a halftime ceremony. The honorees were Steve Young, Jim McMahon, Steve Sarkisian, Robbie Boscoe, Ty Detmer, Marc Wilson, Virgil Carter and Gifford Nielsen. But no Sheide. He received an invitation — to buy a ticket and attend the banquet like everybody else

***BYU Great Quarterbacks Left to Right:** Virgil Carter ('63-'66), Gifford Nielsen ('73-'77), Marc Wilson ('77-'79), Jim McMahon ('77-'81), Steve Young ('80-'83), Robbie Bosco ('81-'85), Ty Detmer ('87-'91). **But: where is Gary Sheide?** (BYU photo)*

Deseret News columnist Lee Benson wrote about that snub and quoted Edwards saying this about Sheide: "He was one of the great ones; in my mind he's in the same category as all of them." Sheide thinks Benson's column is probably the reason BYU has finally decided to induct him into the Cougar Hall of Fame.

"I think Lee stirred the pot," says Sheide. "I loved it. Maybe that got the ball rolling."

Benson should know something about the subject. He wrote a book about BYU quarterbacks in 1988 — "And They Came to Pass." The first chapter was about Sheide.

Even before taking over as head coach, Edwards had determined that the only way the Cougars could win consistently was via the pass. During his first year, he used a running attack to utilize the skills of Pete Van Valkenburg, the nation's leading rusher, and the Cougars had a rare winning season (7-4). But a year later, he installed a pass attack with Sheide at quarterback. That launched the Cougars into a new era of winning football teams and prolific quarterbacks; they've never been the same since then. Sheide was the test pilot that proved the air game could win games nearly four decades later, the school has finally decided to induct him into its Hall of Fame. Sheide, a junior high P.E. teacher and business owner who lives in Highland, is clearly pleased by this turn of events. He has invited family members, friends and former teammates for the event, including former receivers Jay Miller and John Betham. Edwards will introduce him. This time he won't have to pay to get in.

PLAYBOOK FUNDAMENTAL THREE:

Build new and enduring capabilities that others don't have.

With Gary Sheide having graduated, the 1975, the Cougars had to manage another transition in its passing game. The downside to having a revolutionary passing game was it took time to get newcomers on board to skillfully make it work. Once again, the Cougars started the season 0-3 with losses to Bowling Green (21-23) at home, 17-21 at Colorado State, and 0-20 to Arizona State at Tempe.

The starting quarterback was returning letterman Mark Giles. Mark's Fiesta Bowl performance showed he was not a great fit with BYU's big-time passing game. Nonetheless, LaVell and quarterback coach Dwain Painter felt Mark deserved a shot at the starting job. Behind him were two inexperienced quarterbacks, sophomores Jeff Duva and Gifford Nielsen.

1975 GAME #4:

BYU 16, New Mexico 15
Date: October 3, 1975 – evening game
Location: Cougar Stadium
Weather: 40s° clear
Attendance: 30,978

First Half

This game began where the first three left off. New Mexico scored first as quarterback Steve Myer guided the Lobos 80 yards in six plays. He was three-for-three passing on the drive for 50 yards, including his 20-yard scoring pass to receiver Preston Dennard. Bob Berg's PAT was good. The **Lobos were up early, 7-0.**

Mark Giles was injured on the Cougars' first possession and was through for the night. Jeff Duva came in to replace him in his first appearance in a BYU game. Jeff also was an option-style quarterback and struggled in his debut, completing only five of 20 passes for 75 yards. He threw two interceptions.

Later in the quarter the Cougars were in punt formation and a high snap sailed into the end zone for a safety. **UNM 9, BYU 0.**

BYU continued to struggle without scoring until halftime. That made seven quarters in a row that the

Cougars had not scored a point.

Meanwhile. New Mexico's Bob Berg kicked a 37-yard field goal.

Halftime Score: UNM 12, BYU 0

Second Half

The BYU defense played a gritty first half and kept the scoreless Cougars within striking distance until late in the third quarter. In desperation the coaches turned to their third-string quarterback, sophomore Gifford Nielsen. "Giff" came on the field for the first time with 4:18 to go in the third.

Provo Herald sports editor Joe Watts described this way what happened next:

"It was almost like magic with Gifford Nielsen as the genie.

"He rubbed the magic lantern and suddenly the lifeless, going-through-the-motions BYU football team became a fighting, scrapping, determined-to-win group of gridders."

- Nielsen's first play was a 20-yard pass to Jeff Nilsson to the Lobo 48-yard line.
- Next, he ran an option play and kept the ball for a seven-yard gain. A UNM penalty moved the ball down to the Lobo 37.
- On the next play Giff scrambled out of the pocket, found running back Dave Lowry wide open downfield and fired a strike to

him. Lowry carried the mail into the end zone. Dave Taylor added the point after. **UNM 12, BYU 7.**

Nielsen was three-for-three, and the Cougars were back in the ball game with only 1:09 off the clock. But Gifford was not a one-drive wonder. Not by a long shot!

The Lobos got the ball next and, in the fourth quarter, moved from their 16-yard line to the BYU eight. The Cougars stiffened and UNM's Bob Berg kicked his second field goal of the night, a 30-yarder to make the score, **15-7,** for the visitors with only 11:48 remaining in the game.

The Lobos' only problem was – Giff would not go away. He moved the Cougars from their 20 to the Lobo 29 by completing two passes to Tom Dignan and two more to Jeff Blanc. Then he dropped back to pass, saw Blanc racing down the sideline behind all defenders, and fired a bomb into the end zone that Blanc grasped with a diving catch for the TD.

Count them: seven Nielsen passes, seven completions, two TDs. **UNM 15, BYU 13.**

Then Nielsen's conversion pass attempt to tie the game fell short. **UNM was still up, 15-13**. Time off the clock on this drive: 3:14. This was really BYU football!

There was still 8:33 left on the clock and the Cougar defenders were still crushing people! The

Lobos went three-and-out, and the Cougars had another chance with 7:09 remaining.

Moving cautiously down the field to the Lobo 13, Giff set the table for kicker Dave Taylor, who split the uprights with a field goal from 30 yards out to give the Cougars their first lead, **16-15,** with 1:46 to play.

Returned missionary Tim Halverson picked off his second Myer pass of the night to give the Cougars the ball on their own 35 with 1:27 remaining. This time the Cougar offense stalled, and the Lobos got the ball back again.

Moving quickly with only 32 seconds left, Myer connected with Gil Stewart on passes of 15 and 23 yards to set up Berg for a try for the game-winning field goal. Berg's kick with 10 seconds left was short of the mark. The Cougars had prevailed!

Final Score: BYU 16, UNM 15

	1st	2nd	3rd	4th	Final
UNM	9	3	0	3	15
BYU	0	0	7	9	16

Team Statistics	BYU	UNM
First Downs	23	19
Total Offense Yards	223	203

Rushing Yards	179	141
Passing Yards	223	209
Passes (Att.-Comp.1nt.)	34-15-2	35-16-2
TDs Passing	2	1
Punts	7-0	8-0
Fumbles – Lost	2-0	2-0
Penalties/Yards	12-92	12-116

UNM coach Bill Mondt said, "In a lot of ways this was the best football game we've played because we moved the ball well. We were just stopped by penalties.

"We only scored one touchdown, and that's not enough. Our pass defense was good, we were all over their receivers. But they just made fantastic catches. Nielsen was really hot and threw it in there.

"I don't think this was a bad game for us. We played hard and we played well, just not enough to win. It was one of those frustrating things. They couldn't stop us, we just stopped ourselves."

"We were beaten by a better football team tonight. BYU came out in the second half and beat us the whole half. Give BYU credit – they played like hell! Brigham Young is the finest team we've played yet.

"Blanc is a super kid, a great runner. He made a great catch on that touchdown."

LaVell Edwards said, "Our game plan was to try and control the ball, and Duva is the same type quarterback as Giles, so it didn't change. But once we got behind, we had to throw and so did they. Our kids were pressing early in the game. We weren't trying to play defensively; we were just too tight.

"(Nielsen) was the key. He did a super job."

Cougar Offense Leaders

- **Gifford Nielsen** was 10 of 12 passing for 148 yards and two TDs.
- **Jeff Blanc** carried 21 times for 106 yards and also caught four passes for 48 yards and one TD.
- **Dave Lowry** carried 10 times for 30 yards and also caught one pass for 37 yards and one TD.
- **Tom Dignan** caught four passes for 46 yards.
- **Jeff Nilsson** caught two passes for 38 yards.

Nielsen's 10 for 12 passing (.833 percentage) was a new WAC record for one game.

Cougar Defense Leaders

- **Stan Varner** had 11 tackles (four solo, two for loss) and one interception.

- **Sid Smith** had eight tackles (four solo).
- **Clark Carlson** had seven tackles (two solo, two for loss).
- **Mekeli Ieremia** had six tackles (one solo) and two pass break ups.
- **Craig Jensen** had five tackles (four solo).
- **Marcus Kanahele** had five tackles, (four solo).
- **Mark Terranova** had two kickoff returns for 64 yards.

Author's Time Out: *The dynamics of this game illustrate challenges facing any system (person, team, or organization): to balance its steady state with the need for change. A steady state is a steady pattern or process that follows a proven, functional routine.*

Our physical bodies balance their steady state (body temperature of 98.6° Fahrenheit) almost automatically. The need for change comes when the body gets too hot (we sweat) or too cold (we seek more warmth).

Now back to BYU football in 1975. The steady state for BYU's new offense system had proven its value in strong passing attacks in '73 and '74. But now in '75:

- The number one and number two quarterbacks weren't good passers. They were option quarterbacks whose strengths were running the ball.

- Their quarterback coach also favored the option offense because he was more comfortable with it.
- LaVell believed in delegating responsibilities to his assistants and supporting their leadership on his staff.

Bottom line: despite BYU's great results of the '73-'74 passing game, those calling the shots in early '75 favored the option offense. They relegated their lone passing quarterback to third string on what was supposed to be a passing attack.

What criteria were these coaches using when they evaluated the three quarterbacks in practices? The best runner? The best passer?

AUTHOR'S NOTE: *This is also an example of a very typical tendency in teams and organizations: When all else fails, people rely on their own comfort zone rather than on a "new order of things." Even though the option offense started off 0-3-1 in 1974 and was 0-3 in 1975 (and even scoreless in its last seven quarters) heading into game number four with New Mexico, the coach's preferred option offense remained the game plan.*

- *Professor Russell Ackoff of the University of Pennsylvania cited research at UCLA, MIT, and Cal-Berkeley that is relevant here. These research findings demonstrated:*

- *Some people may not see the pattern (or steady state) in the current order of things.*
- *Some may insist the real pattern is what they see (or want to see), not what is actually there.*
- *Some may ignore the real pattern when it is revealed – especially if it disturbs their comfort zone.*

One commonly cited definition of insanity is, "Doing the same thing over and over again and expecting different results." While not exactly medically accurate, this saying does describe why many of our endeavors fall short. "Doing the same thing over and over again" is a steady-state process. But if it no longer delivers proven, functional results, a "new order of things" might be required.

I have seen this happen all too often with some of my business clients in different industries and nations. Some were stuck in process and culture patterns that were causing them to lose in the marketplace. When we introduced methods to help them define "a newer and better order of things," some managers were uncomfortable with our recommendations. But those, who applied what we suggested, often saw their results improve to be better than they thought was possible.

Consider what happened after a great passer (Gifford Nielsen) became the full-time starter, not only leading the Cougars to win six of their last eight games in '75, but also in his two years in '76 (9-2) and '77 (9-2) when he was named an All-American.

What BYU needed was to expand the *process* into a *system* that could roll on so that one quarterback's absence wouldn't derail it.

The next time the Cougars needed a replacement quarterback (1977), they would have another passer-in-waiting who was able to step up. And that inaugurated the improved *system* – the "factory" that earned BYU the reputation as "Quarterback U."

LaVell "supervises" his Quarterback Factory.
(Mark Philbrick BYU photo)

Now, to put a few finishing touches on 1975.

GAME #5:

BYU 28, Air Force 14

Date: October 11, 1975
Location: Cougar Stadium
Weather: Temperature low 60s with occasional gusty winds
Attendance: 30,246

The visiting Falcons tested the resolve of both the BYU players and their fans. Air Force was yielding only 64.7 passing yards/game and a total passing yardage of 259 yards in their three previous games. Gifford Nielsen gained 229 yards in this game alone. But the BYU fans were in suspense until the fourth quarter before the Cougars posted their first lead on the scoreboard.

First Half

In the first quarter Air Force moved 52 yards in nine plays for its first touchdown. Ken Wood ran the ball in from the five-yard line and Dave Lawson added the extra point for a **7-0 Air Force lead** with 9:16 left in the first quarter.

BYU had three valiant efforts to erase the Falcon lead, but a pass interception at the goal line, and a missed field goal kept them behind until Jeff Blanc scored on a seven-yard run to tie things up at **7-7**.

Ken Wood scored another TD for the Air Force

to give it a **14-7** halftime lead. But that was the last bright spot for the visitors in this game. Gifford Nielsen and the Cougars were going to bust things wide open in the second half.

Second Half

In his first quarterback venture as the Cougars' full-time starter, Gifford Nielsen came roaring back like he did the week before against New Mexico.

Early in the third quarter Stan Varner recovered a Falcon fumble at the AFA 43-yard line. Dave Lowry and Jeff Blanc combined for 14 yards on the ground and Giff connected with Jeff Nilsson first for 18 yards and then for the final 10-yard touchdown. Dave Taylor's PAT was good. **Game tied at 14 all.**

In the fourth quarter Jeff Blanc was sidelined with an injury and Charlie Ah You filled in capably on two short TD runs to make the **Final Score: BYU 28, Air Force 14.**

	1st	**2nd**	**3rd**	**4th**	**Final**
AFA	**7**	**7**	**0**	**0**	**14**
BYU	**0**	**7**	**7**	**14**	**28**

Team Statistics	**BYU**	**AFA**
First downs	**20**	**24**

Total Offense Yards	355	344
Rushing Yards	126	259
Passing Yards	229	85
Passes (Att.-Comp.1nt.)	19-14-229	23-8-3
TDs Passing	1	0
Points	2-78	3-148
Fumbles – Lost	1-1	2-1
Penalties/Yards	10-74	7-65

Cougar Offense Leaders

- **Gifford Nielsen** was 14-19-1 passing for 229 yards and one TD.
- **John VanDerWouden** caught five passes for 109 yards.
- **Jeff Nilsson** caught seven passes for 95 yards and one TD.
- **Jeff Blanc** had 18 carries for 75 yards and one TD.
- **Charlie Ah You** ran for two TDs.

Cougar Defense Leaders (not available)

GAME #6

BYU 33, Wyoming 20
Date: October 25, 1975
Location: War Memorial Stadium, at Laramie
Weather: Temperature 32°; winds of 18-25 miles per hour
Attendance: 16,297

First Half

Despite the clear, sunny skies overhead, the field was frigid and icy with wind chill below freezing for most of the game. But the first quarter gave the impression the game would be a hot offensive show. Wyoming actually led the Cougars 20-13 at the end of the first quarter. The Cowboys scored on their first three possessions.

Cornerback Sam Martin got the Cowboys started early when he intercepted a Gifford Nielsen pass near the Wyoming 20 and then returned it 58 yards to the Cougar 32. Freshman quarterback Don Clayton ran two keepers to score Wyoming's first six points. Joe Marion added the extra point, and it was, **7-0** for the Cowpokes.

Not to be outdone, BYU marched 80 yards in nine plays, the key being the 41-yard pass from Nielsen to flanker John VanDerWouden. Shortly thereafter, the Nielsen-VanDerWouden connection struck again for an eight-yard TD. Dave Taylor's PAT tied the score **7-7**.

Clayton was off to the races again for Wyoming as he hit split end John Arnold on a 71-yard scoring pass, set up by runs on the previous four plays. Marion's kick was good again for the **Cowboys' 14-7 lead.**

The Cougars kept pace with the fireworks. Dave Lowry broke loose for a 57-yard run to the Wyoming 18. A couple of plays later, Jeff Blanc scored from the UW 4. The PAT was no good due to a fumbled snap. **Wyoming 14, BYU 13**.

Now it was Clayton's turn to work some magic, and he was not to be outdone. He mixed six running plays from the Wishbone formation and then sprung the surprise – a wide-open running back Andy Dixon in the left flat. Dixon took Clayton's pass and then raced 41 yards for the touchdown. Marion's PAT was wide, leaving the **Pokes' lead at 20-13**.

And that's the way the first quarter ended.

The Cougars failed to move the ball as the second quarter opened. Mark Giles punted the ball to the Wyoming 18. A few plays later the versatile Clayton fumbled the ball on his own 36 and BYU linebacker Sid Smith smothered it.

From there Jeff Blanc carried the load, carrying the ball five straight times and scoring from the one-yard line. Taylor's PAT was good, and it was **20-20.**

Then the Cougars did enough to salt away the victory. Blanc scored on a seven-yard run and Dave Taylor kicked a 35-yard field goal.

Jeff Blanc was unreal in this half. He ran for 158 yards on 25 carries and scored three TDs. He also caught two passes for 29 yards.

Halftime Score: BYU 30, UW 20

The only score by either team in the second half was Taylor's third quarter, 27-yard field goal.

Final Score: BYU 33, Wyoming 20.

The Cougars evened their season record to 3-3 and their WAC record to 2-2.

This was truly a historic win – only the second BYU win in Laramie since World War II.

	1st	2nd	3rd	4th	Final
BYU	13	17	3	0	33
Wyoming	20	0	0	0	20

Team Statistics	BYU	Wyoming
First Downs	26	14
Total Offense Yards	557	329

Rushing Yards	398	167
Passing Yards	159	162
Passes (Att.-Comp.1nt.)	19-9-1	12-6-2
Tds Passing	1	2
Punts	4-150	5-192
Fumbles – Lost	3-2	7-4
Penalties/Yards	7-89	5-19

Cougar Offense Leaders

- **Jeff Blanc** carried 36 times for 215 yards and three TDs and also caught two passes for 29 yards.
- **Gifford Nielsen** completed nine of 19 passes for 159 yards with one interception and one TD.
- **Dave Lowry** rushed nine times for 101 yards and caught two passes for 48 yards.
- **John VanDerWouden** had two catches for 49 yards and one TD.
- **Todd Christensen** carried 10 times for 48 yards and also caught one pass for 15 yards.

Cougar Defense Leaders

- **Sid Smith** had nine tackles (four solo, one for loss), one sack and one fumble recovery.
- **Blake Murdock** had eight tackles (four solo).
- **Craig Jensen** had seven tackles (five solo).
- **Dana Wilgar** had six tackles (three solo).
- **Bill Rice** had six tackles (one solo).
- **Mekeli Ieremia** had four tackles (one for loss) and one sack.
- **Gary Shaw and Mark McCluskey** each had one interception.

GAME #9:
BYU 51, Utah 20
Date: November 15, 1975
Location: Cougar Stadium
Weather: Temperature 47° clear
Attendance: 28,265

The annual duel to determine bragging rights in this lopsided rivalry showed, in the words of Provo Herald Sports Editor Joe Watts, *"Now the lop is on the other side."*

The Cougars established new records in some important categories:

- They won their fourth straight game against the Utes.

- The 51 points scored by the Cougars was the most they had ever scored against the Utes – *and more than they had tallied in the first 16 years of the rivalry.*
- The 51-20 was the widest victory margin.
- This year's 51 points was more than either of the two previous wins (46 and 48).

Here are some of the details behind this memorable game:

First Half

Gifford Nielsen started off the juggernaut with a 46-yard touchdown pass to John VanDerWouden. After that, senior Mark Uselman added the extra point and kicked back-to-back 47-yard field goals. It was, **13-0, for BYU** after one quarter.

In the second quarter the Utes fumbled the ball away three times inside their own 25-yard line. The grateful Cougars scored each time. Stan Varner scooped up the first one at the one. Jeff Blanc scored on the Cougars' first play. Uselman's PAT was no good. **BYU 19, Utah 0**

A few minutes later, Utah fumbled again, and Cougar Bill Rice recovered on the Utes 23. Flanker Bob Biddy scored after recovering teammate Brian Billick's fumble–in the air and running it in from the 11. The two-point PAT attempt was good on Nielsen's pass to Billick. That made the score **27-0.**

Another Utah fumble was recovered by Varner at the Utah 18 and with only 48 seconds on the clock. Uselman kicked his third field goal – this one was "only" a 44-yarder.

Halftime Score: BYU 30, 0 Utah 0

Second Half

The Cougars didn't slow down any in the second half. They moved 52 yards in nine plays to open the third quarter. Nielsen scored from the one. The PAT was good, increasing the BYU advantage to **37-0**. Midway through the third quarter Varner intercepted a pass that was batted in the air and BYU took over at the Ute 19. Charlie Ah You scored from there. Uselman added the extra point for a **44-0** lead.

The Utes answered by putting quarterback Homer Warner into the game. A slim 5'10" 165 lb. sparkplug, Warner passed and scrambled the Utes to two quick touchdowns to bring them closer, **44-14,** at the end of the third quarter.

The Utes scored again in the fourth quarter when Kevin Harrison blocked a Cougar field goal and ran it back 86 yards for a touchdown. The two-point PAT failed, leaving the score, **44-20**.

Then BYU freshman Clay Blackwell capped off the day for the Cougars with a seven-yard TD run. Uselman's PAT was good. (Clay was the first black player in BYU history to score a touchdown.)

Final score: BYU 51, Utah 20

	1st	2nd	3rd	4th	Final
UTAH	0	0	14	6	20
BYU	13	17	14	7	51

Team Statistics	BYU	Utah
First Downs	21	15
Total Offense Yards	412	231
Rushing Yards	250	14
Passing Yards	162	217
Passes (Att.-Comp.1nt.)	21-12-2	29-15-4
TDs Passing	1	1
Punts	4-150	5-192
Fumbles – Lost	3-2	7-4
Penalties/Yards	7-89	5-19

BYU Offense Leaders

- **Gifford Nielsen** completed 10 passes in 15 attempts for 150 yards with one interception and one TD.
- **Charley Ah You** carried 16 times for 77 yards and one TD.
- **Jeff Blanc** carried 13 times for 65 yards and one TD.
- **John VanDerWouden** caught four passes for 73 yards and one TD.
- **Brian Billick** caught two passes for 27 yards.
- **Mike House** caught two passes for 26 yards.

BYU Defense Leaders

- **Stan Varner** had six tackles (two solo, two for loss), two fumble recoveries, and one interception.
- **Chuck Carlson** had five tackles (four solo) and one pass breakup.
- **Steve Dewey** had five tackles (two solo).
- **Blake Murdock** had four tackles (three solo) and one fumble recovery.
- **Phil Jensen** had three tackles (two solo) and one pass breakup.
- **Gary Shaw** had two tackles (one solo) and two interceptions.

PLAYBOOK FUNDAMENTAL FOUR:

Solve problems at their source

At the end of the 1975 season, one of LaVell's top priorities was to address the mismatch between his quarterbacks/receivers coach Dwain Painter and the BYU passing game plan.

LaVell did this the way you might hope he would: he supported Dwain in finding another program that was more in tune with his preferences. Dwain was hired as the quarterbacks and receivers coach at UCLA, a team geared around an option-type offense. Both Dwain and the Bruins benefitted from the move.

Next, BYU needed to solve the passing game problem at its roots. With the benefit of 20-20 hindsight, LaVell learned the selection process to fill the gap left by Dewey Warren's departure didn't dig deep enough to discover someone whose passions really were connected with the BYU aerial attack.

Author's Note: *I once was talking to a prospective employee about joining our firm in a leadership position. I asked this candidate what he thought about our firm's flagship brand. He replied, "I don't have a* *problem with it." This reply was not good enough. We didn't hire the candidate.* ***"Not having a problem" is a much weaker position than having a deep passion.*** *Such a weakness at any point in the chain weakens that chain.*

When you are in the early, formative stages of building a new innovative system, you have to make sure that new associates are as passionate as you are about the "new order of things."

LaVell began his search for a coach who identified deeply with the BYU offense. This search led him to Doug Scovil, a coach who was from a branch on the same coaching tree that shaped LaVell's program.

Doug coached Navy quarterback Roger Staubach in 1963 when Staubach won the Heisman Trophy. From 1971-75 Doug was the quarterback coach for the NFL's San Francisco 49ers who were coached by Bill Walsh. Walsh, you remember, was an early collaborator with BYU's coach Dewey Warren, the originator of the BYU approach.

It didn't take long for LaVell to know Doug was the right one to be the new BYU offensive coordinator/quarterback coach. Doug knew LaVell had a great quarterback and had developed a team waiting to soar with the right coaching.

Digression: the realities of being a head football coach

Forgive this digression, but *solving problems at their source* was very crucial in this phase of LaVell's leadership. Occasionally you may see a head coach who appears to be the hub of every action in a football game: giving assistant coaches their priorities for the upcoming game, personally huddling with the players on the sidelines, calling the plays, making substitutions, and evaluating past games.

Contrast this with LaVell's actions during a game. Most of the time he was on the sideline wearing his famous "LaVell Face." Occasionally he was involved in discussions between an assistant coach and a player. He might confer with his assistants in the press box via a headset or on the sideline. He might give some instructions to one player.

But the assistant coaches were the highly active ones as the game progressed.

The point is the game had become much more complex – with sophisticated changes and swift position adjustments required – that one coach couldn't do it all like a head coach could in the 1930s. The coaching *team* now became essential for a winning program. Each assistant had to be able to solve problems at their source.

Development must take place at *all levels* on a team:

(Player by Player)

(Position by Position)

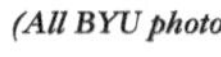
(All BYU photos)

(Play by Play)

(Aligning functions with each other)

Author's Note: *In 1972 I interviewed LaVell and each of his assistant coaches at the beginning of his inaugural season as head coach. One thing each assistant mentioned to me was how much they appreciated LaVell giving them real responsibility to develop their strategy, to coach their function and develop their players – and to get agreement from the coaching team in building an overall team plan. LaVell also was known for keeping his assistants for a number of years. Most of his departures only left when greater opportunities came their way.*

BYU alum and NFL vet Brad Oates told me, "One of the things that always impressed other head coaches about LaVell was that he let his assistant coaches do the coaching. It was one of his hallmarks to 'surround yourself with people who are better than yourself.' That's why his coaching tree is so robust."

LaVell's Assistant Coach Mainstays

Great coaches who stick together for many years can solve problems that might block others. Here are some of LaVell's assistant coaches who were on his staff for several years:

Dave Kragthorpe: offensive coordinator/ offensive line/assistant coach 1972-79

Dave Kragthorpe

Coached All-American Gordon Gravelle, All-WAC players Paul Howard, Brad Oates, Lloyd Fairbanks, Orrin Olsen, Dave Hubbard, Lance Reynolds, Keith Uperesa, Tom Bell, Al Gaspard, Nick Eyre, Danny Hansen, and Scott Nielson.

After BYU: Head coach at South Dakota State (1981 Division I-AA national champions), Idaho State, and Oregon State

Dick Felt: defensive backs, defensive coordinator 1972-93

- Coached 22 All-Conference players: Dave Atkinson, Dan Hansen, Gary Shaw, Dana Wilgar, Jason Morrell Coloma, John Neal, Bill Schoepflin, Mark Brady, Tom Holmoe, Jon Young, Kyle, Rodney Thomas, Troy Long, Rodney Rice, Eric Bergeson, Brian Mitchell, Dewey Gray, Patrick Mitchell, Tim McTyer, Omarr Morgan, Brian Gray, and Jared Lee.

Tom Ramage : defensive line 1973-2000

Coached 23 All-Conference players: Keith Rivera, Paul Winford, Bill Rice, Mekeli Ieremia, Mat Mendenhall, Ross Varner, Glen Titensor, Brad Anae, Chuck Ehin, Mike Morgan, Brandon Flint, Jim Herrmann, Jason Buck, Shawn Knight, David Futrell, Rich Kaufusi, Lenny Gomes, Randy Brock, John Raass, Henry Bloomfield, Darren Yancy, Byron Frisch, and Setema Gali.

Norm Chow: recruiter, quarterbacks& wide receivers, offensive coordinator, assistant head coach 1975-99

Coached Heisman Trophy winner Ty Detmer and Davey O'Brien award winners Ty Detmer, Steve Young, and Jim McMahon.

Coached All-Conference receivers Brian Billick, Mike Chorister, Lloyd Jones, Clay Brown, Dan Plater, Gordon Hudson, Glen Kozlowski, David Mills, Mark Bellini, Trevor Molina, Chuck Cutler, Andy Brice, Byron Rex, Chris Smith Eric Drage, Chad Lewis, Itula Mili, and Margin Hooks.

Named top assistant coach of the year by the American Football Foundation.

Roger French: offensive coordinator/ offensive line: 1980-2000

Coached 29 All-Conference players: Clay Brown, Nick Eyre, Calvin Close, Gordon Hudson **Coached**, Bart Oates, Lloyd Eldredge, Vince Stroth, Rex Burningham, David Mills,, Dave Wright, John Borgia, Brian White, Chris Smith, Neal Fort, Robert Stephens, Bryan May, Byron Rex, Garry Pay, Mike Empey, Evan Pilgrim, Chad Lewis, Larry Moore, Itula Mili, John Tait, and Matt Johnson.

- Mo Elewonibi won the Outland Trophy.
- 46 of Roger's players went into the NFL.

Doug Scovil: offensive coordinator, quarterbacks 1976-77, '79-80

Coached 1963 Heisman Trophy winner Roger Staubach at the U.S. Naval Academy.

Coached BYU All-Americans Gifford Nielsen, Marc Wilson, and..Jim McMahon.

aubach at the U.S. Naval Academy.

Mike Holmgren: quarterbacks 1982-85

Coached BYU's passing game to the NCAA football title in 1984. He helped develop two future NFL quarterbacks Steve Young, Robbie Bosco. He also mentored graduate assistant Andy Reid.

Lance Reynolds: running back, offensive coordinator, assistant head coach 1979-2000

Coached All-Conference running backs Lakei Heimuli and Jamal Willis.
Coached..11 NFL players.
Coached four 1,000 yard rushers: Ronney Jenkins, Brian McKenzie, Jamal Willis and Vai Sikahema.

Ken Schmidt: linebackers, defensive coordinator, assistant head coach 1982-2000

Coached 13 All-Conference players:Todd Shell, Marc Allen, Kurt Gouveia, Leon White, Thor Saldona, Bob Davis, Alema Fitisemanu, Rock Biegel, Shad Hansen, Todd Herget, Shay Muirbrook, Rob Morris, and Justin Ena.
Coached eight NFL players.

Mel Olson: running backs, offensive line, academic coordinator: 1972-1989

Coached All-Americans Trevor Matich and Bart Oates.

Once again, LaVell was ahead of his time – this time by building a strong coaching team.

Solving problems in real time

Sometimes there might be a situation that requires a "modification" of the formation or play that was called in the huddle. One possible modification is to call an audible – changing the play based on what you see the defense (or offense) is planning to do.

I saw a situation years ago that called for an audible. In those days the Cougars' tendency was to open their first drive in the second half with a fullback draw. This play was very effective against a hard charging pass rush, but often a real loser against a normal defense. I was seated in a booth in Cougar

Stadium as the BYU offense began its first drive of the second half. Hoping in my mind that the Cougars wouldn't call the draw, I heard a former Cougar and NFL star sitting in our booth predict loudly, "Fullback draw."

Sure enough, it was a draw and the defense pounced on the runner and dropped him for a loss. I asked the NFL star: "Now, if you knew it was going to be a draw play, and the defense obviously knew it was going to be a draw, why did we run the draw?"

He said, *"In the huddle in those situations we would tell the quarterback, 'Audible out! Audible out!' But we never did."*

Coaches understandably are uncomfortable when others second-guess their play calls. But we all have myopic blind spots – even great coaches like LaVell Edwards, Doug Scovil, and Norm Chow.

Jim McMahon tells of one such situation in the famous 1980 "Miracle" Holiday Bowl against Southern Methodist University.

Jim McMahon "audibled" in the fourth quarter:

"We're down 19 points…and there are about nine minutes left in the game. We're fourth and one around midfield. We hadn't really stopped them all night long. Eric Dickerson and Craig James both had big nights.

"And they (BYU coaches) send the punting team

in… I said, 'If we kick now, we've got no shot.' I'm not going out just giving up…I wouldn't get off the field. I told the offense to huddle up. We had to burn a timeout because I wouldn't come off the field.

"And when I did, I remember calmly (?) explaining to the coaching staff what was going on. I said, 'At least give us a shot to do something.' And I remember LaVell and Doug Scovil looking at each other like they didn't know what to do. I said 'OK, we'll take care of this.' It was fourth down and one. If you can't make one yard, you don't deserve to win."

LaVell's report of the conversation to reporters was slightly different than Jim's: "What Jim said you couldn't print. We talked about it and decided to go for it."

Jim again, "I called the play at the line of scrimmage. *And for some reason they're not covering Clay Brown, the best tight end in the country.* He's got a linebacker over him and that's it."

McMahon hit Brown for 12 yards and the first down. The Cougars went down and scored a touchdown.

As you probably remember, there was much more that happened in the last four minutes of that pulse-pounding game. But McMahon's audible sparked the flame that fueled the "Miracle."

Author's Note: *The BIG question: who is in the best position to call such an audible?*

Should a coach allow a player to call an audible? There is no automatic answer to this question. It's a judgment call –more art than science.

In most business circles, the person at the top of the organization has the "authority" to make the decision. For some problems the needed knowledge and experience to solve them are only at the top – making the "top-down" decision the best choice. But the source of many other problems might be far lower in the organization. Those at the top may not have the necessary knowledge and experience to solve **those problems***. Thus, some "bottom-up" decisions (like McMahon did in the Miracle Bowl) offer better solutions.*

This is one of the great frustrations with a bureaucracy: too often it moves decisions far away from those who really understand and have a "feel" for the problem and puts those decisions in the hands of those who are in reality less experienced and skilled in solving **those problems** *– but may be at the top of the decision-making chain.*

Football coaches are no different than corporate CEOs. Fortunately, none of these executives today need rely solely on their own judgment to solve sticky problems.

Analytics Comes to Football

In recent years a new technology has been proving to be very valuable. This is the technology of analytics: a field of computer science that uses math, statistics, and machine learning to find meaningful patterns in data. A data pattern may highlight a top-down, or bottom-up, or some totally new alternative.

For example, one of my friends and colleagues has become one of the world's leading experts in the field of analytics. He has taught courses on it in top business schools and has done work with many large organizations. Two examples he related to me:

- Analytics of a city's traffic patterns can predict with 95 per cent accuracy where and when the next serious automobile accident will occur in that city.
- Working with government agencies, analytics consultants were able to identify and eliminate 200 terrorist cells before they could strike.

Such tools can help football coaches anticipate what the other team will do and consider how to counter their moves. BYU, like many other NCAA schools, now employs analytics coaches to help their teams better understand and adjust to what their opponents are doing.

Coaching the 1976 Season

Doug Scovil was the missing piece to the puzzle that would make a difference in BYU's fortunes in 1976.

What happened when devotee Scovil was matched with future All-American quarterback Gifford Nielsen? Like most new start-ups, it didn't make headlines right out of the starting gate, but soon thereafter it became a roaring success.

1976 Game #1: Kansas State 13, BYU 3

Date: September 11, 1976
Location: KSU Stadium @ Manhattan
Weather: Temperature 80s° and very windy
Attendance: 27,100

The Cougars traveled to Manhattan, Kansas for their opener with the Kansas State Wildcats. The BYU team certainly had been giving full attention to restoring its passing attack, but that didn't mean it would be in place completely for the first game.

And it wasn't.

Kansas State's defense frustrated the Cougars all day and a constant 25 miles-per-hour wind impeded the BYU passing attack. Gifford Nielsen competed 15 of 29 passes for 142 yards and no touchdowns. He had two passes intercepted. KSU's linebackers were dropping back and helping to blanket the BYU receivers.

While Nielsen and the offense were struggling when they had the ball, they also gave two gifts to Kansas State's offense that put 10 points on the scoreboard. First, on a fourth-down Cougar punt attempt, the snap was low, and freshman Perry Winder was hit as he scooped up the pigskin at the Cougar one, turning the ball over to KSU. The Wildcats' Tony Brown took it in on the first play. Bill Sinovic added the extra point to make it **7-0** and the home crowd was going wild!

In the second quarter with the wind at his back, Sinovic attempted a 58-yard field goal. The ball flew toward the goal post, hit the cross bar, and flopped over the top for another three points, **10-0,** for the Wildcats. And that was the ball game.

BYU's Dave Taylor kicked a 23-yard field goal in the third quarter for the Cougars' only points of the day.

Sinovic then made his final great contribution with a 48-yard field goal.

Final Score, KSU 13, BYU 3

	1st	2nd	3rd	4th	Final
BYU	0	0	3	0	3
KSU	7	3	0	3	13

Team Statistics	BYU	KSU
First Downs	12	7
Total Offense Yards	219	155
Rushing Yards	77	137
Passing Yards	142	18
Passes (Att.-Comp.1nt.)	29-15-2	7-3-0
TDs Passing	0	0
Punts	7-237	11-404
Fumbles – Lost	2-2	3-1
Penalties – Yards	4-36	7-76

This outcome was the farthest thing from what the Cougars had expected to experience.

Gifford Nielsen summed up his feelings in the Cougars' post-game locker room, "I can't tell you what happened today, but I still think we have a very good offense. Next week will be different. Next week we are going to make up for today. Next week we are going to put some points on the board against Colorado State."

P.S. Footnotes: How would you feel if you knew at the time that KSU would win only *this one game* in 1976? Could you have predicted then that this BYU team would post the most wins (nine) in one season in BYU history?

Based on the results of this season opener, these two outcomes were totally unpredictable!

And that's why they *play* the game.

Cougar Offense Leaders

- **Dave Taylor** had a 23-yard field goal.
- **Gifford Nielsen** completed 15 of 29 passes for 142 yards with two interceptions and no TDs.
- **Todd Christensen** had 35 yards rushing and six catches for 24 yards.
- **Johnny VanDerWouden** had three catches for 47 yards.
- **Roger Gourley** had 35 yards rushing.
- **Jeff Blanc** had 30 yards rushing.

Cougar Defense Leaders

- **Mekeli Ieremia** had 11 tackles (one solo, one for loss).
- **Bill Rice** had 10 tackles (four solo).
- **Ross Varner** had nine tackles (one solo, two for loss).
- **Markus Kanahele** had nine tackles (two solo)
- **Dana Wilgar** had eight tackles (two solo).
- **Blake Murdock** had seven tackles (two solo).
- **Rod Wood, Larry Miller, Steve Dewey, Gary Kama, and Marc Swenson** each had one tackle for loss.

Game #2:
BYU 42, Colorado State 18
Date: September 18, 1976
Location: Cougar Stadium – evening game
Weather: Temperature 60s° and clear
Attendance: 33,013

Colorado State was next on the Cougar schedule. LaVell Edwards had never beaten the Rams' coach Sarkis (Sark) Arslanian since taking over the helm at BYU. After the frustrating loss to KSU the week before, many wondered how the team would respond.

The night before the game, Cougar running

backs Jeff Blanc and Dave Lowry walked into a BYU Hall of Fame banquet on campus and announced:

"Things are going to be different this week. We are really ready for Colorado State," Blanc said.

Then it was Lowry's turn, *"We are ready. We are really ready for them."*

A record home-opener crowd of 33,013 was on hand the next night in Cougar Stadium. Everyone wanted to see the predictions fulfilled on the scoreboard by the end of the night.

First Half

BYU started on its own 20-yard line after receiving the opening kickoff. The offense machine went 80 yards in 15 plays and drew first blood when Gifford Nielsen hit Jeff Nilsson with a nine-yard touchdown pass. Dave Taylor kicked the extra point and the Cougars were up, **7-0**.

Then it was Déjà vu all over again as CSU struck back and took the lead. Jeff Blanc fumbled a punt later in the first quarter and the Rams recovered it on the BYU 38. They moved toward the end zone, helped substantially by a Cougar pass interference penalty. Tailback Mark Davis scored from the six. Then the crafty Arslanian called for a very unconventional extra point try.

CSU's kicking team was positioned on the far side of the field away from kicker Tom Drake and his holder. A bewildered BYU defense lined up across from the kicker. The ball was then snapped clear across the field to quarterback Dan Graham, who ran untouched into the end zone for a two-point conversion. CSU was in the lead, **8-7**!

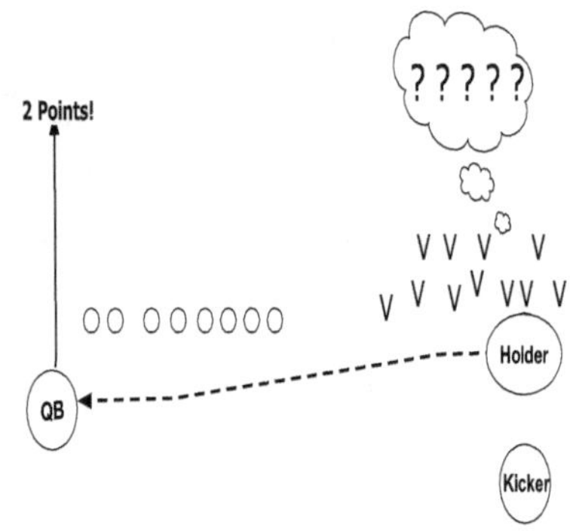

Late in the second quarter, another Cougar fumble led to a CSU score. A bad pitch to Blanc caused his fumble and the Rams' Keith King recovered it on the BYU 22. Another pass interference penalty gave the Rams the ball on the one. Halfback Ron Harris scored, and Drake's "conventional" extra point was good for a **15-7** lead with 4:30 to go in the half. Now it was time for Dave Lowry to put up or shut up. Dave kept his word with a stunning 59-yard kickoff return to the CSU 35-yard line. From there, Nielsen found flanker Johnny VanDerWouden open for a touchdown. He also hit Mike Chronister for the two-point conversion to tie things up, **15-15**.

But the Cougars weren't resting at that point. They forced another CSU punt in the waning minutes of the half and moved 65 yards in nine plays for another touchdown. The Cougars were on fire! Nielsen hitting Chronister for 11 yards, Lowry running for nine, Nielsen finishing the drive with two passes to VanDerWouden: a 14-yarder to the 26 and then the TD pass from there. Taylor's PAT was good.

Halftime score: BYU 22, CSU 15

Second Half

Dave Taylor and Tom Drake traded field goals in the third period. Taylor's 38-yarder moved the score to **25-15 for BYU**. Drake's 42-yarder tightened things up at, **25-18**, but that finished the scoring for the Rams. But the Cougars reloaded and had a big fourth quarter:

- VanDerWouden caught Nielsen's 10-yard toss and Taylor's PAT made it, **32-18.**
- Taylor's field goal (21 yards this time) widened the gap to **35-18 for BYU.**
- Then VanDerWouden finished his BYU record-setting night (four TD receptions in one game) catching backup quarterback Terry McEwen's 17-yard touchdown pass. Taylor's PAT rounded out the scoring for the night.

Final Score: BYU 42, CSU 18

	1st	2nd	3rd	4th	Final
CSU	8	7	3	0	18
BYU	7	15	3	17	42

Team Statistics	BYU	CSU
First Downs	17	20
Total Offense Yards	306	259
Rushing Yards	03	114
Passing Yards	213	145
Passes (Att.-Comp.Int.)	37-16-1	29-10-4
TDs Passing	5	0
Punts	8-366	6-237
Penalties – Yards	10-127	13-101

LaVell Edwards had finally beaten his nemesis, and his Cougars were 1-0 in the new conference season.

CSU coach Sark Arslanian said, "BYU was ready to play, and we weren't. They have an excellent team.

They will, without a doubt, be a contender for the Fiesta Bowl."

LaVell Edwards said, "The two touchdowns at the end of the first half really turned things around and Lowry's return was key. It feels very good to beat Sarkisian, but more than that, we really needed this one. The kids have been under a lot of pressure because so much has been said of our slow starts."

The Cougars' next game was in Tucson to take on the Arizona Wildcats, one of the teams favored to win the WAC that season.

Game #3:
BYU 23, Arizona 16
Date: September 25, 1976
Location: Arizona Stadium @ Tucson
Weather: Temperature 60s° and rainy
Attendance: 31,000

Normally a late September night game in southern Arizona would be a dry, pleasant experience. But not this time. For this year's BYU-Arizona football duel, the weather dialed up a steady rainstorm that started an hour before the game and continued to the final gun with only a few very short pauses.

A slippery time was had by all.

Weather notwithstanding, the game was a real nail biter dominated by kicking rather than other offensive tools – except for the grand finale.

First Half

Arizona had a three-and-out after taking the opening kickoff. Wid Knight's punt of only 31 yards gave the Cougars the ball on their own 41. After a few short plays, surrounding Jeff Blanc's 32-yard run, Dave Taylor kicked a 36-yard field goal for the Cougars' first lead, **3-0**.

Two plays after Taylor's field goal, Arizona freshman quarterback Jim Krohn fumbled the ball at the Wildcat 27 and Steve Dewey recovered for BYU.

The Cougars couldn't do much, however, so the reliable Taylor kicked another field goal–this one from 38 yards for a **6-0** lead with 8:41 left in the first period.

Arizona moved the ball on its next possession – just far enough for kicker Lee Pistor to boot a school record 53-yard field goal to make it, **6-3**. And thus, the kicking duel was initiated between Taylor and Pistor, with each kicking three field goals before the final gun.

The Cougars took the Arizona kickoff and launched their first touchdown drive, moving 53 yards in eight plays. Roger Gourley started things off with an 11-yard run. Then Nielsen hit Johnny VanDerWouden for 10 yards. Two short runs gave them a third and five. Then, from the Arizona 20,

Nielsen connected with tight end Brian Billick who was all alone on a post pattern at the seven. Billick went into the end zone for the score. Taylor added the PAT and the Cougars extended their lead, **13-3**.

Arizona scored its only touchdown in the second quarter. Krohn hit receiver Charles Nash with a 31-yard TD strike. Pistor's kick made the score, **13-10**.

BYU's Taylor added his third and final field goal of the game, a 39 yarder, to end the half.

Halftime Score: BYU 16, Arizona 10

Second Half

Pistor had two more field goals in the second half to match Taylor's three for the game. His second goal in the third quarter salvaged a failed Wildcat drive that couldn't punch through the Cougars' goal line stand. Still **16-13** for the Cougars.

Then another Arizona drive stalled in the fourth quarter, so Pistor came in again. His third field goal tied the game, **16 all,** with only 4:10 left to play.

But the Cougars couldn't do anything and punted back to the Wildcats. The Wildcats were stymied again as well by the Cougar defense, so Wid Knight went back to punt from his own 25. The wet ball slithered off Knight's foot, traveled a mere 18 yards, and gave BYU possession on the Arizona 43 with 14 seconds to play.

An ecstatic, but exhausted LaVell Edwards

described what Giff was supposed to do. "The call on the last play was 'throw underneath' the coverage and get an extra 10 yards. We still had a timeout remaining. Our receivers were well-covered and George Harris, who hasn't played much for us this year, kept going deep."

Giff, finding no target receivers open, dodged an onrushing defender, ran to his right and lofted the ball toward the end zone where Harris seemed to be boxed in by two Arizona defenders. But Giff's pass cleared the two Wildcats, who collided on the play, and fell into Harris' hands at the two-yard line as he crossed the goal line with three seconds to play. (Remember, Cougar fans, this play was in a rainstorm and was four years **BMB** (**B**efore the **M**iracle **B**owl)! Giff had almost 11 seconds to release the ball!

Dave Taylor still had enough leg strength on this very busy night to add the extra point.

Final Score: BYU 23, Arizona 16.

	1st	2nd	3rd	4th	Final
BYU	13	3	0	7	23
Arizona	3	7	3	3	16

Team Statistics	BYU	Arizona
First Downs	14	12
Total Offense Yards	313	252
Rushing Yards	113	194
Passing Yards	200	58
Passes (Att.-Comp.1nt.)	28-18-1	9-3-1
TDs Passing	2	1
Punts	6-239	7-276
Penalties – Yards	10-127	13-101

Arizona coach Jim Young said simply, "It was a tough game to lose."

LaVell Edwards said, "This was a very big win for us. It puts us in good shape in the league and gives us a lot of momentum. We felt like we outplayed Arizona, and it would have been very frustrating to lead all the way and then have to settle for a tie."

"A key play was our goal line stand inside the five which forced Arizona to settle for a field goal. Our kids pulled together and didn't quit, which makes me very happy.

(About Nielsen's game-winning pass): "There's no way we should have completed the winning pass against Arizona (43-yard TD pass in a rainstorm with :03 left on the clock), except the guy is a winner. He scrambled until he found a receiver, knew exactly where the line of scrimmage was, then put the ball right where it had to be at the precise moment. If there's one guy you'd like to have when the going is tough, it's Gifford."

Cougar Offense Leaders

- **Gifford Nielsen** was 18 for 28 passing for 200 yards with one interception and two TDs, including the game winner.
- **George Harris** led all receivers with 43 yards gained – on one big TD reception!
- **Jeff Blanc** had 15 carries for 62 yards.
- **Dave Taylor** scored 11 total points: three field goals and two extra points.
- **Todd Christensen** had eight carries for 28 yards and one TD, and six catches for 29 yards.
- **Brian Billick** had three catches for 39 yards and one TD.

Cougar Defense Leaders

- **Bill Rice** had 11 tackles (six solo, two for loss).
- **Larry Miller** had nine tackles (six solo) and

- **Marcus Kanahele** had nine tackles (four solo).
- **Mekeli Ieremia** had eight tackles (four solo).
- **Dana Wilgar** and **Rod Wood** each had seven tackles and (four solo each).
- **Steve Dewey** had four tackles (two solo), one tackle for loss, and one forced fumble.
- **Tony Hernandez** had one tackle and one pass interception returned for 29 yards.
- **Marc Swenson, Craig Jensen, and Ross Varner** each had one tackle for loss.

The Cougars were on a roll with two impressive wins in a row. Then they were in two squeakers in successive weeks:

- They beat a San Diego on the road, **8-0.**
- Then, in a topsy-turvy game with Wyoming in Provo, the Cougars couldn't make anything happen in the first three quarters and trailed, **27-7**. Then they woke up in the fourth and scored 22 points. But the Cowboys scored once more and came away with the **39-34** victory.

The Cougars regrouped and had two blowout wins in Provo:

- A **63-19** win over Southern Mississippi that more than made up for their loss to the Golden Eagles in 1975. BYU gained 718 yards total offense, paced by Gifford Nielsen's 515 yards through the air and four touchdowns.

- A **45-14,** romp over Utah State. Led again by Giff with 468 yards passing and five TDs.

Then the Cats hosted Arizona State, and everybody knew this one would be no walk in the park. They were right.

Game #8:
BYU 43, Arizona State 21
Date: October 30, 1976
Location: Cougar Stadium
Weather: Temperature 59° and hazy
Attendance: 29,854

With the WAC football championship race entering its final four weeks, four teams were still in the running: Wyoming (4-0), BYU (2-1), Arizona (1-1), and Arizona State (2-1). BYU had already played two of the other contenders. Every game, every point, every twist of fate: all were critical in this tight field. This week BYU and ASU were squaring off against each other. The winner would still be in it; the loser probably was out of it.

Frank Kush's ASU Sun Devils had tradition on their side. ASU had won three of the four previous titles ('72,'73, and '75). Remember that BYU bested the Sun Devils in '74 to take home the trophy. The

Cougars' impressive wins in the previous two weeks, however, had them confident they could hold their own against their southwest neighbors from Tempe.

Cougar Stadium was full of very vocal fans, the weather was pleasant, and both teams were ready.

First Half

The Cougars drew first blood early in the first quarter as linebacker Larry Miller intercepted Sun Devil quarterback Dennis Sproul's short pass at the ASU 21 and returned it down to the 'Devils' 10. First-and-goal for the Cougars – right in their lap.

Jeff Blanc gained seven yards on the first two plays. Then Gifford Nielsen's first pass was incomplete. Fourth-and-three. Dave Taylor came in for the field goal attempt. Piece of cake, right?

The Sun Devils should have scouted a trick play Colorado State used in a similar situation in BYU's first home game of the season. As baseball Hall of Fame great Yogi Berra would say, "*You can observe a lot by watching.*") scooped up the ball and tossed it over to the far side of the field to speedy receiver Johnny VanDerWouden. Johnny raced into the end zone for a touchdown before the bewildered defenders knew what hit them! The kicking team was already on the field, so the PAT was quick and good. **BYU up, 7-0.**

Arizona Republic sportswriter Bob Eger called

the play the *"Trick AND Treat"* on the eve of Halloween. But the Sun Devils weren't going to go quietly. After receiving the kickoff, Sproul hit his flanker Larry Mucker on a catch-and-run for 80 yards and the tying score. **BYU 7, ASU 7.**

Dave Taylor kicked a 21-yard field goal on the next exchange. **BYU 10, ASU 7** .

Sproul and Mucker also connected on their next possession for 43 yards and another touchdown. Dan Kush added the extra point. **ASU 14, BYU 10.**

The momentum shifted again as the Cougars drove 72 yards in eight plays with Giff hitting George Harris with a 35-yard TD pass. Taylor's PAT made it **BYU 17, ASU 14.**

ASU continued the see-saw contest with a drive of 80 yards in nine plays. Sproul dove over the goal line from the one as the wild first quarter ended. With Kush's extra point it was **ASU 21, BYU 17**.

The scoreboard remained the same until late in the second quarter when Dave Lowry's two-yard plunge and the PAT closed the first half.

Halftime Score: BYU 24, ASU 21

Second Half

The Sun Devils opened the second half by moving the ball steadily down the field until BYU cornerback Tony Hernandez intercepted a Sproul pass at the goal line and returned it to the 10. Two plays later Giff hit flanker Mike Chronister with an 81-yard strike for six points. The PAT made it **31-21 for the Cougars**.

Dave Taylor booted a 40-yard field goal to stretch the Cougar lead to, **34-21,** with 4:02 left in the third quarter.

Later in the same period, the Cougars went 42 yards in four plays with fullback Todd Christensen running the ball in from two yards out. The pass for two extra points failed, leaving the score, **40-21**.

It stayed that way until 8:43 left in the game when Taylor kicked a 44-yard field goal to make the

Final Score: BYU 43, ASU 21.

	1st	2nd	3rd	4th	Final
ASU	21	0	0	0	21
BYU	17	7	16	3	43

Team Statistics	BYU	ASU
First Downs	21	20
Total Offense Yards	471	454
Rushing Yards	105	81
Passing Yards	366	373

Passes (Att.-Comp.1nt.)	**41-22-2**	**35-17-3**
TDs Passing	**2**	**2**
Punts	**5-215**	**8-341**
Penalties - Yards	**10-76**	**10-128**

The final statistics were much closer than the final score. BYU had 471 yards total offense; ASU had 454. Gifford Nielsen had 366 yards passing; Dennis Sproul had 373. But ASU scored all of its 21 points in the first quarter and were blanked across the final three quarters.

ASU coach Frank Kush said, "Give the credit to BYU. Nielsen gave us fits. We tried to mix it up – put pressure on him by blitzing and then dropping back and trying to get double coverage whenever possible, but nothing worked. He's the best quarterback we've seen this season."

LaVell Edwards said, "This was one of the best wins we've had at BYU. The offense kept us in the game in the first quarter and then both the offense and defense did a super job. For our defense to give up 21 points in the first quarter against a team like Arizona State and then pull together and play a game like this is tremendous."

The Sun Devils continued to struggle the rest of the season, posting Frank Kush's first losing season

(4-7) at ASU.

Cougar Offense Leaders

- **Gifford Nielsen** was 20 of 37 passing for 339 yards with two interceptions and two touchdowns. He completed passes to 10 different receivers.
- **Dave Taylor** scored 13 points on three field goals and four extra points.
- **Jeff Blanc** carried 20 times for 82 yards.
- **Todd Christensen** carried five times for 11 yards and one touchdown and also caught six passes for 42 yards.
- **Dave Lowry and Johnny VanDerWouden** both scored one touchdown.
- **Mike Chronister and George Harris** both caught one touchdown pass.

Cougar Defense Leaders

- **Rod Wood** had 18 tackles (nine solo, three for loss) and three pass break ups.
- **Mekeli Ieremia** had 12 tackles (five solo, one for loss), two sacks, and one QB hurry.
- **Bill Rice** had eight tackles (one for loss), two sacks, and seven QB hurries.

- **Marcus Kanahele** had seven tackles (two solo, one for loss), one sack, one pass break up, and two QB hurries.
- **Craig Jensen** had five tackles (two solo), one forced fumble and one pass break up.
- **Larry Miller** had five tackles (two solo) and two interceptions.
- **Tony Hernandez** had four tackles (three solo) and one interception.
- **Ross Varner** had two tackles (one solo and one QB hurry.

Game #12

BYU 34, Utah 12
Date: November 20, 1976
Location: Rice Stadium @ Salt Lake City
Weather: Temperature 56° and clear
Attendance: 30,503

Optimism was high for both teams as they entered into this big rivalry game. BYU, with a record of 8-2 coming into the game, was cruising toward the conclusion of its most successful season ever. Utah, fresh from victories over New Mexico and Arizona State in the previous two weeks, felt it was ready to trade punches with the Cougars despite the Utes' 3-6 record. Utah's optimism faded fast despite a capacity home crowd and a perfect fall afternoon.

Both teams punted after their first series. Then BYU got down to business, scoring on its second possession. A short Utah punt gave the Cougars the ball on the Utah 39. On the first play Gifford Nielsen was sacked for a loss of eight. So, technically, the Cougars went 47 yards in nine plays for the touchdown. Key plays in this drive included:

- Jeff Blanc ran up the middle for 12 yards.
- Giff hit tight end Brian Billick for 12 yards.
- A 10-yard pass completion to Johnny VanDerWouden.
- Giff's keeper where he rolled to the right, faked a pitchout, then cut inside to score from the six for the touchdown. Dave Taylor's PAT made it **7-0 for the Cougars**.

The Cougar defense held again, and Utah's punt gave the Cats the ball on the Ute 48. This time BYU scored in five plays:

- Billick caught a pass for 12 yards.
- Todd Christensen caught one for eight yards.
- Dave Lowry ran for seven.
- George Harris caught one for 18 to put the Cougars first-and-goal on the three.
- Nielsen then hit Mike Chronister in the end zone for the score. Taylor's PAT was no good.

BYU up 13-0 with 8:44 to play in the half.

Utah got its first touchdown with 5:49 to go in the second quarter when running back Steve Peake went over from the three. The PAT was no good. **BYU 13, Utah 6.**

The Cougars punted on their next series and the Utes started to move the ball but stalled at the BYU 35. With 1:30 to play in the half, the Utes went for it on fourth and three. They were short by inches. Ball over to BYU.

The Cougars needed only 43 seconds to up their lead. Nielsen connected on three consecutive passes:

- He hit Johnny VanDerWouden for 30 yards,
- Then an 11 yarder to Christensen.
- Finally, a 25-yard TD pass to George Harris. The PAT was good.

Halftime Score: BYU 20, Utah 6

There wasn't much doubt what would happen in the second half. In the third quarter the Cougars scored two more touchdowns:

- Blanc caught a 19-yard TD pass from Nielsen. Taylor's PAT was good for a **27-6** BYU lead.
- Later in the third, Lowry scored from two yards out. The PAT was good. It was **34-6** for BYU.

LaVell rested his heroes in the fourth quarter, letting the reserves finish up the most successful regular season in BYU football history.

Utah did score one final touchdown in the final period: Richard Graham caught a three-yard touchdown pass from Patrick Degnan. The pass for the two-point conversion failed.

Final score BYU 34, Utah 12

	1st	2nd	3rd	4th	Final
BYU	7	13	14	0	34
UTAH	0	6	0	6	12

Team Statistics	BYU	UTAH
First Downs	25	23
Total Offense Yards	567	355
Rushing Yards	152	65
Passing Yards	415	290
Passes (Att.-Comp.1nt.)	39-25-3	52-21-1
TDs Passing	3	1
Punts	7-250	7-273
Penalties – Yards	10-128	4-20

This was the Cougars' fifth win in a row over Utah. Moreover, this year BYU tied for the WAC championship with Wyoming. In short order they would be invited to play in Florida's Tangerine Bowl (Florida Citrus Bowl today).

Cougar Offense Leaders

- **Gifford Nielsen** was 25 for 35 passing for 415 yards, with three interceptions, and three touchdowns and also scored one rushing TD.
- **George Harris** caught six passes for 134 yards and one TD.
- **Johnny VanDerWouden** caught five passes for 89 yards.
- **Mike Chronister** caught three passes for 59 yards and one TD.
- **Brian Billick** caught three passes for 60 yards.
- **Jeff Blanc** caught one pass for 19 yards and one TD and ran five times for 32 yards.
- **Todd Christensen** ran eight times for 53 yards.
- **Dave Lowry** ran seven times for 33 yards and one TD.

Cougar Defense Leaders

- **Rod Wood** had 12 tackles.
- **Blake Murdock** had eight tackles and one interception.

- **Marcus Kanahele** had eight tackles.
- **Tony Hernandez** had seven tackles.
- **Bill Rice** had seven tackles.
- **Craig Jensen** had four tackles and one pass break up.

The 1976 Tangerine Bowl

Oklahoma State 49, BYU 21
Date: December 18, 1976
Location: Citrus Bowl Stadium at Orlando, FL
Weather: Temperature 66° and clear
Attendance: 37,812

In an era when the number of bowl games was not comparable to the number of confetti bits thrown at a New Year's Eve celebration, BYU felt fortunate to be invited to play in the Tangerine Bowl in Orlando, Florida. Their opponent was none other than Oklahoma State - their 1974 Fiesta Bowl opponent. Both teams were stronger this year than their 1974 editions. BYU was ranked #17 in the Coaches Poll; Oklahoma State was ranked #14 in the AP Poll.

First Half

The outcome of the game could be summarized as follows: *BYU's error-prone offense vs. Oklahoma*

State's Terry Miller and its opportunistic defense.

On the BYU side, All-American quarterback Gifford Nielsen had to scramble on most plays as the Cowboy defenders were in the BYU backfield constantly. Defender Philip Dokes said, "He (Gifford Nielsen) is a real good passer. We didn't expect him to scramble so much or to be so hard to catch. If he had been able to sit in the pocket he would have picked us apart."

BYU's defense forced the Cowboys offense to punt twice. However, BYU kicker Dave Taylor missed two field goals. On the third Cougar possession, Dokes batted a Nielsen pass right into the hands of teammate Chris Dawson, who returned it 36 yards for the first score of the game. **OSU 7, BYU 0.**

Then it was the Cougars' turn. Mark Terranova returned the following kickoff 33 yards, and the Cowboys were assessed a 15-yard personal foul penalty, putting the ball on the OSU 45.

From there, Giff threw incomplete before hitting Jeff Blanc on the OSU 31 and Todd Christensen on the 25 for two first downs. Dodging the Cowboys defenders, Giff then found an open Tod Thompson on the one-yard line. That ended the first quarter.

On the first play of the second quarter Christensen was stopped inches short of the goal line. But he made it into the end zone on the next play.

Dave Taylor's PAT tied things up, **7-7**.

The Cowboys' next drive ended with running back Terry Miller's fumble and Bill Rice's recovery for BYU on the BYU 38. Things seemed to be going the Cougars' way. But then Giff missed and overthrew his first pass. OSU safety Gary Irions intercepted it and ran for 44 yards to the BYU 16. A penalty on BYU put the ball on the eight. Three plays later quarterback Charlie Weatherbie scored from the two. The PAT was good, and the Cowboys took the lead, **14-7**.

The Cougars were driving again before defender Milton Kirven intercepted a Nielsen pass and returned it 14 yards to the BYU 34. The Cowboys moved deeper into Cougar territory, culminating with Terry Miller's three-yard TD run. That made it **21-7** for the Cowboys.

The Cougars' next series yielded their second touchdown, moving 69 yards in nine plays. The big plays were passes from Nielsen to Mike Chronister (for eight), Brian Billick (for nine), and Christensen (for eight, then for 12) to put the ball on the Cowboy 27. The next play was Giff's pass across the middle to tight end Thompson, who caught the ball on the 17 and ran it into the end zone. That made it **21-14** with two minutes to go in the half.

But the Cowboys' Miller wasn't ready to take a break. Instead, he had a breakaway 78-yard TD run (a Tangerine Bowl record).

Halftime Score: OSU 28, BYU 14.

Here's what the two marquee players delivered in the first half:

- Oklahoma State's Terry Miller had 13 carries for 124 yards and two TDs.
- BYU's Gifford Nielsen completed 14 of 19 passes for 161 yards and one TD.

Second Half

BYU's next bang came with the second half kickoff. Dave Lowry took the kick two yards deep in his end zone, ran up the middle, then cut quickly to the left, and outran everybody to the end zone. This 102-yard gem was another Tangerine Bowl record. Before you knew it – BYU was right back in it, **28-21**. What made Lowry's run even more remarkable was the fact that he had undergone surgery for appendicitis just eight days before the game.

Then the next OSU thunder struck. The Cowboys scored three times in the third quarter:

- Robert Turner scored on a one-yard run (he gained 80 in the game).
- Terry Miller scored on a six-yard run.
- Miller again on a one-yard TD run.

And that concluded the scoring for the night.

Final Score: Oklahoma State 49, BYU 21

	1st	2nd	3rd	4th	Final
BYU	0	14	7	0	21
OSU	7	21	21	0	49

Team Statistics	BYU	OSU
First Downs	14	18
Total Offense Yards	255	402
Rushing Yards	46	375
Passing Yards	209	27
Passes (Att.-Comp.Int.)	34-23-4	10-2-0
TDs Passing	1	0
Punts	5-172	5-204
Penalties - Yards	6-67	7-56

Cougar Offense Leaders

- **Gifford Nielsen** completed 23 of 34 passes for 209 yards with four interceptions and one TD.
- **Dave Lowry** had a 102-yard kickoff return for a TD.

- **Tod Thompson** had three catches for 63 yards and one TD.
- **Todd Christensen** had six catches for 53 yards.
- **Brian Billick** had four catches for 37 yards.

(Defense Stats not available)

Oklahoma State's Terry Miller finished the night with three Tangerine Bowl records:

- His 78-yard TD run
- His 173 yards for most yards gained in the game
- His four TDs for the game tied another Tangerine Bowl record.

Author's Personal Note: *One of my work colleagues, Robin, was a graduate of Kansas State and a real sports junkie. He used to tease me with the comment, "Do they play football at BYU?"*

After the Tangerine Bowl, the next time he saw me, Robin said, "BYU's quarterback really was very good!"

PLAYBOOK FUNDAMENTAL FIVE:

"Handle" whatever the competition throws at you.

On the heels of its most wins in a season (9), but still 0-2 against Oklahoma State in bowl games, the Cougars knew they still needed some improvements

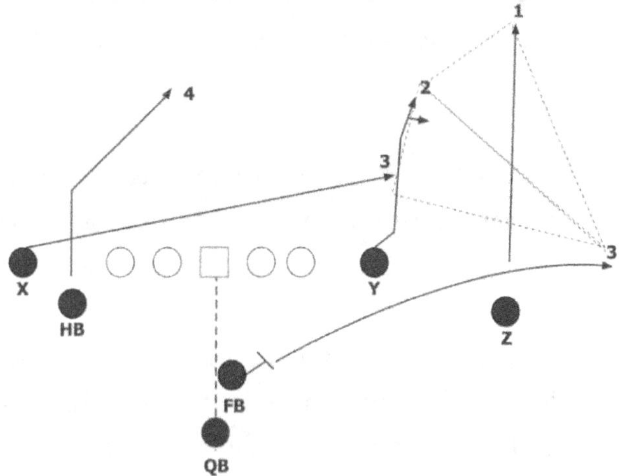

in their game. BYU was advancing in the college football ranks and would be facing increasingly greater competition year by year. They needed greater skills and capabilities to answer these challenges.

LaVell's passing game strategy already called for several players to expand their capabilities:

- Halfbacks (HB in the diagram) had to be able to run a variety of pass routes and catch all kinds of throws. And they still had to be great runners when called on.
- Fullbacks (FB) had to expand from just blocking and short runs to becoming another "wide receiver."
- Tight ends (Y), formerly used primarily as an additional blocker for runners, also had to be able to catch passes all over the field.
- Quarterbacks (QB) had to see the whole field as the pass play unfolded, not just its "assigned" receivers. They also had to become more adept at dodging heavy blitz attacks that increased as the passing game took its toll on opponents.
- Offensive linemen had to adjust far more frequently between run and pass blocking and also communicate faster with each other when doing so.

One tangible measure of the changes the BYU offense injected into the players: in the Tangerine Bowl, BYU's top receivers were two tight ends (Tod

Thompson and Brian Billick) and a fullback (Todd Christensen).

Who caught the most passes during the 1976 season? Fullback Todd Christensen with 51 receptions for 510 yards. This was only the beginning for a career shift for Todd. (See the special piece about him at the conclusion of this section.)

What about the defense?

A subtle but very real additional advantage the BYU offense had on the team was the improved play of the defenders. In practice scrimmages the defense had to learn to handle all those crazy receivers stretching the play horizontally and vertically at the same time.

In other words, virtually every new member of a LaVell Edwards team on offense and defense had to grow new skills and capabilities when they came into the BYU football program.

1977 Season

The largest opening-game crowd ever at BYU saw the Cougars start off running while the visitors were still in the starting blocks.

The *Manhattan* (Kansas) *Mercury* Sports Editor Dave Wright said it best, "*Whatever frustrations Brigham Young suffered in a 13-3 loss last season in*

KSU Stadium were more than made up for here (Provo) Saturday night."

Wright continued his summary, "*Before retiring to the bench midway through the fourth quarter, Nielsen, who already holds all the Western Athletic Conference passing records, completed 28 of 45 passes for 318 yards and two touchdowns.*"

First Half

The slaughter began on the game's first play when KSU sophomore tailback Ken Lovely fumbled and BYU's Ross Varner recovered on the KSU 19. The Cougars couldn't cross the goal line, however, so kicker Dev Duke (recently returned from a mission) kicked a 23-yard field goal to give the **Cougars a 3-0 lead.**

The Cougars held the Wildcats on the next exchange. Punter Don Birdsey kicked to BYU's Jason Coloma and KSU players interfered with Jason's called fair catch. The penalty gave BYU the ball at K-State's 41.

Nielsen & Co. only needed five plays to score the season's first touchdown. The big plays were Giff's pass to Tod Thompson for 26 yards and a 10-yarder to Roger Gourley. KSU was offsides on the next play, putting the ball on the three. Gourley finished the drive by sweeping left for the TD. Duke's PAT made it, **10-0, for the Cougars.**

K-State couldn't do anything on offense and punter Birdsey fumbled the snap and only managed to get off a two-yard punt. BYU called on Duke again, and he nailed a 37-yard field goal to up the Cougar **lead to 13-0**.

After another K-State fumble (this one recovered by Rod Wood), BYU was back in business again at the Wildcats' 21. Giff passed to Thompson for 18. Gourley moved the ball to the one. Then Giff faked one play into the line and lofted the ball over to Mike Chronister in the end zone for six. A two-point conversion failed, leaving the first quarter with the score: **BYU 19, KSU 0**.

Second Quarter

The Cougars were far from finished in scoring. They added 13 more points in the second quarter. On their second possession of the quarter, the Cougars went 60 yards in seven plays. Giff's four passes made the difference:

- A pass to VanDerWouden for 12 yards,
- One to Chronister for eight,
- A screen pass to Gourley for 13,
- A 34-yard bomb to VanDerWouden for the TD.
- Then the Nielsen-to-Chronister connection was good for two points. **BYU 27, KSU 0**.

The next BYU score was another Dev Duke field

goal from 26 yards. **BYU 30, KSU 0.**

Finally, the defense decided it was time for it to add some points. Senior middle linebacker Gary Kama tackled Wildcat punter Birdsey in the end zone for a safety to make the

Halftime score: BYU 32, KSU 0.

There was only one TD in the second half. But it was significant. Giff had gone to the bench for a well-deserved rest. Redshirt sophomore Marc Wilson, a highly valued recruit from Bremerton, Washington, took over and maintained the pounding offensive pulse: eight completions in nine attempts for 101 yards – the last completion a 32-yard touchdown to Chronister. Duke's PAT yielded:

Final Score: BYU 39, Kansas State 0.

	1st	2nd	3rd	4th	Final
KSU	0	0	0	0	0
BYU	19	13	0	7	39

Team Statistics	BYU	KSU
First Downs	24	8
Total Offense Yards	492	267

Rushing Yards	**73**	**77**
Passing Yards	**419**	**190**
Passes (Att.-Comp.Int.)	**54-35-0**	**28—12-1**
TDs Passing	**3**	**0**
Punts	**7-273**	**9-334**
Penalties - Yards	**11-110**	**11-108**

Kansas State coach Ellis Rainsberger said, "We started off poorly and continued to play poorly. We were outhit throughout the ballgame. Brigham Young was ready to play. Nielsen was super and his receivers are too."

LaVell Edwards was exuberant and said, "It's just as I've said all along. We've had a great fall. The kids worked extra hard to be ready for this game. Our kicking game was superb. Our backs ran well, and the offensive and defensive units just played excellent ball.

Cougar Offense Leaders

- **Gifford Nielsen** completed 27 of 45 passes for 318 yards with two TDs.
- **Marc Wilson** completed eight of nine passes for 101 yards and one TD.

- Kicker **Dev Duke** scored 11 points on three field goals and two extra points.

12 different receivers caught passes, including:

- **Mike Chronister** with seven for 85 yards and two TDs.
- **Johnny VanDerWouden** with six for 114 yards and one TD.
- **Tod Thompson** with five for 62 yards.
- **Todd Christensen** with five for 24 yards.
- **George Harris** with three for 46 yards.
- **Roger Gourley** with three for 32 yards.
- **Bill Ring** with two for 29 yards.
- **Casey Wingard** with one for 27 yards.
- **Richard Jones** with one for nine yards.
- **Lynn Zwahlen** with one for seven yards.
- **Stan Younger** with one for seven yards.
- **Scott Phillips** with one for four yards.

Leading rushers included:

- **Roger Gourley** with 11 carries for 34 yards and one TD.
- **Casey Wingard** with two carries for 27 yards.
- **Scott Phillips** with two carries 18 yards

Cougar Defense Leaders

- **Mekeli Ieremia** had 10 tackles (three for loss) and two QB hurries.
- **Gary Kama** had six tackles (one for loss) and a safety.
- **Ross Varner** had six tackles (one for loss) and one pass breakup.
- **Gary Peterson** had six tackles and one forced fumble.
- **Danny Frazier** had six tackles.
- **Rod Wood** had six tackles.
- **Tony Hernandez** had four tackles (one for loss) and one pass breakup.
- **Bob Prested** had three tackles and one pass breakup.
- **Doug Stromberg** had two tackles (one for loss) and one forced fumble.
- **Tom Enlow** three tackles and one QB hurry.

Game #2

BYU 65, Utah State 6

Game #3

BYU 54, New Mexico 19

Game #4

Oregon State 24, BYU 19

Date: October 8, 1977
Location: Parker Stadium @ Corvallis
Weather: Temperature 56° mostly sunny
Attendance: 33,965

This is one of those games that everyone in Cougarville wished could be a *"Do Over."*

It was one of the Cougars' two losses on the season; it was one of Oregon State's two victories for the year. Gifford Nielsen only threw three interceptions in the entire season; all three were in this game and two of them provided the Beavers with 14 points and the win.

Most devastating was Giff's severe knee injury was that ended his BYU career.

First Half

The game started innocently enough with the Cougar offense wasting no time putting up a lead on the scoreboard. The Beavers received the opening kickoff. On their first play from scrimmage, BYU's Ron Velasco intercepted John Norman's pass at the OSU 37-yard line.

From there Nielsen moved the Cougars in for a quick score. He completed three of four passes:

- One to Todd Christensen for seven yards.

- Then two to Roger Gourley (for 12 yards and the 18-yard TD). Dev Duke's kick made it, **7-0,** for BYU.

Both teams traded punts until late in the second quarter when the Cougars moved 80 yards in eight plays. The big gainer this time was a 30-yard halfback option pass from freshman Scott Phillips to Mike Chronister. Then Giff connected with Gourley for 10, to Chronister for 14, to Christensen for 16, and to Chronister for the final three yards and the touchdown. Duke missed the PAT. The score was **BYU 13, OSU 0** with 2:32 left in the half.

Despite the offense's heroics, the real stars of the first half were the BYU defenders. These Cougars held Oregon State scoreless with only 43 yards rushing and 32 yards passing. The Beavers only got as far as the BYU 49 twice in the half.

Second Half

And the BYU fireworks erupted again with the second half kickoff. Junior defensive back John Neal took the kickoff from his four-yard line and returned it 60 yards to the Beaver 24. The Nielsen-to-Chronister connection struck again on the first play from scrimmage as Giff found Mike all alone in the end zone and hit him for the TD. Duke's PAT was off the mark, but the Cougars led, **19-0**.

Those were the last points BYU would score in

this game. The Oregon State defense was throwing multiple formations at Nielsen & Co. Up front the Beavers rushed at times with five or six defensive linemen. In the backfield they went man-to-man and zones of five, or six backs. The combinations were switching constantly.

Shortly after the Cougars took the 19-0 lead, Oregon State struck for its only offensive touchdown in the game. Receiver Dwayne Hall caught a 40-yard bomb from QB John Norman to cut the Cougar lead to **19-7**. Craig Fertig, the Beavers' coach, said they decided to try a long pass because ace Cougar cornerback Tony Hernandez had gone out with an injury.

From there the Beavers clawed back: Kent Howe returning a Nielsen interception 32 yards for a score. The PAT made it, **19-14**. Then a 37-yard field goal by Kieron Walford made it, **19-17,** with 2:08 to play in the quarter.

Then Eugene native Todd Christensen returned the OSU kickoff 25 yards to the BYU 39. Christensen next ran for 16 yards to the OSU 45. Gourley picked up four and Christensen went again for seven. After two incomplete passes Giff hit Christensen with a 17-yard pass and a first down at the Beavers' 17 with 35 seconds to play in the third quarter. Nielsen threw two incompletions and then dodged the blitzing Beavers and ran *"about"* 10 yards. The ball was spotted inches short of the seven. On fourth down Giff ran a QB sneak and disappeared in the huge pileup. The final measurement put the ball one inch short of the first down. *One inch!* That ended the third quarter.

In that traumatic fourth quarter Oregon State had the ball but had to punt to the Cougars. Starting at the OSU 46 with 14 minutes to play. The Cougars started to move the ball. Christensen ran twice for 19 yards. Nielsen hit Gourley for 12 to the OSU 16.

Then came the final blow to the Cougars. Giff dropped back to pass, had to dodge multiple blitzers yet again and was hit just as he was trying to throw the ball away. At that moment he was hit again from behind and the ball floated up – and into the arms of linebacker Gene Dales. Dales returned the ball 79 yards for what proved to be the winning touchdown, **24-19**, for Oregon State.

Somewhere in all of those plays, blitzes, and hits, Giff's medial collateral ligament in his left knee had been torn away from the bone. The knee didn't feel right, but he stayed in the game for several more plays before telling the coaches he couldn't walk.

It was very little consolation to the Cougars to learn they weren't alone that "Upset Saturday." Oklahoma lost to Texas, Southern Cal lost to Alabama, and California lost to Washington State,

The Cougars' All-American quarterback was

finished for the season and two of their toughest conference rivals – Colorado State and Wyoming – were next on their schedule.

	1st	2nd	3rd	4th	Final
BYU	7	6	6	0	19
OSU	0	0	17	7	24

Team Statistics	BYU	OSU
First Downs	21	14
Total Offense Yards	329	218
Rushing Yards	45	128
Passing Yards	284	90
Passes (Att.-Comp.1nt.)	49-23-3	21-9-1
TDs Passing	3	1
Punts	8-315	12-451
Penalties – Yards	8-89	12-137

Cougar Offense Leaders

- **Gifford Nielsen** completed 22 of 48 passes for 255 yards with three interceptions and three TDs.
- **Todd Christensen** caught six passes for 89 yards and carried 13 times for 45 yards.
- **Roger Gourley** caught six passes for 58 yards and one TD and carried eight times for 29 yards.
- **Mike Chronister** caught four passes for 70 yards and two TDs.

Cougar Defense Leaders

- **Rod Wood** had 12 tackles.
- **Mekeli Ieremia** had eight tackles (one for loss) and one sack.
- **Mat Mendenhall** had five tackles (one for loss), three sacks, and one pass break up.
- **Mark Bernsten** had eight tackles.
- **Ron Velasco** had seven tackles and one interception.

BYU 63, Colorado State 17

Date: October 15, 1977

Location: Hughes Stadium @ Fort Collins

Weather: Temperature 57° partly cloudy

Attendance: 29,110

Out of the ashes of the Corvallis loss, the Cougars faced a second straight game on the road.

This time the opponent was the 5-0 Colorado State Rams. The CSU fans, encouraged by BYU's fresh loss to Oregon State and the loss of Gifford Nielsen for the year, had their own visions of WAC domination and a potential bowl game bid at the end of the rainbow. The home crowd of 29,110 fans for this contest was the second largest in CSU history.

Just getting to this game was a journey of disjointed episodes for the Cougars. For starters:

- The bus taking the BYU team to the Salt Lake airport was late picking them up in Provo.
- Then their airplane to Denver was an hour late arriving.
- On the lunch flight there were not enough meals to go around. Some players went hungry.
- The bus taking them to Fort Collins broke down and everyone had a long wait sitting on the bus while it got fixed.
- LaVell Edwards addressed the team once they got into their locker room at Hughes Stadium and said in all seriousness, "Now that you've had a great trip here, I want you to settle down and concentrate on the game."

A question you might ask yourself at this point

might be, "How many teams in NCAA football history have lost their All-American quarterback for the season and then had any hope of beating a strong conference rival on the road the following week? Especially if the new starting quarterback was a redshirt sophomore with little varsity experience prior to that season?

Enter Marc Wilson, coming from the frying pan into the fire – but surrounded by great teammates and mentored by the best quarterback coach in the nation.

First Half

BYU won the coin toss and kicked off to the hometown Rams. The locals picked up three first downs before having to punt the ball away.

BYU started from its own eight-yard line. Marc calmly directed the Cougars, covering 79 yards in six plays. *He connected with tight end Tod Thompson for the final 38 yards and a touchdown.* Dev Duke's PAT (his first of nine for the day) made it, **7-0**, for the Cougars.

Now it was the Rams' turn to flex their muscles. Ron Harris took the Cougar kickoff and zipped 100 yards for a touchdown. The PAT knotted the score, **7-7**.

On the following kickoff BYU's Jason Coloma returned the ball 13 yards before he was hammered and fumbled. CSU recovered at the BYU 21. The Cougar defense was absolutely awesome, limiting CSU to two yards in three plays. The Rams' 39-yard field goal attempt was wide. **Still 7-7.**

BYU started at its 20. Wilson was sacked on first down for a loss of nine. On the next play Wilson's long pass was picked off and returned to the Cougar 43.

Once again, the Cougar defense was immovable, yielding only three yards. On fourth down the Rams lined up for a field goal attempt. At the snap, holder Mike Deutsch stood and threw a pass to Chuck Kovac – good for only two yards. The Cougars took over again.

The Cougars then scored twice more in the opening quarter.

- They drove 75 yards in four plays with *Wilson hitting George Harris with a 25-yard TD strike.* Duke's PAT made it **BYU 14, CSU 7**.
- *Wilson sneaked for one yard and the TD* after the Cougars recovered a Ram fumble on the CSU nine. The PAT again was good: **BYU 21, CSU 7**.

The Rams scored first on a 47-yard field goal to make it, **21-10**, for BYU.

Then the Cougars scored three more times to take a **42-10** halftime lead:

- *Wilson passed eight yards to Tod Thompson* to make it, **28-10**.
- *Wilson to Thompson* again, this time from 33 yards out. BYU up, **35- 10.**
- *Wilson to George Harris* for 22 to make it, **42-10, at the half**

Second Half

- *Wilson passed to Todd Christensen*, who broke two tackles to finish a 28-yard scoring play. **BYU 49, CSU 10.**
- *Wilson to Johnny Van*DerWouden from eight yards out. **BYU 56, CSU 10.**
- Scott Phillips ran it in from the 10 to close out the Cougars' score at **63-10.**

CSU scored on an eight-yard Dan Graham to Chuck Kovac pass with four seconds remaining in the quarter.

Neither team scored in the fourth quarter.

Final Score: BYU 63, CSU 17.

	1st	2nd	3rd	4th	Final
BYU	21	21	21	0	63
CSU	7	3	7	0	17

Team Statistics	BYU	CSU
First Downs	26	20
Total Offense Yards	527	307
Rushing Yards	149	207
Passing Yards	378	100
Passes (Att.-Comp.1nt.)	31-20-2	26-13-3
TDs Passing	7	1
Punts	4-144	3-127
Penalties – Yards	13-90	10-69

Colorado State coach Sark Arslanian said, "If you had blank jerseys on both those kids you couldn't tell them apart…I was sorry to see Gifford Nielsen get hurt. I think he deserves the Heisman Trophy. But it wouldn't have been any worse today with Nielsen playing. These two are as good as any quarterbacks in the country."

Then the coach added, "Boy, I'm glad that this one's over… BYU is well deserving of a national ranking."

After the game LaVell Edwards shared his perspective on this big win, "When you win, **63-17**, it is hard to convince fans and the media that it is the defense that makes us so good. But that is the case.

You take the first quarter. We score a touchdown, and they run the kickoff back 100 yards to tie the score. Then we fumble the ball right to them on our 21. And our defense stops them without giving up a point. Then we turn around and give them the ball right back again and the defense shuts them off. They were the plays that made it possible for us to win."

Cougar Offense Leaders

- **Marc Wilson** completed 15 of 25 passes for 324 yards with one interception and **seven TDs (new BYU and WAC record).**
- **Johnny VanDerWouden** had five catches for 120 yards and one TD.
- **Tod Thompson** had three catches for 78 yards and three TDs.
- **George Harris had** three catches for 61 yards and two TDs.
- **Todd Christensen** had three catches for 58 yards and one TD and four carries for 22 yards.

Cougar Defense Leaders

- **Gary Peterson** had 11 tackles (one for loss).
- **Gary Karma** had nine tackles and two pass break ups.
- **Mekeli Ieremia** had six tackles (two for loss).
- **Dave McKee** had six tackles (one for loss) and one interception.

- **Tony Hernandez and Bob Prested** each had one interception.

Dave McCann Aug 7, 2022 Deseret News

New kid in town

Marc Wilson made his Provo debut in August 1975.

"I was scared to death!" he said. "For one, I had never thrown a leather football. Growing up in Seattle, we used rubber balls. I hated the feel of these leather footballs. Just trying to get used to that was enough, not to mention that we had this offense to learn. It was nerve-wracking. It really was."

Wilson didn't suit up his freshman season and redshirted the following year. At some point during that second year, equipment manager Floyd Johnson tossed him a No. 6 jersey. Wilson asked him, "Why 6?" He had never worn that number in all his years of football.

"You are from Seattle, right?" Johnson asked.

"Yes."

"There was a great player who played for the (Washington) Huskies, do you remember Sonny Sixkiller?" Johnson said.

"Yeah, he was our hero growing up," said Wilson.

"Well then, you have to wear No. 6," Johnson said.

Wilson's number still honors Sixkiller, his beloved equipment manager who gave it to him, and his head coach as it hangs in retirement from the press box at LaVell Edwards Stadium.

Game #6
BYU 10, Wyoming 7
Date: October 22, 1977
Location: Memorial Stadium at Laramie
Weather: Temperature 47° partly cloudy
Attendance: 25,398

BYU was ranked 17th in the AP poll heading into this game with a Wyoming team that was much stronger than its 2-2-1 record would indicate. The play by both teams defied all pre-game predictions. The 14 turnovers in the game (six by the Cougars, eight by the Cowboys) foiled the performance by both teams.

Perhaps the biggest surprise of the day was the six interceptions thrown by BYU quarterback Marc Wilson after throwing a WAC record seven touchdown passes the week before. The six interceptions were also a WAC record for one game.

Wyoming had two weeks to prepare for the Cougars' aerial-circus offense. And they prepared very well. Dropping eight men back into zone coverage, they left Wilson very little margin for error with his passing. "They did a good job of falling back," Marc said, "and I foolishly tried to force the ball through them. That's how they got the interceptions."

When the dust finally settled, BYU had scored 10 points in the second quarter. Wilson directed a drive of 84 yards in eight plays. Most of the damage was done as follows:

- With starting fullback Todd Christensen on the bench with a knee injury, reserve back Bill Ring ripped off three runs for 25 yards.
- Wilson passed to Roger Gourley for five yards,
- Then to Johnny VanDerWouden for 14,
- And finally to tight end Tod Thompson for 13 yards and the touchdown.
- Dev Duke added the PAT, giving the Cougars a **7-0** lead with 11:15 to play in the second quarter.

Later in the same quarter the Cougars got their final points from a Cowboy fumble. Defensive end Mat Mendenhall fell on Wyoming QB Marc Cousins' fumble on the Cowboy 11. Three plays advanced the ball to the nine, inviting Duke to come in and boot home the winning points with a 27-yard field goal. **That made it, 10-0, at halftime.**

The Cowboys scored a touchdown in the third quarter after two 29-yard passes from Don Clayton to Doug Wilson and Vic Baginski. Myron Hardeman (who led the Wyoming ground attack with 16 carries for 98 yards) ran the ball in from the 11 for the TD. Mike Smith added the PAT to finish the game scoring – **a 10-7 hard-earned win for BYU.**

	1st	2nd	3rd	4th	Final
BYU	0	10	0	0	10
WYO	0	0	7	0	7

Team Statistics	BYU	WYO
First Downs	14	17
Total Offense Yards	234	304
Passing Yards	138	233
Rushing Yards	96	71
Passes (Att.-Comp.1nt.)	26-10-6	11-4-1
TDs Passing	1	0
Punts	5-202	5-179
Fumbles – Lost	2-0	9-7
Penalties – Yards	9-93	8-79

Wyoming coach Bill Lewis said, "Our defense played one of the finest games that I have ever seen in my 13 years at the college level. It was a frustrating loss, but I can't fault our defense."

About his offense, Lewis said, "When we weren't making mistakes, we were moving the ball well. Those turnovers took all the continuity away from our offense."

LaVell Edwards said, "This is the wildest game I've ever been in as far as turnovers go. It was a real tough, hard-fought game, but the turnovers came so fast and furious it seemed we were spending most of the day changing units. This was by far our toughest game of the year. Wyoming was extremely well prepared. Give credit to them. The eight man drop worked well. They got into so many defensive sets Wilson had never seen before and he wasn't ready for them. He has seen that type of defense now and he'll be ready for them."

The final game statistics bore out LaVell's statement about what a wild game it was. The Cougars won, yet:

- BYU was outgained in total offense 304 to 234.
- The Cougars had only 96 yards passing.
- Wilson had only 10 completions in 26 attempts – and those six interceptions.
- The defense got the gold stars for this one!

More damaging to the Cougars than any of these

statistics were two Cougar injuries:

- Fullback Todd Christensen's knee injury
- Defensive tackle Mekeli Ieremia's reinjured separated shoulder

Cougar Offense Leaders

- **Marc Wilson** completed 10 of 26 passes for 96 yards with six interceptions and one TD.
- **Tod Thompson** had three catches for 25 yards and one TD.
- **Bill Ring** had 21 carries for 91 yards.
- **John VanDerWouden** had two catches for 34 yards.
- **Dev Duke** scored four points (the margin of victory) on one field goal and one PAT.

Cougar Defense Leaders

- **Rod Wood** had eight tackles (6 solo) and one interception.
- **Ron Velasco** had seven tackles (four solo).
- **Ross Varner** had seven tackles (four solo).
- **Gary Peterson** had six tackles (two solo, three for loss).
- **Mark Bernsten** had five tackles (four solo), one fumble recovery, and one pass break up.
- **Jason Coloma** had five tackles (three solo and one pass break up.

Todd Christensen: A Cougar for All Seasons

Todd was a typical fullback at 6'4" and 222 lbs. He was a good runner for the Cougars, but an even better pass receiver:

- In 1976 his 51 receptions led the team. He gained 510 yards receiving and three TDs.
- His 1977 totals were nearly identical: a team leading 50 receptions for 603 yards and five TDs.
- He was All WAC first team in 1977
- He finished #5 in BYU career receptions with 152.

But Todd's expanded capabilities led to a 10-year NFL career *as a tight end*, highlighted by:

- Two Super Bowl titles in 1980 and 1984
- Three times All-Pro first team and two times All-Pro second team
- Five times a Pro Bowl selection (1983-87)
- Two times NFL receptions leader in 1983 with 92 and 1986 with 95.

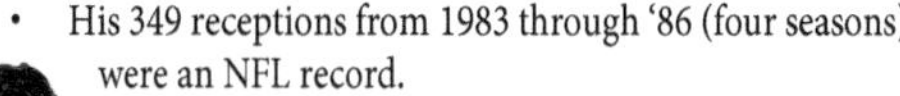

- His 349 receptions from 1983 through '86 (four seasons) were an NFL record.

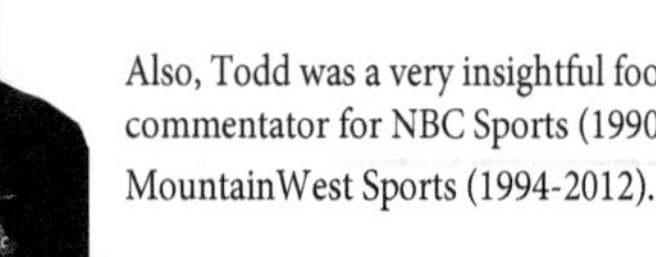

Also, Todd was a very insightful football commentator for NBC Sports (1990-94) and MountainWest Sports (1994-2012).

Published Aug 3, 2014

Toby Christensen gives tribute to his father Todd Christensen

By Toby Christensen

CougarNation.com Senior Analyst

At Brigham Young Todd immediately made an impact. He started at fullback as a true freshman and held the spot for four years, leading the team in receiving three times and helping the Cougars play in four straight postseasons. Along the way he also met and married the beautiful, and talented, Kathleen Simmons.

After his BYU career, the Dallas Cowboys chose Todd in the second round. After a year he found himself fighting to stay in the NFL bouncing from the New York Giants to the Oakland Raiders. It took him a couple of years to escape the shadow of Raider great, Dave Casper, but eventually he made a name for himself as a tight end. As a Raider, he won two Super Bowls, led the entire NFL in receptions twice (one of only two tight ends in NFL history to do that), and was the first NFL player to have 80 or more receptions in four seasons. His first season leading the NFL in receptions by a tight end was in 1983. He then broke his own record three seasons later…

Todd would stay close to football after his playing

days, joining the broadcasting ranks in many different capacities for the next 25 years. He worked NFL games with NBC. He was involved in the 1992 Olympics in Barcelona working multiple events and venues. He worked with ESPN, the Mtn Network, and CBS College Sports doing college football games and was well known for his wit and massive vocabulary.

His professional life is well chronicled. What many people may not know is that he was a father of four and grandfather of six. His four sons all graduated from BYU just as he did. He and Kathy were full-time care givers for their fourth son who was born with spinabifida.

He spent hundreds of hours volunteering with charity groups such as the Childrens Miracle Network, Athletes for Youth, and the Special Olympics. He was a regular visitor at elderly homes and care centers, often times singing for residents just to see them smile. He opened his home to strangers at Christmas and Thanksgiving. He served and volunteered in his church his entire life.

He gave hundreds of speeches to youth groups, church groups, and businesses.

He's a member of the Utah Sports Hall of Fame, Oregon Sports Hall of Fame, Nike Hall of Fame, Sheldon High School Hall of Fame, and BYU Hall of Fame. He coached youth sports and spent countless hours with hopeful high school athletes, hopeful college athletes, and hopeful NFL athletes, helping them hone their skills.

So, Todd should be celebrated as one of the greatest Raiders of all-time, one of the greatest Cougars of all-time, and one of the greatest fathers of all-time.

PLAYBOOK FUNDAMENTAL SIX:

Develop True Partnerships

Leaders who are models of great things develop other leaders who also do great things. In this review of Fundamental Six we will review four examples of how LaVell Edwards earned trust and respect from some of the game's Hall of Fame coaches and how his values rippled through to others who have done some wonderful things.

Partnering #1: LaVell Edwards earns the respect of other Hall of Fame coaches and other greats. (Deseret News Dec. 29, 2016 Dick Harmon)

The late Penn State coach **Joe Paterno** called LaVell one of the "*true giants in our game,*" and praised his integrity. "*He is a magnificent human being and has done a fantastic coaching job. We have* *had some great games. We beat them up here, and they kicked our ears out there. When you played him, you played against a man in the program that had a lot of class."*

Grant Teaff, former Baylor coach and past executive director of the American Football Coaches Association, called Edwards *"an icon in coaching...I've said this to anyone who will listen to me: LaVell Edwards is one of the top five coaches to ever coach the game of football. If you don't believe me, just look at his record. But beyond that, and far more important to me, LaVell Edwards is one of the top five men I've ever known...."You can't separate the coaching from the man."*

Florida State legend **Bobby Bowden** said, *"LaVell was always one of my favorites... We had a lot of nice times together...I don't know anyone who didn't like or love LaVell..."We were pretty close when he was in the game. Now that he's out, I don't see him much anymore. I miss him."*

Former USC and UNLV coach **John Robinson** said, *"I think he's one of those people who are the foundation of college football. That's in terms of what he stands for, who he is, the consistency with how he's done his job. He's one of those guys you say, 'Hey, the game is better because he's in it."*

Former Super Bowl champion Green Bay Packers head coach **Mike Holmgren** said, *"LaVell*

Edwards has been one of the most influential men in my coaching career. He gave me my first Division I job as quarterback coach at BYU. More importantly he taught me how to treat people. He was generous, consistent and a model for all young coaches in keeping your life in perspective. To be a part of the 1984 season – with the players and coaches at BYU – will always be something very special."

Former University of Utah coach **Ron McBride** said, *"LaVell's consistency from one year to another has been incredible and unbelievable."* LaVell and Ron became lifelong friends despite being in a rivalry that has been heated and called toxic by some.

"He is like a father to the players," said **Steve Sarkisian**, who quarterbacked Edwards' 1996 team to a 14-1 record. *"He really cares about us individually, and while he's low key and sometimes looks like he's bored in games, nobody wants to win more than he does. He has a fire inside of him and he loves the game."*

Former "nemesis" **Barry Switzer** the Oklahoma coach who loudly challenged whether the 1984 BYU team deserved to be No.1: *"Their schedule was an easy thing to disparage," he said, "and I did it to make us look good... "(Speaking of LaVell) We always got along great," Switzer said. "We'd go on those Nike cruises in the summer and have a good time. He was a good coach who had a very good football team. They* *were throwing the football and doing it well. I had no problem with LaVell. I don't know anyone who ever did."*

"LaVell's service as a bishop was very influential in his ability to connect with players," said **Brad Oates**, All-WAC at BYU and NFL veteran.

LaVell Edwards and Grant Teaff: parallel paths traveled by two "one in a million" leaders. Consider:

LaVell Edwards	*Grant Teaff*
▪ *1972: Became the head coach at BYU.*	▪ *1972: Became the head coach at Baylor.*
▪ *BYU was at the bottom of the Western Athletic Conference.*	▪ *Baylor was at the bottom of the Southwest Conference.*
▪ *1974: BYU won the WAC championship.*	▪ *1974: Baylor won the SWC championship.*
▪ *Reversed BYU's 5-38-4 record with Utah to 22-7.*	▪ *Reversed Baylor's 1-29 record with Texas to 10-11.*
▪ *Served as bishop of a BYU ward.*	▪ *Taught a weekly Sunday School class for years (never absent, never late).*
▪ *His team rallied in the final minutes to defeat Utah in his last game as coach.*	▪ *His team rallied in the final minutes to defeat Texas in his last game as coach.*

Partnering #2: Jim McMahon Partners with Former Teammates. (This episode was not about what LaVell did to be a partner, but what Jim McMahon did as he followed the example of his coach. Leader-partners influence other partners.)

"Jim McMahon not the greatest? You might want to reconsider."

By Vai Sikahema (Oct 2, 2014 DESERET NEWS)

I was inundated with emails about my piece on Jim McMahon's graduation, jersey retirement and induction into BYU's Hall of Fame from a few weeks ago. The response was overwhelmingly positive, but I expected some would maintain McMahon isn't worthy of recognition, even with his challenge of early-stage dementia as he labored to earn his BYU degree.

One of those detractors came from a BYU grad, former professor at Utah State and former mission president. He wrote, "I appreciated what you wrote about Jim. I don't doubt his right to be included in the BYU Hall of Fame but let's not go overboard on the accolades. Jim was OK and had some brilliant moments but the 'greatest?' Independent reviewers didn't honor him with the Heisman nor did they give him serious consideration."

He cited a former BYU basketball player with whom he roomed and had a similar reputation for carousing and frequenting bars up and down Utah Valley but "neither received significant discipline because if you were really good in those days folks tended to turn a deaf ear to what you were doing. I believe that statistics would support the premise that there have been many records broken before Jim and since. His bad language and antics even to this day are pretty much a mockery to the way football is conducted at BYU today."

Well sir, one reason I go overboard on the accolades is specifically because of sentiments like yours. I will do so again today, with anecdotes of private time spent with Jim that in its entirety, gives a more balanced view of who he is. So much of what we know about McMahon is of his many antics, which he often does deliberately and never denies. Like him or not, he's no hypocrite. Jimmy Mac loves cold beers, is profane and flawed in so many ways. But he has a soft side that he carefully guards. Our mutual friend, Charles Barkley, likes to say there are two kinds of athletes: those who are jerks privately but publicly portray they're good guys; and those who are good guys but are publicly portrayed as jerks. Mac and Chuck are both in the latter category.

"Jim was OK"?? Are you kidding me? He set 32 NCAA records in 1980, including single season records for total offense (4,627), passing yards (4,571), touchdown passes (47) and passing efficiency (176.9). Those numbers reflect games in which he mostly sat in the fourth quarter, sometimes most of the second half. At the end of his career, he left BYU with 70 NCAA records. Had he played in South Bend or Ann Arbor or Tuscaloosa, the New York Athletic Club would've Fed-Exed its trophy to his dumpy apartment, but BYU and the WAC were still widely considered eight-man

flag football by Heisman voters. McMahon finished an embarrassing fifth — FIFTH!!! Quarterback Mark Herrmann of Purdue, who threw 24 fewer touchdowns, even finished ahead of him, as did Pitt DE Hugh Green.

Jim did a little better his senior year, moving up two spots to finish third to USC's Marcus Allen. This, of course, was at a time when Heisman voters were enamored with running backs and regarded quarterbacks as simply "facilitators" who handed the ball to record-breaking tailbacks.

My last column dealt with our first meeting and how our relationship developed my freshman year. But it was my father, of all people, who cemented our bond through three-plus decades and teammates in college and the NFL, in a fight, of all things.

It happened my sophomore year and Jim's senior year. We traveled in mid-October 1981 to San Diego to play the Aztecs. The last time the Cougars played there was 1979 and Marc Wilson embarrassed the Aztecs in front of a national television audience by throwing four touchdowns on his first three attempts. It turned into a slaughter. Their new head coach, Doug Scovil, had been our offensive coordinator the previous year and publicly stated he was the secret ingredient to our success and vowed to crush BYU. Jim had gotten hurt two weeks before in Boulder against the University of Colorado and Steve Young had come in to finish the game; Steve then started the previous week in a loss to UNLV in Provo. The Aztecs were frothing at the mouth for a chance to finally give us our comeuppance. Their fans, even more so.

Unbeknownst to us on the field, two burly, probably drunk college-age men sat in the BYU family section and from the opening kickoff, relentlessly cursed and screamed obscenities at the team but specifically McMahon. In that setting, players' families who were mostly LDS, simply tried to ignore them. My dad, however, who was a young and fit 42 and a former professional boxer in Tonga, had had enough. Dad rose from his seat and made his way towards the two men. He asked them to stop and motioning towards Jim's parents, told them to have respect for the McMahons. Predictably, both men rose to their feet and cursed at Dad.

The skirmish didn't last long. Dad knocked them both out, and when they awoke, paramedics and security surrounded them but no perpetrator. Dad quickly scooted out of a portal and to the parking lot, where he listened to the rest of the game on the car radio. As investigators asked for witnesses, the BYU family section collectively became Sargent Schultz: "I know nothing! I see nothing! I hear nothing!"

After the game, when Jimmy Mac heard from his parents what happened, Dad became Jim's best buddy. As they both wore size 12, Jim made a habit of bringing dad into the locker room after games to give him shoes. Even when we were Eagles' teammates in Philly. To this day, Dad still has a pile of Jimmy Mac turf shoes, some of them autographed.

You didn't always have to do something for Jim for him to acknowledge you.

As Eagles, we rode a bus down I-95 for our divisional game in D.C. against the Washington team. We always sat together on the plane and bus trips, though we weren't roommates. As we pulled into our hotel, he asked what I had planned. I told him I didn't know anyone in D.C., so I was free. He proceeded to tell me of a former teammate we had at BYU who was in the D.C. area but had fallen on hard times. In fact, he was in a rehab center for drug abuse. I was shocked. Jim asked if I wanted to accompany him to the rehab facility to see him. We agreed to check into our room and within a half-hour, we'd meet in the lobby and share a cab to the facility.

When we arrived, it was clear Jim had been there before because everyone knew him — and not just because he was a famous NFL quarterback. We visited our teammate for an hour and lifted his spirits. On our return, Jim confided in me that our former teammate's life spiraled downward when he failed two attempts to make an NFL roster and this was his third time in a facility. Knowing neither the teammate nor his family were in a position to pay for what appeared to be a swanky residential treatment center, I asked Jim who was paying for it. Reluctantly, Jim admitted he had paid for all three of his stays.

That same season, we flew to San Francisco to meet the 49ers in a Monday night showdown. I had barely laid my bag down on my hotel bed when the phone rang. It was Jim.

"Kid, come to my room, 2090." And he hung up.

When I knocked on his door, he answered with a grin that showed a big chaw of tobacco. "Come in."

In his room was a guy who looked vaguely familiar, sitting on a chair while his three sons, 6, 8 and 10, sat on a bed. Jim asked, "Remember this guy?"

I was stumped. Jim re-introduced me to a freshman classmate who only lasted at BYU for a semester. He was a non-LDS kicker who came highly recruited to BYU as a scholarship athlete. Sadly, he didn't live up to the hype, which was exacerbated by the fact a walk-on from Texas named Lee Johnson was kicking the cover off the ball. I hadn't seen this guy since the Miracle Bowl 12 years before, when he didn't return for winter semester. Turns out, he returned to California, straightened his life out, got married and had a family. He called the Eagles' office the week before and left a message for Jim. Jim returned his call and invited him to the hotel. We laughed, told old stories, took pictures with his kids with a camera he brought and before he left, Jim produced an envelope with four tickets and handed it to him. I watched a grown man, once a cocky and proud 18-year-old, reduced to tears.

In a game with such diverse backgrounds, from Polynesia to inner-city to country bumpkins, from Mormons to Muslims, Jews and atheists, Jimmy Mac had a way of uniting people for a common cause because he was so honest. Oddly, he could say things that people were thinking but no one dared utter. The year we played together in Philly, the Denzel Washington movie "Malcolm X" debuted and was enormously popular among the black players in the Eagles' locker room. Understanding the power of the NFL and its players, Warner Brothers sent a box of T-shirts and hats hoping players would wear them during interviews on ESPN. Nearly every African-American player on our team wore a T-shirt and hat that simply had "X" on it.

Tired of the hype, McMahon started wearing a hat and T-shirt with a big "O" on it — a silent, contrarian protest to all the hype. When a reporter asked him if he opposed the movie, McMahon replied, "No dude. A locker room has X's and O's. If the Bruthas are into X's, I'm into O's. Football is about X's and O's."

No one laughed harder than Reggie White, Randall Cunningham and Seth Joyner.

Among the reasons Jimmy Mac was so popular on every team he played was his penchant to say things to coaches, management and ownership no one dared say. He famously sparred with Bears coach Mike Ditka in Chicago, but today, Ditka loves him like a son. Had he not scolded LaVell for wanting to punt late in the SMU game, BYU would not have won that game. LaVell and Patti Edwards love Jim like their own son.

...This weekend, finally, the prodigal son returns. BYU will kill the fatted calf. They'll put rings on his fingers and a robe on his back. I am not missing this party.

Partnering #3: How LaVell recruited partners to prevent what could have been the biggest failure of his coaching career.

The year was 1978 and Gifford Nielsen's BYU career had been terminated by his serious knee injury. Quarterback coach Doug Scovil also was missing – gone to coach quarterbacks with the Chicago Bears in the NFL. Marc Wilson was the returning quarterback for the Cougars.

Once again LaVell was on the hunt for a new quarterback coach. One of his contacts was Tommy Hudspeth, LaVell's predecessor as head coach at BYU. Tommy was the head coach of the NFL's Detroit Lions. He and his entire coaching staff were fired in January of '78 after two losing seasons. His quarterback coach was Wally English. After reviewing his needs with Hudspeth, LaVell hired Wally to coach BYU's quarterbacks.

As we saw with the earlier transition from the BYU's 1973 passing playbook to different versions installed by new coaches in '74 and '75, the '78 offense underperformed against everyone's expectations. For comparison:

- Team: 1978's 2,858 passing yards and 14 TDs in 13 games (compared with 1976's 3,386 passing yards and 31 TDs and 1977's 3,758 passing yards and 41 TDs).
- Individuals: Marc Wilson's individual statistics in 1978 (1,499 yards passing and eight TDs) compared with 1977 (2,418 yards passing and 24 TDs) in only seven games as a starter.
- Jim McMahon's 1978 statistics were 1,307 yards passing and six TDs in only nine games.

An additional change in the system was coach English's frequent switching between Marc Wilson and sophomore Jim McMahon. Both quarterbacks shared playing time in eight of the 12 1978 games. Platooning Wilson and McMahon regularly was rough on both of them.

Sportswriter Vince Langford of the El Paso Times wrote:

The big question for Brigham Young University's football team after Saturday afternoon's methodical

44-0 victory over injury-riddled University of Texas at El Paso might be: what do you do with Marc Wilson?

You may remember Marc Wilson, a nice guy with a problem. He was the Western Athletic Conference back of the year last season when he passed BYU to a WAC co-championship.

Here Saturday, however, Wilson didn't make his first appearance until late in the third quarter, and then all he had to do was hand off to fullback Bill Ring, who burst three yards for his second touchdown on a cool, cloudy day to give the Cougars a 30-0 lead.

As an example of Wilson's pain:

Against Hawaii and UNLV Wilson played both games (McMahon out with an injury) and did well, passing for 478 yards and five TDs.

But McMahon started the next game against Navy in Holiday Bowl I. One columnist wrote after that game, "BYU, switching two quarterbacks all night, finished its year 9-4."

In the Holiday Bowl, BYU lost to Navy, 23-16. McMahon and Wilson combined for 16 completions in 34 attempts for 181 yards, with two interceptions and one TD. BYU averaged only 5.3 yards/pass attempt. Definitely not BYU's norm.

BYU was outscored 13-0 in the fourth quarter.

The Cougars finished the year with a bitter taste in their mouths as they left San Diego. There was great foment swirling beneath the surface of the waters in Cougarville.

So, how did LaVell spend the off-season after winning has latest conference championship? Certainly not by just sitting around, enjoying the holiday goodies, and watching other teams play in bowl games. He had a lot of work to do; preparations to make; personal discussions to conduct; and demotivated players to inspire. After some weeks, he was ready to rebuild his team.

"LaVell was a crafty, smart guy," Wilson said. "He went to the NCAA Coaches Convention and talked up English and got him hired at Pittsburgh."

Marc Wilson recounted how deep the chasm was:

(Excerpted from "Marc Wilson recounts how LaVell Edwards avoided a mutiny after '78 season" By Dave McCann, Deseret News Aug 7, 2022):

"It was just a miserable year. Not just for me, it was miserable for Jim," Wilson said. "It was miserable for everybody... "I was done. I talked to my dad over Christmas and said, 'I can't go through another year like this. I'm just gonna finish my classes, graduate, and move on to law school.'"

Wilson's father supported him but asked that he do one thing first — go talk to Edwards.

"I waited two weeks because I was too scared to tell him, but I walked in and finally said, 'LaVell, I've got

to tell you, I'm not coming back. I'm gonna graduate and go to law school.'"

Edwards sat and listened and then pointed out, "You don't need to decide that today. There is no reason you have to decide that today. Wait two or three months and see how it feels and come talk to me."

Wilson watched Edwards pull out a manila-colored legal pad and he wrote down his name. "I was at least 20 guys down on that legal pad," Wilson said. "Twenty guys had gone in there before me and said the same thing, so I wasn't the only one who felt that way."...

LaVell knew what he had to do, both for the current team and his future.

"LaVell was a crafty, smart guy," Wilson said. "He was not very often wrong...He was a very, very smart, intuitive guy. He was very sensitive to his feelings about things and he was, in most cases, always right and we could trust that."

BYU football didn't have team meetings in February, so when LaVell called the players together for a special meeting in the Richards Physical Education Building in February of 1979, all team members were present and accounted for.

"We are all sitting there not knowing what was going on because it was such a strange, out-of-nowhere meeting," Wilson said.

LaVell stood up and took charge.

"I want the defense to go down the hall and for the offense to stay here," said the sixth-year head coach. The defensive guys got up and walked out.

Looking at the offense, Edwards said, "There is someone I want you to meet." He then turned to the door and walked out of the room leaving the players in a quiet quandary.

A moment later the door opened and in walked Doug Scovil, back from his one-year work with the Chicago Bears, and he had a message for the kid from Seattle and his teammates who wanted to quit.

"Doug was so funny," Wilson said. "He walks in and says, 'We've got a guy sitting in this room (referring to Marc) that is better than anybody I had last year in Chicago. I don't know what happened this year, but we are going to get back to work!"

Scovil turned to the door and walked out of the room and the meeting ended.

"When that happened all of us guys said, 'We are in!' Wilson said. 'We are not going anywhere.'"

With Scovil's offense back, the Cougars would go from 9-4 in 1978 to 34-4 over the next three seasons. Three years after that, with Scovil gone but his offense still in Provo, the Cougars would win the 1984 national championship...

"I think the biggest thing LaVell learned was that never again would he allow that offense originated by

Doug to leave Utah County, no matter who the offensive coordinator was," Wilson said. *"And over all the remaining years, he never did."*

Author's Note: *You can see how critical culture is: culture can motivate or demotivate people even more than results. There were 20+ members of a team that had won three consecutive WAC championships with nine total wins each year – yet all were ready to quit the team.*

What about Jim McMahon?

Not to be forgotten in all this euphoria was the "other" Cougar quarterback, Jim McMahon. LaVell took him aside and enlisted his support for a plan: Marc would be the starter in 1979; Jim would redshirt the season, letting his injured knee heal completely, and preserve his last two years as the starter.

What was Jim's reaction to LaVell's plan? *"Marc was a hell of a player, and I think LaVell was smart for doing that,"* McMahon said. *"But at the time I was 19 or 20 and I wanted to play. I knew we were going to be good, and Doug (Scovil) had just come back. I wanted to play. That was a really rough year for me."*

But Jim agreed to the plan. One reason he bought in was that he also understood the deep hurt Marc had just endured by the season of "quarterback musical chairs." So, Jim stood by his coach and his teammate when they needed his support.

Many years later in an interview with *the Deseret News' Dick Harmon, Marc was asked the question, "You and fellow College Football Hall of Fame quarterback Jim McMahon shared playing time in 1978. What do you remember about playing with McMahon?"*

Marc answered, "I loved playing with McMahon. Jim was a great player and teammate. The thing I love the most about Jim is during my junior year (in 1978), Wally English was coordinator, (and) it was a rough year...One thing he wanted to do is change the quarterback. I've often thought about it. Jim was a young guy, and he didn't want to sit on the bench. It would have been so easy for Jim to fall into that, but he'd have nothing to do with it; he recognized it for what it was, and he didn't want any part of it. I've always loved him for that."

Author's Personal Note: "I heard it through the grapevine…"
While living in Georgia, many miles away from all this drama, I spoke with the father of one of the BYU players as the 1979 fall camp opened. "My son says that coach Scovil is back, and everyone is so excited. He says this is going to be a great season!"

Partnering #4: LaVell's former quarterback helps orchestrate an "unimaginable partnership."

In the late '60s racial unrest in America was at the boiling point. Demonstrations to protest racial discrimination grew in frequency and intensity in communities, in the 1968 Olympics, in other various sporting events, and eventually targeted BYU athletic teams. BYU was targeted due to the church policy at the time of ordaining its priesthood to male members – except to those of black African lineage.

Milestones:

Spring 1968: the U.S. Department of Health, Education, and Welfare (HEW) sent a five-person team to BYU to "determine whether (it is) complying with the [1964] Civil Rights Act."

November 30, 1968: seven black football players at San Jose State University boycotted their home game with BYU. A crowd of only 2,875 spectators watched the Spartans defeat BYU, 25-21.

March 27, 1969: regional director Hollis Bach of the Denver branch of the Office for Civil Rights wrote to BYU President Ernest L. Wilkinson, "This letter is your notification from the Office for Civil Rights that, as a result of our review on your campus and your response to our report, the Brigham Young University is deemed to be in compliance with Title VI of the Civil Rights Act of 1964.

"Since our visit to your campus last spring, we have visited a number of institutions of higher education. We think you might like to know that we still consider Brigham Young as being one of the very finest schools we have visited."

The Wyoming "Black 14" Episode

Then the most publicized event aimed at BYU was in October 1969 at the University of Wyoming. This event has been widely reported and too often distorted through the years. Here are the facts of this episode as documented (Wyo. History.org, November 8, 2014) by those who were actually involved in it:

Wyoming coach Lloyd Eaton warned Wyoming's tri-captain Joe Williams about his rule prohibiting participation by athletes in any demonstrations. Williams conveyed this information to his fellow black players that night, and they decided to meet with Eaton to discuss the issue after practice the next day (October 16).

Williams said later, *"We wanted to see if we could wear black armbands in the game, or black socks, or black X's on our helmets. And if he had said "no" we had already agreed that we would be willing to protest with nothing but our black skins."*

About 9:15 a.m. on Friday, the 17th, the 14 black players gathered at Washakie Center in the dormitory complex. They donned black armbands and walked to Memorial Fieldhouse where Eaton had his office, hoping to persuade the coach to allow them to show some solidarity with the Black Student Alliance call for a protest.

Seeing them together, wearing armbands, Eaton led them into the upper seating area of the fieldhouse and, according to the players, immediately told them, *"I can save you a lot of time. You are all off the team."* After that, a witness overheard the coach insulting the players in an angry manner, which further polarized the situation.

"It was pretty belligerent talk," the witness said. *"I felt embarrassed for the young men hearing this tirade."*

The unsettled feelings and issues were sidelined as were the "Black 14" (as the players came to be known).

The next day it was time to play football.

Wyoming 40, BYU 7

The Date: October 18, 1969

The Place: War Memorial Stadium, Laramie Wyoming

Weather: temperature 31 degrees: cold and windy

Attendance: 14,993

First Half

The Cowboys were red hot to start the game and the Cougars were sloppy, giving up five first-half turnovers inside their own 35-yard line on the cold and muddy field.

Wyoming's first two touchdowns came after Cougar turnovers on the BYU 17- and 3-yard lines. Frosty Franklin and Gary Fox both scored on one-yard runs. Bob Jacobs kicked the two PATs. It was **14-0** for Wyoming, a lead it would never surrender. That set the tone for the rest of the contest.

BYU lost another fumble on its own 14-yard line and Wyoming's Bob Jacobs kicked a field goal to make it **17-0**. Thus ended the first quarter.

The Cougars scored their lone touchdown in the second quarter. Defensive lineman Gerald Meyer batted a pass, caught it, and advanced the ball to the Wyoming 47. The Cougars then marched 47 yards in 10 plays to the end zone with quarterback Marc Lyons running the ball in from four yards out. **Wyoming 17, BYU 7**. But that was it for the Cougars.

The Cowboys, however, were far from being done. Just a few minutes after BYU's score, Wyoming quarterback Ed Synakowski hit receiver Bill Kyranakis for a 70-yard touchdown to make the score **24-7**.

Wyoming's Jacobs actually missed a field goal late in the second quarter, but two plays later the Cougars coughed up the ball again at their own 25 with 12 seconds left. Seven seconds later Jacobs again trotted onto the field and kicked a field goal to make it **27-7** at the half.

Second Half

Neither team scored in the third quarter. Wyoming closed out the scoring with two touchdowns in the fourth quarter. Ed Synakowski got his second touchdown of the game on a five-yard run. Then Larry Suganuma caught a nine-yard pass from Wayne Wells for a score. Jacobs made one of two PAT attempts.

Final Score: Wyoming 40, BYU 7

	1st	2nd	3rd	4th	Final
BYU	0	7	0	0	7
Wyoming	17	10	0	13	40

Statistically, Wyoming, the nation's leader in the fewest rushing yards allowed, held BYU to 16 yards rushing for the game. But the Cougar rushing defense was also strong, holding the Cowboys to only 42 yards on the ground for the game.

Cougar Offense Leaders

- **Marc Lyons** was 10 of 25 passes for 113 yards with three interceptions and also carried 11 times for a net of minus 14 yards and one TD.
- **Wes Homolik** had five catches for 63 yards.
- **Kip Jackson** carried 21 times for 42 yards and also had two catches for 21 yards.

Cougar Defense Leaders

- **Rick Dixon** had 12 tackles (seven solo).
- **Gerald Meyer** had nine tackles (six solo) and one pass interception.
- **Dennis Watford** had eight tackles (seven solo).
- **Jeff Slipp** had eight tackles (six solo) and one pass break up.
- **Chris Farasopoulos** had seven solo tackles.

Aftermath: The Cowboys also won the next week against San Jose State. Then their 6-0 record plummeted, losing their last four games to Arizona State, Utah, New Mexico, and Houston.

Ultimately, everyone in this scenario lost big time:

- The Black 14 lost their Wyoming careers.
- The Wyoming team lost its perfect season.
- Lloyd Eaton lost his job at the end of the 1970 season.

- The Universities at Wyoming and BYU both lost in the court of public opinion.
- The Church of Jesus Christ of Latter-day Saints lost because its reputation as an alleged racist institution persisted despite the HEW investigation's positive findings.

Out of the Wounds: "An Unimaginable Partnership"

Deep wounds to the body, mind, or spirit seldom heal quickly. Those living in and associated with the football fortunes in Laramie and Provo had to be skeptical that the wounds from their 1969 episode would ever heal.

But the remarkable thing about human beings is that they can climb out of such periods of despair through their personal commitments and collaboration/teamwork even with former adversaries. When such collaboration between BYU and Wyoming actually unfolded, outsiders could not believe it was possible. Both parties contributed greatly to the outcomes.

One person deeply involved in the healing process was one of LaVell Edwards' gifted quarterbacks, who had been called to serve in the Church of Jesus Christ of Latter-day Saints as a general authority: Elder S. Gifford Nielsen, who called the progress, "*an unimaginable partnership.*"

A Historic Revelation comes to President Spencer W. Kimball of the Church of Jesus Christ of Latter-day Saints

First and foremost, the source of the contention between the two schools was the Church of Jesus Christ of Latter-day Saints' policy of not ordaining black men to the priesthood. This policy was ended by the same source that instituted it. A revelation was received by President Spencer W. Kimball as he reported on June 8, 1978:

"Witnessing the faithfulness of those from whom the priesthood has been withheld, we have pleaded long and earnestly in behalf of these, our faithful brethren, spending many hours in the Upper Room of the Temple supplicating the Lord for divine guidance.

"He has heard our prayers, and by revelation has confirmed that the long-promised day has come when every faithful, worthy man in the Church may receive the holy priesthood, with power to exercise its divine authority, and enjoy with his loved ones every blessing that flows therefrom, including the blessings of the temple."

Making an announcement (even about a revelation from God) is one thing, actually changing centuries of culture is quite another. The following experiences have brought the revelation to life.

BYU Experience

In 1970 Ron Knight, BYU's first black football player, transferred from Northeastern Oklahoma A&M College (NEO). Ron was a defensive back who helped NEO win the NJCAA national championship. He played for BYU his final two years. Many other blacks have followed in Ron's footsteps and today are on teams in most major sports.

Churchwide Experience

Black men and women have been called to and are serving in leadership positions in ward congregations, stakes, regional areas, and as general authorities and church officers. Churchwide statistics in 2025 showed a total of 933,511 members living in black African nations. And the church has 29 temples in those nations either built, under construction, or announced. These temples will enable African members to receive the church's most sacred ordinances near their own home

Author's Personal Experience:

At the time this revelation was received, our family was living in Albany, Georgia. There was one street in Albany (Slappey Blvd.) that divided white neighborhoods from black neighborhoods. Previous attempts by black families to live on the "wrong" side of Slappey Blvd. had failed.

A history of racial prejudices wasn't erased overnight, but in our ward congregation alone, out of 100 new converts in the 12 months following the revelation to President Kimball, 50 of them were black. A strong, common faith united all members as they worshipped together in the same meetinghouse on the "white" side of Slappey Blvd. and moved forward. Black members have served and continue to serve in key leadership positions.

The Rebirth of the Black 14: *"We wanted our legacy to be more than a confrontation."*

At the same time major changes were rolling forward in the Church of Jesus Christ of Latter-day Saints as well as in the Black 14:

- 10 of the 14 men earned college degrees.
- The University of Wyoming officially apologized to the Black 14 on May 21, 2019.
- Also in 2019, the Black 14's 11 surviving members organized The Black 14 Philanthropy. The Philanthropy's mission is to educate, feed, and serve underserved communities.

May 21, 2019, the University of Wyoming officially apologizes to the Black 14. Present for this occasion were eight members of the Black 14. Front: Mel Hamilton. Back left to right: Tony Gibson, John Griffin, Lionel Grimes, Ron Hill, Tony McGee, Ted Williams, Guillermo Hyshaw. (Carey Hamilton photo)

Mel Hamilton (offensive lineman) and John Griffin(wide receiver) both had helped launch the Black 14 Philanthropy. They knew that the University of Wyoming had set up a campus food bank during the Covid 19 pandemic for students who couldn't get home and didn't have enough to eat after the university shut down in-person classes in March. The Black 14 wanted to help.

Mel developed an ongoing relationship with the LDS church's religious instruction institute on the Wyoming campus and with local church leaders in Laramie that led to connection with Elder S. Gifford Nielsen. In early 2019 Mel told Laramie Wyoming Stake President Cory Allen that Black 14

Philanthropy was about to receive official nonprofit status.

"Is there more we can do together?" President Allen asked.

"I'll call Gifford Nielsen," Mel said.

Mel spoke with Elder Nielsen, who helped arrange the donations with approval of the First Presidency.

"When I "first met Mel we had this instant connection," Elder Nielsen said, "because I'm a quarterback and he's an offensive lineman, and we know how closely you have to work together to accomplish a common goal, and that is to win. So, I thought to myself, 'Well, how do we make this a win-win situation?' I didn't know about the Black 14 Philanthropy foundation."

"Mel Hamilton spent over 15-plus years engaging with the Church and also gaining respect from the elders," Griffin said. "The fact that they respected us, and we've gained that respect for them made them interested in grabbing that olive branch with us and doing something for the greater good for us and for the greater good of The Church of Jesus Christ of Latter-day Saints. That's where we are today. That helps with the healing process overall because it brought everything full circle."

In 2019 Mel and John were invited to Church headquarters, where they first saw the epicenter of the Church's food distribution operation

The Church of Jesus Christ of Latter-day Saints and the Black 14 Philanthropy begin a partnership (2020).

"When I became acquainted with Mel, I was deeply moved knowing the Church could offer its resources to help the Black 14 provide education and nourishment for those in need," Elder Nielsen said. "We have become dear friends and close allies in a unified purpose — helping our brothers and sisters. We are honored to partner with them, assisting in the health and development of children. Significant changes are happening from our shared vision."

After working with church leaders, Elder Nielsen told Mel the church was prepared to donate 180 tons of goods to food pantries in nine cities near the homes of Black 14 members throughout the United States to help people in need. Church officials said that a single full truckload contains about $45,000 worth of food.

The news stunned Hamilton. He managed to whisper two words: "Sweet Jesus."

The first of several deliveries took place November 16, 2020, at Cathedral Home for Children and the University of Wyoming Food Share Pantry.

These organizations then distributed the food to families and students in the greater Laramie area. The other eight locations to receive food were:

- Baltimore, Maryland
- Battle Creek, Michigan
- Boys Town, Nebraska
- Charleston, South Carolina
- Denver, Colorado
- Ethete, Wyoming
- Pittsfield, Massachusetts
- Wilmington, North Carolina

The second delivery was unloaded the next day, Nov. 17, 2020, at the Salvation Army's Emergency Service Center in Aurora, Colo. The food was redistributed to a number of charities in Colorado. John Griffin helped organize the donation and was on hand to share his thoughts, "Families, little kids will have food in their bellies for Thanksgiving. I get a little emotional."

The deliveries are being made in the name of Black 14 Philanthropy and the Church. In the future, annual food drives will help address

food insecurity. Mel stressed "the loving relationship that the Black 14 and The Church of Jesus Christ of Latter-day Saints are trying to initiate. I want people to realize "that we're working together, and will continue to work together, to strengthen the love between people—even people with differences."

In the fall of 2022, Mel invited some church leaders to a Wyoming dinner honoring the Black 14 because he felt there could be no celebration without the church. Laramie Wyoming Stake President Cory Allen bought 100 Black 14 T-shirts for Latter-day Saints to wear to the game the next day in honor of the players. He reserved one shirt for himself.

Two weeks after the dinner, Mel was in Salt Lake City with his son Malik and their wives Carey and Melissa to meet three of the church's apostles: Elders Gary E. Stevenson, Ronald A. Rasband, and Dale G. Renlund — as well as Elder Nielsen.

The Hamiltons (Left to right: Mel,Carey , Melissa, and Malik) (Carey Hamilton photo).

Later that month, healing for a university, a game, and an institution finally came. Mel and John were the featured guests of a weeklong series of events honoring the Black 14:

- Lectures involving the BYU football team and students from across campus
- The Sept. 23, 2022 premiere of the BYU student-made Documentary Film **"The Black 14: Healing Hearts and Feeding Souls."**

(available on YouTube).

(BYU photo)

- "The film was created, produced, shot, written, and edited by BYU students Elisabeth Ahlstrom, Abigail Gunderson, Carly Wasserlein, and Shyler Johnson. with the help of faculty and staff mentoring them," BYU Adjunct Professor Melissa Gibbs said.
- They worked for over a year to gather the story of The Black 14 in collaboration with Black 14 members John Griffin, Mel Hamilton, Tony Gibson, and Tony McGee. Their travel included eleven states in ten days and hundreds of hours of research, interviews, and edits.
- All this hard work brought together details of a profound story.

L to R: Mel Hamilton, John Griffin, & Elder S. Gifford Nielsen (Deseret News photo)

And for Griffin, the healing came full circle as he sat in front of a sold-out theater on campus to explain the mission of Black 14 Philanthropy and a partnership with the church to eradicate food insecurity in underprivileged areas.

"I think a lot of healing has been done prior to this," said John, who with Mel, received a standing ovation from BYU students, faculty and administrators after the premiere of the documentary. "That was a wonderful affair. They did what they had to do to mend some open wounds.

“But I can draw parallels between that and what I've experienced this week; it's a healing process, and this has been a week of fellowship; bringing two entities, even three entities together: Wyoming, BYU and the representatives from the Mormon Church who are now brothers — not adversaries, but brothers and sisters. It's been one heck of a journey.

It's been a journey of fellowship, it's been a journey of recognition, and it's been a journey of something that is going to grow and be even more special that we thought it would be before."

Mel Hamilton's Experience

Mel Hamilton's son, Malik, who wasn't even born when his father was dismissed from the Wyoming football team, joined The Church of Jesus Christ of Latter-day Saints while studying culinary arts at Utah State and worked for a while as a chef at BYU. Malik's experiences as a member of the church exposed Mel to people and aspects of the church's culture that further impressed him.

"Never did I hate the people of the Latter-day Saint religion," Mel said. "It was a mission of mine to ... speak out wherever I went to clarify we don't hate people. We just wanted that one policy changed. And thank God, there was a revelation that changed it."

"I must do everything I can to plaster all the cracks made in the walls of that relationship. [It] was a rift, not a hate," Mel says. "My mom said, 'God will tell you what to do. All you have to do is listen.' So, I'm listening."

And so, Mel's journey and listening have continued to this day. After his experiences with Malik's family, in 2024 Mel came to the decision to become a member of the Church of Jesus Christ of

Latter-day Saints.

The Character of The Black 14

To be clear: *The Black 14 never demonstrated against BYU.*

President Allen, the church's Laramie stake president, described Griffin and the other members of the Black 14 as enduring examples:

"It says a lot about who they really were as young men to have the courage to stand up in 1969, and then it says more that they continue to strive for the less fortunate and those stuck in poverty," he said.

"The Black 14 always wanted to make something useful out of the incident in 1969," Mel told the Deseret News in 2020. "We didn't want to take on a bitter and negative connotation. We wanted to do something to improve the look of our legacy by helping other people…I am a Christian, so I do know the Lord had his hand in this. I know the Lord is guiding this, and we are connected from now on. I hope we do great things together."

"The grace of God is all over this. If we didn't have that grace in play, this probably never would have happened," said John, a devout Catholic.

"It is remarkable," John continued. "This is an American story. Nobody could have written this 50 years ago, 10 years ago, two years ago. They can now. And it's a heartwarming story. It's not spin. It's real.

It's in the hearts of all of us. If I passed away tomorrow, I have lived a full life. I have been a part of something that's much bigger than me."

John added, "People will say, 'What happened? You joined with your so-called adversary to do all of this?' I want to be a part of that. How could I get involved? … I can't think of a better Thanksgiving story than this. This is a story of joy; this is a story of gratitude. This is an answer to prayer."

John's grandmother always taught him that God works in mysterious ways, which he has seen proved true again and again.

"Now we're partners with the church," he said. "We might have different faiths, but it's all about humanity and how we can reach out, how we can work together. I'm grateful for this opportunity, for both us and the church."

"The partnership is a modern tale of forgiveness," Elder Nielsen said as he watched the food loaded on trucks at the Bishops' Central Storehouse in Salt Lake City: "We can forgive and move forward. It's up to each one of us to make that decision. In this particular case, Mel and John have made that decision and those members of the Black 14 that are with them have made that decision, which puts us in a position where we can really help them. That's why we have what we have here today."

"Especially now," Mel said, "in this climate that

we have, this polarizing climate of love and hate, I don't want to be on that hateful side, and I don't want people to think that the Black 14 is on that hateful side. We certainly are not."

John said the joint food deliveries will become legacies of the Black 14 and the church. "It's gratifying to us to have the ability to give back at our ages," he said. "Thank God I'm still here to be able to experience this. It's a wonderful day. We're moving mountains of food, and those mountains of food are going to be consumed by people who need it. …For us to be able to do that, that just makes me happy!"

"Never be defined by an incident – you can overcome that." – John Griffin

References

LDS scriptures, *Doctrine & Covenants, Official Declaration 2.*

The Black 14: Race, Politics, Religion, and Wyoming Football. *WyoHistory.org*, Nov. 8, 2014.

The LDS Church and Black People, 1969 Office for Civil Rights Study of BYU

BYU to honor 'Black 14' football players kicked off Wyoming's 1969 team, *Deseret News, Sept. 22, 2022.*

The Black 14: Healing Hearts and Feeding Souls – Documentary private screening honors two Black 14 members, *The Daily Universe, Sept. 22, 2022.*

BYU to honor the Black 14, a group of former

Wyoming football players who once protested LDS church policy, *ESPN, Sept. 24, 2022.*

Healing hearts: 53 years after dismissal, BYU honors members of Wyoming's 'Black 14', *KSL.com, Sept. 24, 2022*

Healing continues as 2 members of "Black 14" light the Y, receive warm reception at BYU-Wyoming game, *Deseret News, Sept. 25, 2022.*

How the Black 14 and church are (still) putting the giving into Thanksgiving, *Deseret News, Nov. 26, 2021.*

Is America Really Interested in Racial Healing?, *C Square Magazine, October 13, 2022*

How the 'Black 14' and Latter-day Saints became partners moving mountains of food to those in need, *Deseret News, Nov. 17, 2020.*

The Church of Jesus Christ Partners With the Black 14 to Feed the Hungry.
newsroom.churchofjesuschrist.org/article/black 14 – partnership

The Corporate World of "Partnerships"

From a different arena, here are two corporate examples of partnerships:

Example #1: Some years ago, a large company *("Alpha")* took out a full-page advertisement in a nationwide newspaper. It opened with this sentence: *"We'd like to thank our best suppliers worldwide."*

Then 152 suppliers were recognized as *Alpha's* Suppliers of the Year. At the bottom of the page, the final sentence read: *"Working together to achieve customer enthusiasm with exciting Alpha products."*

The casual reader might have been impressed with this company's recognition of its best suppliers. But those who knew the background smiled at the advertisement's irony.

Just two years before this recognition, *Alpha* had torn up its contracts with many of these suppliers and demanded the terms be renegotiated with significant across-the-board savings to *Alph*a. One of *Alpha's* suppliers asked this author, "How do we know they won't do the same thing six months from now? They tore up a legal contract and made us bid lower. They could do it again. They've destroyed our trust in them."

Despite its resentment, this company and most of *Alpha's* other suppliers swallowed hard and lowered their prices. But the suppliers compensated in their own way as one of them explained, *"I can tell you how we and everyone else will make up some of the loss. We'll dilute the quality of our materials."*

And an industry observer added, *"I don't know of any major supplier who will take a new design to Alpha today, because, in the end, they will give it to the lowest bidder."* *(Some partners, huh?)*

Example #2: At a different company *("Bravo")*, the leaders were committed to shape true partnerships in the automobile industry. They had periodic meetings with various dealerships who sold their cars to see how their partnership was progressing.

At one such meeting the dealers wanted to know how soon they could get more cars to sell. "We never have enough cars," lamented one dealer. "We have sold out all of the cars on our lot. The only test drive car we have is my own personal car. Then, our customers have to wait weeks to take delivery of their car."

Bravo's president explained the parent company would not allow them to start a third shift until *Bravo* was in the black financially. "We are right on track with our commitment to our owners, but it will take us another year to get there."

One of the dealers asked, "How much money do you need to get into the black?"

"About $13 million," the president replied.

After doing some quick calculating of annual sales, the dealers stated, "That's about $140 per car. If we rebate back to you $140 per car, can we get our third shift?"

The president readily agreed and also got the parent company's agreement. The third shift was organized, sales volume accelerated accordingly, and the voluntary dealer rebate moved *Bravo* into the black one year ahead of projections. (*Some **real** partners, eh?*

PLAYBOOK FUNDAMENTAL SEVEN:

Adapt to changes in your world

We are all, too often, creatures of habit. Routines make our lives easy… We like our comfort zones…It irritates us when something forces us out of our routine... We get stuck and feel like we are just treading water until we can get back to normal.

Teams are the same. So are organizations. Work in organizations is done by the bureaucratic code defined at the outset of the Industrial Revolution around 1760. One tenet of that code is: *"Do a task exactly the same way every time."*

In my business experience with clients, this is still one of the universal organizational rules. One criticism of modern organizations is they are too bureaucratic: they perform in a steady-state whether it is too fast or too slow – at least it's steady. Many translate the bureaucratic rule to mean – "go by the book" – even when the situation may call for a different plan. This is the blessing and the curse of the steady state.

One executive of a large U.S. company described what he found when he toured some of his company's manufacturing plants, seized by the East German government at the end of World War II, and returned to his company's possession after the fall of the Berlin Wall.

"It was eerie," said this executive. "It was a time warp. Here were plants still operating in pristine condition – with vintage 1940's equipment. Everything had been repaired "by the book" but not modernized one bit. The 1940's standards of proficiency were totally inadequate by today's standards. It was more cost effective now to raze each facility rather than to modernize it."

Another example of the bureaucratic code was "the book" on warfare at the time of the American Revolution. The British army was a world power, fighting battles based on what made them successful on the battlefields in Europe. You've seen "the book" in action in a number of Revolutionary War era movies: each army lined up in a horizontal line (or lines) across from each other and fired guns and artillery at each other until one of them retreated or surrendered.

But the American colonists, because they were usually outnumbered and strapped for cash, invented some different ways of fighting:

They changed many battlefields from flat plains and meadows to the wild terrain of the new, untamed American landscape. They fought on uneven ground with rocks, trees and bushes to impede the use of artillery. They hid behind those natural shields and spread out all over the place. They attacked the enemy from all different sides. They borrowed some new weapons designed by native Americans for hand-to-hand combat.

Adapting the Steady State

So, today we work hard to maintain our steady state, but the outside world does not force-fit itself to our system. We are surrounded by a variety of demands and expectations. If you respond to all of them in the exactly the same way, you may win some and lose some.

Fundamental Number Seven is all about adapting to improve your team's results. This requires:

- Understanding the current order of things: what customers want, what opponents are doing now…and which of these elements are affecting your success?

- Adapting and adjusting so that you continue being successful. Do you need to change something in your playbook because of what key stakeholders are expecting *now*? Or do you need to change a specific game plan for one opponent?

Here are eight examples of such adaptation from the LaVell Edwards years:

#1. The invention of LaVell's earnestly sought game changer: the BYU passing attack first initiated by Dewey Warren. This adaptation has not only transformed the culture and results at BYU, but also has led to a different NCAA football scenario from the old days of "three yards and a cloud of dust." The BYU playbook itself has been modified at times when needed, but the roots have been preserved.

#2. Offensive coordinator/quarterback coach Doug Scovil adapting the playbook to better fit a change of quarterbacks. (Dick Harmon, Deseret News, July 1, 2013)

Marc Wilson and Jim McMahon sat behind Gifford Nielsen on the depth chart in 1977. But when Nielsen suffered a season-ending knee injury at

Oregon State during the fourth week of the season, Wilson was called into Scovil's office.

"Doug put his playbook down in front of me with a stack of sticky notes and said, 'I want you to put a note on every play you like in this offense because Marc, you are not Gifford and it doesn't make sense for me to call plays that Gifford liked if you don't," Wilson said.

The eager quarterback put sticky tabs on all of the roll-out plays, plays that Scovil never called for Nielsen. Doug preferred to keep his quarterbacks protected in the pocket.

"Doug looked at me and said, 'What's with all these roll-out plays?'" Wilson said. "I grew up as a little kid playing two-man touch in the street and I'm a lot more comfortable running around."

Scovil listened to the skinny sophomore from Seattle and changed the entire offense. The following Saturday, with Wilson rolling out all over the place, the Cougars stunned Colorado State 63-17. Wilson threw a Western Athletic Conference-record seven touchdown passes in his first full game of action since the second week of his senior season at Shorecrest High.

Marc was awestruck: "Think about that. We are leading the nation in every offensive category with Gifford as quarterback and this is a great offensive coordinator and I'm a nobody going into this game.

He was willing to throw out everything we had been doing and design a set of plays for a nobody, a backup quarterback who hadn't done anything and was going to play his first game."

"That was Doug Scovil and that's why Scovil was great with Roger Staubach, Gifford and me, Jim McMahon and everybody because Doug was willing to do that."

"After doing that I thought, 'This isn't that hard. I'm just gonna keep setting WAC records...And I did the following week at Wyoming,'" Wilson said with a hint of sarcasm. *"I continued my WAC record-setting pace with six interceptions."*

#3. Jim McMahon's "Miracle Punt"

Background: The Cougars were playing at Hawaii in the seventh game of the year on October 25, 1980. The Cougars were coming off a brutal physical battle at Utah State in which a number of players had been injured.

Most serious of these injuries was quarterback Jim McMahon's shoulder separation on his passing arm. Jim did not practice during the week and was still questionable until kickoff time. LaVell Edwards said, "We talked about (the injury) before the game. I told him, 'If at any time that arm doesn't feel right, you let me know and you're coming out.'"

The injured shoulder was heavily taped, so heavy in fact, that McMahon couldn't raise his arm up to a normal throwing position. He improvised a side-arm motion that could zip the ball short distances. But he couldn't throw long with the sore shoulder.

McMahon grabs a high snap with his wounded arm. (*Honolulu Advertiser photo by Ron Jett.*)

Provo Herald sports editor Marion Dunn's memorable tribute was, "*What he (McMahon) did that night should have its own special place in BYU's athletic Valhalla.*"

The miracle:

With 13:50 to play in the second quarter, and the Cougars facing a fourth and six on the Hawaii 36, McMahon, who did the short yardage punting for the Cougars, pulled off the punt of the century.

He was back to punt when the ball was snapped and soared high over his head. He jumped for the ball and somehow managed to raise his heavily-taped and injured right arm and got his hand on the ball and brought it in. With his back to the onrushing Rainbows, Jim turned around to face one defender right in front of him. His punt certainly would be blocked.

But his punt was not blocked! His competitive instinct kicked in and Jim fooled everybody by kicking the ball with his *left* foot. The ball landed inside the Rainbows' 10, took a high bounce toward the end zone but was grabbed by BYU's Tom Holmoe at the one.

The Cougars stopped Hawaii inside the seven and took over on the Rainbow 41 after their punt.

It is also worth mentioning that McMahon threw 60 passes that night, completing 31 for 389 yards with three interceptions and two TDs. Jim certainly showed his sore shoulder who was boss that night!

#4. BYU changing its defensive scheme from the 4-3 formation to a 3-4 for some opponents or specific plays.

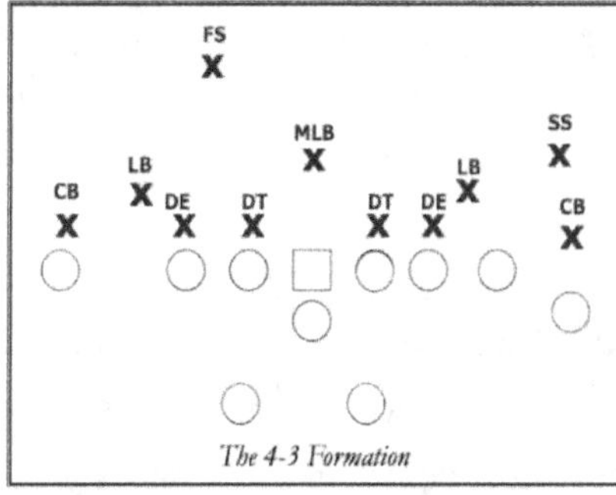

The 4-3 Formation

The 4-3 defense was the standard at all levels of football in the '70s. It was a good fit for teams who primarily ran the football.

The four down-linemen and three linebackers were all close to the line of scrimmage and in position to crunch a runner for little or no gain. Two cornerbacks and two safeties in the backfield gave protection to an occasional pass play.

BYU also employed the 4-3 defense until a painful loss to UNLV, 45-41, in 1981. The Cougars were frustrated that their 511 yards of total offense and 41 points were not enough to overcome the Rebels' 45 points and 628 yards of total offense. The Rebels actually had more passing yardage than the Cougars by a margin of 473 to 269.

The newer 3-4 formation (three down linemen and four linebackers) was employed to negate those teams who sought to emulate BYU's passing game. The four linebackers could use their speed to stop runners *or* to strengthen the pass defense. The flexibility of the linebackers would confuse the opponents. BYU worked on perfecting this defense.

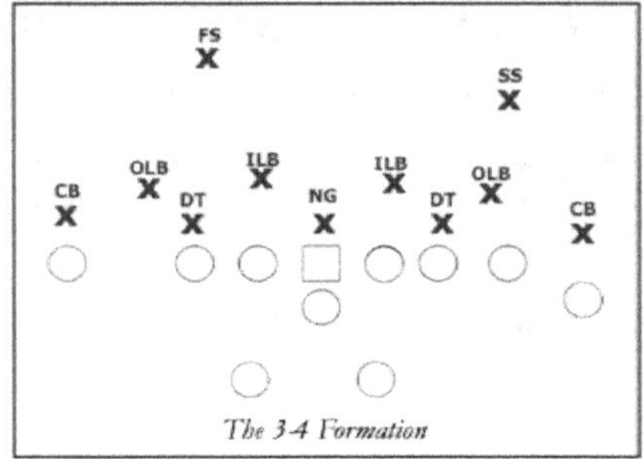

The 3-4 Formation

BYU first unveiled its 3-4 defense for the 1982 season opener. The Cougars were in Las Vegas on a scorching hot day (108 degrees) for a rematch with UNLV.

The new defense worked perfectly: the mighty Rebels gained only 15 yards rushing and 145 yards passing for the entire game. No wonder the Rebels were shut out, 27-0! It was the first shutout UNLV had suffered in 45 straight games. For BYU, it was its first defensive shutout in 44 games.

In the future BYU would carefully consider the right defense to use to actually "attack" what an opponent was doing.

#5 Defender Kyle Morrell's goal line somersault tackle

Background: September 22, 1984, Saturday night in Honolulu (wee hours of Sunday morning in Utah). BYU's march to an undefeated season and national championship was almost over before anyone even suspected it had begun.

Trailing, 12-10, Hawaii had the ball third down and six inches from the BYU goal line with just seconds remaining in the third quarter. The two teams lined up and BYU safety Kyle Morrell called an audible – for himself – and he began a charge from deep in the formation, leaped over both his defensive linemen teammates and Hawaii's offensive linemen, and grabbed quarterback Raphel Cherry by the jersey and shoulder pads and dragged him down behind his line.

Kyle Morrell stops Hawaii QB Raphel Cherry short of the goal line (Mark Philbrick BYU photo)

No touchdown! The Rainbows had to settle for a field goal by Richard Spelman, and Hawaii took the lead, 13-12.

Then BYU received the following kickoff and rode Robbie Bosco's arm for three completions and a score. Facing third and 21 from the Rainbow 25, Bosco hit Glen Kozlowski breaking on a post pattern for the winning touchdown.

The Cougars pulled this one out and went on to their date with destiny for the Holiday Bowl and the national championship.

Kyle Morrell was named a first-team All-American that year. Well-deserved, Kyle!

#6: November 20, 1993: Freshman Chad Lewis abandoned the "cordial host" protocol to defend the BYU goal post.

The visiting Utah team beat BYU, 34-31, in Provo for only the third time in the last 22 games. The Utes' emotions were "over the top."

Some Utes tried tearing down the north goal post in Cougar Stadium to "rub it in" the faces of the BYU fans. The traditional home crowd protocol for BYU football games is to show only respect and hospitality to the visitors.

So, what should any loyal Cougar do when members of the Ute clan start to destroy your school's property?

A loyal Cougar fan recorded the moment: "*I was walking down the stairs in the north end zone and seeing the Utah team trying to tear down our goalposts. Depression turned to anger at the thought of those guys thinking it was cool to tear down our goal posts. Then, like out of a movie script, I noticed Chad Lewis, seeing the Utes beginning to commit their crime, and he sprinted directly into the swarm of Ute players and caused the greatest human domino-effect the world has ever seen. Like a true superhero he thwarted the Utes' plans and saved the goal posts. It was awesome!*"

#7: A players-only meeting that was a "rededication" that ignited the 1974 WAC title drive.

Background: The 1974 BYU football team, with its new passing game posting four landslide victories in the last five weeks of 1973, had high hopes for its first WAC title since 1965. But the Cougars lost their first three games and tied Colorado State in their first conference game. The hoped-for title seemed to be a longshot with a strong Wyoming team coming to Provo.

The team was frustrated and upset by the situation. The team's three captains Brad Oates, Keith Rivera, and Gary Sheide led a players-only meeting and then met with LaVell and asked him to support some changes: (1) they wanted to reinstate the 1973 playbook that had unleashed the dominating passing game. The new offensive coach had installed his run-pass option playbook that wasn't delivering. (2) Keith Rivera personally spoke with each team member in the team meeting and got their commitment to practice and play by the playbook.

Notice where the call for change came from in this tense situation: *The team asked the boss to change the plan*. This is what we in industry call "bottom-up leadership" – those at the bottom of the organization see things that need to be done that the top leaders don't see.

No matter how skilled or charismatic the top leaders may be, the catalyst for change often is much lower in the system. "Bottom-Up," or "Self-Governance," is where the magic often happens. Both are essential, but total alignment and commitment are built best from the "Bottom-Up."

Notice how the "boss" at the top of the football team responded to the captains' "call for change." LaVell did what I have seen too few business leaders do when such "Bottom-Up" commitments come their way. He supported the call for change and set the example to make sure it succeeded.

Brad Oates concluded, "*The '74 team changed the arc on BYU football. Our passing could compete. The culture we shaped after that players meeting has endured with us even to today. Many of us hadn't seen some of our teammates for those many years, but when we had the 50-year reunion for that team (in 2024), we all came together and still felt as close to each other as when we were playing. It was truly magical."*

#8: Going to the shotgun formation on offense

In both 1989 and 1990 the Cougars had been ambushed in Hawaii by the Rainbow Warriors. What do these numbers tell you?

1989: Hawaii 56, BYU 14

- Ty Detmer was sacked 10 times and intercepted twice.

1990: Hawaii 59, BYU 26

- Detmer sacked three times and intercepted four times.
- **Two-year bottom line: the Heisman Trophy winner was sacked 13 times and gave up six interceptions.**

1991 the Cougars used a new offensive formation – the shotgun – with Ty standing a few yards behind the offensive line to take the direct snap from center. Ty said he didn't like the change at first, but as he got used to it, he said he could see everything better in front of him, including finding some outlet receivers on the blitzes. Here are the results of this first game in the shotgun:

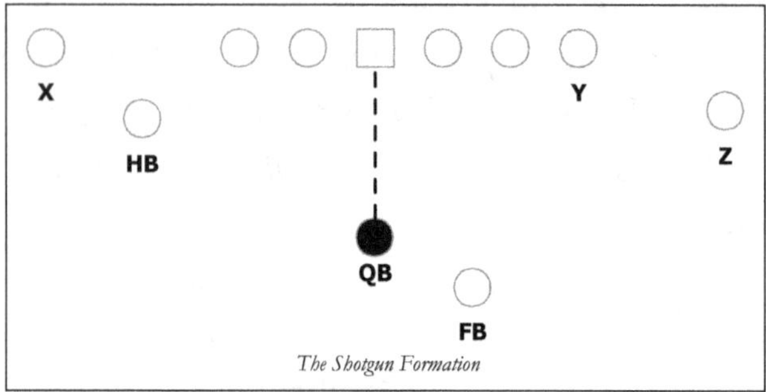

The Shotgun Formation

1991Key Passing Stats:

- **Detmer 14 of 20 for 225 yards with no interceptions, two sacks, and three TDs.**
- **Key Total Offense Stat: BYU 443 yards, Hawaii 454 yards**
- **Key Turnovers Stat: BYU 2, UH 5**

Reading between the lines, the shotgun allowed Ty to blunt the Hawaii crazy blitzing defense…And the BYU defense caused five Hawaii turnovers.

FUNDAMENTAL NUMBER EIGHT:

Never "write off" an individual.

This is a profound fundamental – one which LaVell demonstrated with a heart and vision that many would not comprehend. To put it very simply, *this is looking beyond the person or team as they appear today and paving the way for them to accomplish even more than they had envisioned.*

Perhaps some real-life examples with living, breathing, complex people can reveal how LaVell "never wrote off" an individual."

Danny Frazier Danny was a 6'5", 221 lb. redshirt sophomore linebacker. LaVell said, "*Athletically, he had it all – height, strength, speed, and quickness…He looked like he had tremendous potential as a football player."* He became a starter in 1979 at weak linebacker. In the first game against Texas A&M in Houston, Danny suffered cracked vertebrae in his neck and was finished for two years.

Danny Frazier 1979 (BYU photo)

So, Danny served a mission to Oakland CA as one of the early black missionaries in the Church. When he returned, he rejoined the Cougars in spring practice with an eye on picking up where he left off.

After a couple of days, LaVell took him aside and coached him, "You're done with football. You don't want to do this. Get on with your life."

As Danny recalls, "Who's going to argue with LaVell Edwards?"

What LaVell knew, that most of us didn't know, was Danny's history as a member of the National Honor Society, senior class president at Tooele High, all-state in track, basketball and football, and one of those glowing personalities that drew others to him.

Doug Robinson's profile in the Deseret News will fill in the blanks for you:

Blessing in disguise: career-ending injury didn't stop BYU athlete

Doug Robinson Deseret News Aug 31, 2011

SOUTH JORDAN —The first thing you notice about Danny Frazier is that he fills a room. He is 6-foot-6, 260 pounds, with wide shoulders and a flat stomach. At 52, he looks like he could still line up for BYU's defense, if not the Pittsburgh Steelers. Then there is his booming laugh, which punctuates every other sentence and is so loud that it used to scare his grandchildren until they realized he is a warm, engaging man who tends to draw people in.

"It's hard to miss him because he's so tall and so loud," says his son Jameson. "You can hear him across the room. He's always been loud, warm, and loving."

Frazier is an attorney with his own private practice — Frazier Law Firm — specializing in criminal defense. But when he is shopping or out in public, here come the questions that come naturally when you are big and black.

"Where did you play football/basketball?"

"I never get mistaken for a lawyer," he says, laughing again.

He played football and basketball at BYU, and the story ends there, although if circumstances had been different, he might have gone much further.

He seemed destined for gridiron greatness when he took the field at starting outside linebacker for BYU as a sophomore, going up against national powerhouse Texas A&M. A lanky and ripped 6-foot-5, 220 pounds, he was a rare combination of speed, athleticism and size. With his instinct for the ball, could the NFL be far behind? He was such an all-around athlete that he played basketball for BYU in 1977, earning mop-up duty at power forward as a freshman (he and Keith Rice were the first blacks to play basketball for the Cougars).

"Athletically, he had it all," says former BYU head coach LaVell Edwards. "He looked like he had tremendous potential as a football player."

And then it was finished.

He broke his neck against A&M and that was that. He will tell you today that it was a blessing in disguise. The injury launched the rest of his life. He became one of the early black missionaries of the LDS Church after the ban against blacks holding the priesthood was lifted in 1978; he went to law school; he married; he started a law firm; he raised a family.

Frazier was equipped to deal with such challenges. Edwards was not only struck by the kid's athleticism, but by his engaging personality, as well. "He was very friendly and very well-liked," says the legendary coach. "He went out of his way to meet and talk to people. Not in a phony way, but a real genuine way. I remember that smile. He was like Magic Johnson that way. He had success written all over him, not just in athletics, but in anything."

After graduating with a degree in accounting in 1986, Frazier was accepted into BYU's law school. He has worked as a criminal defense attorney for 21 years.

Looking back now, he calls the neck injury "the best thing that ever happened to me. I say that mostly because of the mission. If I hadn't gotten hurt, I wouldn't have served a mission. Here's the deal, man. I played football from junior high all the way until I got hurt, and I was good at it, but I didn't know how to do anything else. All I did was work out. I didn't think I could do anything else. I really believe I'd be in a world of hurt if I hadn't gotten hurt. I got into academics. I learned the importance of education. I moved on with life. I actually enjoyed it more. I had to change my life. Reality sets in sooner or later."

His son Jameson notes that his father didn't

discuss regrets about his football career when he discussed his life with his children. "He mainly focused on his mission and how much he loved it," says Jameson. "It was never, 'Oh, man, I wish I hadn't gotten hurt.' It was about his mission and how he came back and did well in school and married my mom. He reminds me all the time that if he hadn't gotten hurt, I probably wouldn't be here. He probably would not have gone on a mission, and he would have played in the NFL and never met my mom."

He met his future wife, Joy Hobbs, a white woman from Canada who was living in Utah, before his mission, but there was no immediate spark. After Frazier returned from his mission, they reconnected at a fireside in which he was the speaker. They dated for 10 days and then eloped…A year later Danny and Joy were married in the LDS Laie, Hawaii, Temple.

Looking back, Danny says, "I wanted to do what I'm doing now. I chase my grandkids around the house, and we go for walks. I'm teaching my granddaughter to ride a bike. This is what it's about. This is what I wanted to do."

Give the final word to Edwards, his old coach: "He had all the athleticism to be a great football player; the accident was tragic that way. But he didn't use that as a crutch. He moved on. A lot of people would have been bitter and let it ruin their lives. Danny never thought that way. He found other challenges. The guy was one of the real choice people you ever work with because of his attributes. Athletically, he had it all, but equally, and maybe even more, was his outlook on life and the type of person he is."

Behind every great Frazier is a great mother... Danny's mother, Shirley Crump, was a single mother with four very lively sons. She was also a faithful member of the Church of Jesus Christ of Latter-day Saints. During the years of controversy about the church's policy of not ordaining black men to the priesthood, Shirley kept the faith, never murmuring. The week after the priesthood revelation was announced, Shirley's sons Danny, Mark, Michael, and Rodney all were ordained to the priesthood. On January 21, 1979, Danny was ordained an Elder. He was the first black member of the church on that '79 team.

Danny Frazier today
(Deseret News photo)

Jim McMahon

Whenever I mentioned Jim McMahon to others about being in *LaVell's Leadership Playbook* I, almost without exception, heard statements like:

- *"Oh yeah, McMahon was a wild man. He violated the Honor Code...hung out in bars...was foul mouthed."*
- *"The coaches looked the other way and let him get away with things because he was a football player."*
- *"He said and wrote derogatory things about BYU after he went to the NFL."*
- *"It isn't right that he was admitted to the BYU Hall of Fame. He was a disgrace to the school."*

Etc., etc., etc.

In FUNDAMENTAL NUMBER SIX you read Vai Sikahema's accounts of Jim McMahon:

- Partnering with others to help distressed former teammates.
- Coming to the defense of the Sikahema family when some rowdy bullies were threatening them at a game.
- Finding ways to bridge gaps between diverse social and ethnic groups.

I find these behaviors strikingly similar to those my church leaders might describe as being a *"peacemaker."*

Now consider that in the discussions about Jim's qualifications to enter the BYU Hall of Fame, (even as he was suffering from early-stage dementia), two leaders who know him best – warts, bad habits, and all, – LaVell Edwards and Tom Holmoe – actively made sure he had support to *legitimately qualify* for the BYU degree.

Here is the eyewitness account from the BYU official who was the proctor for Jim's work and progress to earn the final two credits for his BYU diploma. (From Vai Sikahema: *"Jim McMahon not the greatest? You might want to reconsider."* Deseret News Oct 2, 2014)

Trevor Wilson was dispatched from BYU to fly to Scottsdale to proctor Jim's final two tests, one of which was an exam on public speaking. A few days after his trip, Trevor sent me (Vai) a long email detailing his experience. With Trevor's permission, here is a portion of his email:

"Jim talked with me about the reasons why he wants to graduate. The roots stem from a promise he made his father that he would complete his degree. He also talked about wanting to finish something he started.

As an educator for over 20 years, I have preached to thousands of people (youths) the importance of an education mostly based on the opportunities it brings for the future. I learned from Jim something deeper; an education meant accomplishing something that represents a challenge. Conquering a mountain you once began to climb and promised people you would.

Jim doesn't need a degree for money. I don't even

think he feels he has to be in the BYU Hall of Fame. I think Jim wants a piece of paper on his wall in his office that sits right next to the hundreds of athletic awards he has won (including a Super Bowl) that right now means more to him than all the others because it was accomplished with his mind — a college degree.

"We reviewed Jim's homework to prepare one last time for his exam. I watched as he painfully studied, frustrated with his own mind that he could not capture everything he wanted. He then took the exam as I nervously watched. I then saw the "game mode" take over. Jim was determined to do this. When he handed me the exam back, he said, 'I think I only missed one.' For a small moment I think he willed his mind to work.

"Vai, on the flight home, I thought about all of this. About BYU and its mission. About all the kids I work with who are not members of the LDS faith and how hard it is for them to fit in at BYU. I saw all the faces of people I want to see finish their degree. Then, I thought about Jim. Jim represents all of those kids. Especially, the nonmember student-athletes who come to BYU and who provide a talent that helps BYU accomplish its mission of sharing its message to the whole world. He represents all of them. For everything some may say Jim did wrong, what he did right overshadows all of it. With the prompting of Tom, Jim's father, his girlfriend Laurie (who is truly a gift to

Jim), and a host of others who helped, Jim McMahon accomplished something greater than any game, any "Hail Mary," and any Super Bowl season. Jim overcame not just a disability, but a stereotype often given to nonmember athletes who don't fit the square peg — he got a degree."

Jim McMahon on Mondays with LaVell

(Dave McCann Sept 2, 2022 Deseret News)

"I had to meet with him (LaVell) every Monday morning for all five years that I was here," McMahon said of his individual sessions with his head coach. This is when Edwards would question reports of McMahon's weekend antics and where the quarterback could defend himself.

"He'd say, just keep, just keep on the straight path," McMahon said. "I'd say, I am on the path coach. I'm on the path that will take me straight to the NFL, hopefully!"

Edwards understood McMahon, but that didn't mean there weren't moments of sharp correction, especially with his swearing. Just moments after stopping practice and demanding that the team "clean it up" McMahon muttered a word under his breath. He had no idea Edwards was right behind him.

"He grabbed my face mask and jerked my head around," McMahon said. "I knocked his arms away and ended up leaving practice. That night I had to go

up to his house and talk to him about it. He knew I just wanted to win. That's all I wanted to do."

*New graduate Jim with LaVell (*Deseret News photo*)*

"The night my name went up in the stadium here, it was awesome!" McMahon said. "I didn't think it would ever happen because I didn't think I'd graduate. I didn't like school when I was here. I was happy with my 2.0 GPA so I could keep playing. It took me 37 years to get that diploma."

"I saw LaVell and he said to get it done," McMahon said. "He said, 'I don't know how much longer I've got left and I want to see your name up there (on the press box)'. I'm glad I was able to do that before he passed."

Jim at LaVell's Funeral: (Dick Harmon Oct 3, 2014)

"As much as I hate funerals, this is one I couldn't miss. He meant a lot to me and my football career and in my life. He was a great person, not only on the football field, but [in] teaching kids about life. I think that's why a lot of these guys showed up. He meant a lot to them."

Tom Holmoe (Dick Harmon Oct 3, 2014 Deseret News)

"Jim is my favorite teammate I ever had from Pop Warner to the NFL. He was so much fun to be around. He was a serious dude, a field general, a smart student of the game who played it to perfection and he had fun doing it. To go out to practice or play with Jim McMahon, it was like sandlot…I've had tears since the day he said, 'I'm done," (he earned his degree). "I've been crying for a month."

Marc Wilson Marc was perhaps the least experienced quarterback to be named a starter in the LaVell Edwards era. In high school he was injured and only played in two games his senior year. At BYU he didn't suit up for the freshman team and redshirted in '76. In other words, he had only played in two high school football games in the three years leading up to the 1977 season.

Late in the fourth quarter of the fourth game that season, Gifford Nielsen, going full speed toward that year's Heisman Trophy, went down with a torn MCL that ended his BYU career.

Marc Wilson (BYU photo)

The Cougars' next two games were against their strongest challengers for the WAC title – undefeated Colorado State and always-combative Wyoming – and both on the road. Outsiders looking at this situation might have urged LaVell not to put the fate of this team in the hands of such an inexperienced quarterback. *"Don't waste the potential of this great team with this move. Gradually break him in, then let him take over!"*

But LaVell looked beyond the logic of the situation and didn't write off the string-bean kid from Seattle. His first three-start results:

- **BYU 63, @Colorado State 17:** Marc completed 15 of 25 passes for 324 yards with one interception and **seven TDs (new BYU and WAC record)**.
- **BYU 10 @Wyoming 7:** he completed 10 of 26 passes for 96 yards with six interceptions and one TD.
- **BYU 34, Arizona 14:** he completed 23 of 43 passes for 334 yards with two interceptions and two TDs.

Marc ended up making LaVell look like a genius!

Marc's 1977 NCAA marks

- Most passing yds. one game – 571
- Most passes completed in one half – 27 (tied)
- Most yds. gained in one half – 339
- Most times total offense exceeded 300 or more yds. in s season (7) tied

Marc's 1979 NCAA marks

- NCAA leader in total offense – 3,580 yds.
- Most consecutive games total offense exceeded 300 yds. or more in a season – 5
- Most times total offense exceeded 300 or more yds. in a career – 13.

Marc was BYU's first consensus All-America quarterback.

Glen Kozlowski *"the punk, fighting kid"*

For those who closely followed the BYU football team, Glen Kozlowski was the successor to Jim McMahon – superstar on the field and often bad boy off the field.

As the youngest brother in his family, "Koz" was often picked on by his siblings. He grew up punching to stand up for himself. Teammates, opponents, strangers in weekend bars – Koz punched them all. His behavior in 1981 as a freshmen led to him being "invited" to take a time out from BYU.

Koz knew he could play at some other university and when he suggested this option to his girlfriend, Julie, she replied, "You can go where you want, I'm going to BYU... You make it right and be a man!"

So, Koz stayed in Provo and had monthly coaching from LaVell during his year on the sidelines.

He returned for three of the greatest seasons in BYU history:

- *1983 (11-1) team ranked (No. 7)*
- *1984 (13-0) team ranked (No. 1)*
- *1985 (11-3) team ranked (No. 16)*

He recalls giving his game gloves after his BYU games "to just a little kid" named Kalani Sitake.

After a super performance in the 1985 season-opening game on national TV (10 catches for 241 yards and one TD) he was poised for a banner year.

Then in the fourth game he suffered a serious knee injury that sidelined him for the next four games.

"I had given up. I'm never gonna play again," he said. Then he got a get-well card from four-year-old Mark Erickson, a handicapped fan. Here was a little guy who had physical problems who got a lot of joy just watching Koz play football.

"That letter changed my life," Koz said.

He was finally cleared to play in the next game with Wyoming. So, he wrote and invited Mark and his father to attend the game as his guests.

Marion Dunn reported:

Koz Converts a Sad Day into a Joyous One:

In the third quarter of the game Glen Kozlowski reinjured his left knee (the one that had sidelined him since the fourth game of the season against Temple). This ended Koz's playing days for BYU. BUT, despite his pain, he escorted his special guest, four-year-old Mark Erickson, around the locker room to meet all the players. Little Mark was thrilled beyond description. His father, Bruce, was there and explained the Mark-Koz connection to the Daily Herald's sports editor Marion Dunn..: "Mark cried when Koz was

NCHS coach Koz
(BYU podcast screenshot)

hurt against Temple. His mother, Joyce, suggested he write a get well note to Glen and wished that he would get better. He did. Glen answered. Then, this week Glen called and invited Mark to be his guest at the game with Wyoming and then join him in the locker room to meet the team. Here we are."

Then Marion Dunn observed, "But watching Koz take the young Mark Erickson around the locker room and introduce him to the other Cougars you wouldn't know anything was bothering him."

Glen Kozlowski 2.0

Wife Julie said, after his NFL days were over and he was seeing success as a high school coach, "In my eyes I think coaching is what really defines who Glen really is at the very core, because he is so wonderful with those young men and making a difference in their lives."

Robbie Bosco described the "new" Koz: "He would go to schools that weren't very good, and he would help them and bring some toughness to that team – and they would go on and win games and win championships. And I think just the love that he has for the game and the toughness that he brings – he instills that."

Koz described how he redefined success as a coach. "If I had a kid that couldn't play, and he improved, and was the best that he could be –that was success for me."

"At North Chicago High School, a minority school, my last year all 18 of my senior kids went to college; 15 on academic scholarships. That had never happened before, in the four years before...We'd did a garden every year. Gave back to the community."

"I'm telling you; he's a sensitive man now," said his son Tyler. "Back in the day, there were stories about him fighting and all of this other stuff. Even growing up, we weren't allowed to cry. Nowadays, he might be the biggest crybaby of us all."

More than anything, Tyler knows what BYU did for his dad.

"When my dad graduated from high school, they were so excited to get rid of him and have BYU take him over so he could be BYU's problem," Tyler says. "When he got here, he was a punk kid. Through LaVell, meeting my mom, and being at BYU, he's changed his life. He served as first counselor in the bishopric. He's been on the high council, and he's put four sons out on missions.

This experience he had at BYU turned him from the little boy that he was into the man he is now."

Brandon Doman: A "running" quarterback at BYU?

Brandon Doman (BYU photo)

The latest member of the BYU football Doman "clan," (older brothers Kevin, Bryce, and Cliff were all wide receivers in the years 1988-'94), Brandon was an option quarterback coming out of Salt Lake City's Skyline High. He was named Utah Player of the Year and highly ranked nationally before coming to BYU.

In 1998 and '99, he was the third string quarterback, throwing only four passes in actual games.

In 2000, it was more of the same as the Cougars were 4-5 on the year and losing big to Colorado State, 45-0, when Brandon was inserted into the lineup for "mop up" duty in the third quarter. Instead of just going through the motions, he sparked the Cougars:

- Passing for a team high 72 yards and one touchdown and
- Rushing for 25 yards in four carries for another touchdown.

The final score: Colorado State 45, BYU 21

Brandon's performance earned him the starting nod for the next game with New Mexico. The Lobos were also in a losing year (5-6), but had the Mountain West Conference's leading defensive team. His statistics in the game belied the fact that it was his first career start: he was 21 for 35 passing for 349 yards and ran nine times for 51 yards and one TD. The Cougars won the game, 37-13, to boost their record to 5-6.

Third-Stringer Doman's Miracle for LaVell

That put Brandon in the driver's seat for the season-ending (and LaVell Edwards' career-ending) game against archrival Utah in Salt Lake City. *(See the game details of this one in the Epilogue game: 2000: BYU vs. Utah).*

Brandon was actually LaVell's "Pay It Forward" gift to his successor, Gary Crowton, as Brandon remained the starting quarterback for the Cougars and led them to a 12-2 record in 2001. He passed for 3,542 yards and 33 TDs and rushed for 503 yards and eight more TDs. He was a unanimous All-Mountain West Conference QB and went on to play three seasons in the NFL.

He tied a BYU school record by winning his first fourteen games as a starter. Not bad for a "running" QB!

Graduate Assistant Andy Reid

KC Chiefs Andy Reid ((thesportingbase.com photo)

A solid backup offensive lineman for the 1979-80 Cougars, Andy was a graduate assistant on LaVell's staff during 1980-81. He since has risen to the top of the NFL coaching ranks, winning three Super Bowls with the Kansas City Chiefs.

But Andy is not only a winning coach, but also a person who doesn't write off a teammate. Deseret News reporter Tad Walch reported about Andy's service to teammate Michael Vick whose fortunes had sunk as rapidly as they had climbed.

Part of their success, Reid said, is the four-part slogan plastered on walls and pillars in the team's building. He said the players have dubbed it "The Formula..."

Reid said he developed "The Formula" when he saw Vick struggling in his return to the NFL after serving a prison sentence. Vick had been the first Black quarterback to be No. 1 in the draft and the first quarterback to run for 1,000 yards in the NFL. He had been to three Pro Bowls in his first six years.

"This guy was the greatest player in the National Football League at one time," Reid said. "He was the leader of the pack. The hugest Nike contract ever went to Michael Vick. He was a hip-hop star. He was it and he was the guy."

Then Vick, who was playing for the Atlanta Falcons, was charged and convicted and sent to prison for 21 months for his part in sponsoring dog fights. While he served his sentence, his grandmother died. He also filed for bankruptcy.

He emerged broken, according to a Washington Post *feature. This electric superstar appeared forgotten and ignored, according to a* GQ *feature.*

"It was all self-inflicted," Vick told the Post*. "I was young. I didn't have (any) guidance. I don't use this as no excuse. I could've said, 'No.' I could've made those right decisions, like, 'This ain't for me.' That's a blemish that I will never be able to erase."*

He didn't know if he'd ever play again.

The second chance

Enter Reid, then the head coach of the Philadelphia Eagles.

"When he comes out (of prison)," Reid said, "he's 20 pounds heavier, his family's abandoned him — other than his wife, his family has abandoned him. All the people that were involved in the situation he had,

abandoned him. (None of them) came to visit him when he was in jail. So now he comes out, and he's wondering, 'Am I ever gonna get back into the National Football League?'"

Reid said he did his homework on Vick and decided he deserved a second chance as a backup.

"When I met Andy," Vick told the New York Post, "I didn't have anything. I won't say anything, I just had my family. I had my family and a sense of hope that I can do it all over again, and I only told two people this post-incarceration —I told my wife, and I told Andy. When he brought me in, I told him I just needed one shot at it. And he gave me that shot."

Vick initially was the backup's backup. He spent a full year as the Eagles' third-string quarterback.

"There probably wasn't a professional quarterback farther from glory in all of football," the GQ feature said.

Reid clearly explained his expectations, which included Vick being a leader in the locker room. Vick told the Post that Reid spoke with the quarterback every week and asked him to check in with the coach regularly. Reid knew what was happening in his life, including who the lawyers were in his bankruptcy case.

Reid wanted to guide him in the right direction, Vick told the Post.

Michael Vick and Andy Reid (NY post.com photo)

"He instantly made me one of the guys, and it made me comfortable," Vick said. "He believes in people, and he gives you opportunity regardless of where you come from, or what you look like. He's always been that way. He's just a guy who was always open, always candid, cared about us as players, cared about us as men. And as long as you give him the proper respect, he'll give you the respect you deserve…Fell in love with him the first time I met him."

'The Formula'

Reid also made Vick laugh, and helped him be comfortable on the team. He also sent him into 12 games in that first season, 2009, even though Vick never threw more than three passes while playing at the end of decided games.

Then, before the 2010 season, the Eagles traded McNabb, elevating Kolb to starter and Vick to backup. Then Kolb got hurt in the first game. Suddenly, Vick was thrust back into the spotlight.

"He's scared to death. He's shaking to play in the game that he once controlled," Reid said. "So, we get

through the game, and he did OK. I mean, he did OK. I sat down with him, and I thought, what can I give this kid? I'm giving him a chance to play, but what can I give him to help him play?"

Reid told the roomful of government and religious leaders at the New York banquet he was doing the same thing they do when they care for the needy.

"What you guys are doing, you're giving people an opportunity," the coach said. "So how do I give him something to help him become the player that he once was?"

Reid said he thought about what Christ's primary characteristics would be if he were a football player and came up with "The Formula":

- ***Eliminate distractions***
- ***Create energy***
- ***Fear nothing***
- ***Attack everything***

"Eliminate distractions, nobody did it better than Christ," Reid said. "...And then create energy. Listen to me, and we all go here: Am I going to be an energy giver or an energy taker? I presume most of the people in this room are energy givers, man. You're going where other people are afraid to go, and you're bringing it every day to this community here. So, am I gonna be an energy giver or an energy taker?

"And then, fear nothing. Well, we all have fears. You know, we all have fears, but are you gonna run

from your fear, or are you going to attack your fear? Are you going to get to the bottom of what that fear is? Are you willing to go there and go in there deep? Are you willing to go there?

"And then, attack that son of a gun, so attack everything."

In 2010 Michael Vick attacked the opposition. *When the Eagles' starting quarterback Kevin Kolb was lost for the season with a major injury, Michael was elevated to starting QB for the Eagles. He led the team to a division title and won the Comeback Player of the Year Award. He was selected to his fourth Pro Bowl.*

Assistants who didn't fit well: Dwain Painter and Wally English

Hiring and releasing other coaches is a tricky and often unrewarding task for a head coach. *How do you release coaching friends without writing them off?*

As we have seen, in the early years of BYU"s passing movement, Dwain Painter and Wally English were two quarterback coaches who had different passions – both favoring a run-pass option offense more than BYU's new passing playbook. But their different passions weakened the BYU team's performance.

So, LaVell helped Dwain connect with UCLA coach Terry Donahue, whose Bruins ran a run-option offense that wasn't shy about passing. It was a good fit for both.

LaVell helped Wally connect with the Pitt Panthers, who also were known for producing great running backs. Another good fit.

Both of these coaches eventually became head coaches in their own right.

Going out on a limb for an "Unknown"

Offensive lineman Brad Oates played on the freshman team for a well-respected eastern university in the early 1970s. But he longed for BYU, where others shared his LDS faith, as he realized he had virtually nothing in common with his teammates, except football. Brad contacted BYU but was told there were no scholarships available. Undaunted, he moved forward with his plans to transfer anyway.

LaVell called Brad's coach. (*LaVell had no previous contact with Brad* – so this is what he said on the phone): *"A member of our faith has reached out and inquired about a transfer. I don't know that we're interested but as a courtesy I thought I would let you know that we're going to talk to him."*

Then the conversation suddenly got ugly. The other coach exploded – yelling, screaming, and cursing at LaVell and threatening to turn him into the NCAA for "poaching" his player. LaVell listened calmly until the coach finished.

Only then did LaVell speak. "Coach," LaVell said softly, "before I called, I didn't have a scholarship. But the longer you spoke, it occurred to me that Brad could easily slip into a scholarship vacated by an outbound missionary."

Then LaVell dropped the hammer.

"I can see that Brad must be a pretty good football player for you to act like this. Before this call I really had no intention of offering Brad a scholarship. But this much is clear...You don't deserve to coach a kid like Brad Oates. I want you to be the first to know that after I hang up the phone, I'm going to offer Brad a scholarship. He'll have to redshirt a year, but we will find a spot for him."

Click...Coach Edwards Over and Out.

Brad did transfer and played for BYU in 1974-75. LaVell and Dave Kragthorpe did indeed find a spot for him on the offensive line. He was a two-year starter and an All-WAC selection at offensive tackle in 1975. He was also named a second team All American that same year.

After graduation Brad was drafted in the third round by the NFL's St. Louis Cardinals. While playing in both the NFL and USFL, he earned a juris doctor degree in the offseason from BYU's J. Reuben

Clark Law School.

Brad, Barry, and Bart Oates (Mark A. Philbrick BYU photos)

Brad's younger brothers Barry and Bart also followed him to BYU. Barry was a solid four-year defensive letterman. Bart was a center, who in 1982 was named to the All-WAC team and also second team All-America. In the NFL he played for the New York Giants and the San Francisco 49ers and was a three-time Super Bowl winner.

Brad summarized this whole series of events, "LaVell was committed to us and we to him."

Returned missionaries

Outsiders would not even notice some other players who had been "written off" before LaVell's tenure as head coach. These were the players who chose to interrupt their athletic pursuits to serve as missionaries for the Church of Jesus Christ of Latter-day Saints.

Two years without intense physical training,

team practices, and game competition left these individuals, – in conventional wisdom – "too rusty and not in shape" – to make the BYU team. This was true not only for football, but also in most other sports. If students did choose to come back to the team after their mission, they were "on their own" to compete with those already in the fold.

One of LaVell's predecessors even made the statement that "if the brethren won't call my players on missions, we will build the Notre Dame of the west."

LaVell *made it his business* to give his players, those who wanted to serve, a legitimate shot at returning to the team after their missions. This is considered normal today, but at the time (1973) when LaVell began this "project," it was deemed by many to be a big mistake. His first "test" case was offensive lineman Lance Reynolds.

Lance was an all-state player who came to BYU out of Granite High School in Salt Lake City. He played on the freshman team (NCAA requirements in those days made freshmen ineligible to play varsity sports). He became a starter on the offensive line as a sophomore in 1973.

Lance told me of his experience as the first player LaVell supported to go on a mission. *"It definitely was not the thing a football player was encouraged to do back in those days," he said. "I was a starter, but if*

I went on a mission I would be gone for two years. My discussions with some members of the BYU program did not paint a very good picture for my return. I decided if I served a mission, I would not return to BYU. Then LaVell called me in and spoke with me. When I told him about my mission plans, he promised me that he would support me and help me be successful after I returned."

That sealed the deal for Lance. In 1973 he accepted a call to the Seattle, Washington mission. He returned two years later and rejoined the team.

"It takes you about a year to get back in shape to play again." Lance said. "You don't have the reflexes, the strength, the moves to fit into the flow of things."

He started working to get back into shape. He earned a starting position again in 1976 and in '77 was named to the All-WAC team. The next year he was drafted by the Pittsburgh Steelers in the NFL.

Lance's experiences paved the way for his four sons to follow in their father's footsteps at BYU: Lance Jr.(2002-05), Dallas (2005-08), Matt, (2008-2011), and Houston (2010-2012). It seemed like *"there was always a Reynolds to fortify BYU's line."*

Lance later was a graduate assistant under LaVell and then a full-time assistant coach for the running backs and offensive line. He understood first-hand the challenges these players – and coaches – faced. *"When Vai Sikahema came back from his mission, he was small and out of shape. But we were patient with each other, and he became a great player in our system... "LaVell was right. Now we have dozens of players on each team who are returned missionaries."*

An imperceptible thread in the culture of BYU football is these missionary-players. They know "in their hearts" not to get down on one another. Others have been patient with them as they overcame their post mission rough spots; they owe it to their teammates to be patient with them. These dynamics build strong team cohesion.

Lance Reynolds Player:

- 1973: started as a sophomore, left guard (6-2, 260 lbs.)
- 1973-75: served a mission to Seattle, Washington
- 1976: (6'2, 265 lbs.) started at left tackle
- 1977: named to the All-WAC first team
- 1978: played with Pittsburgh and Philadelphia in the NFL

Coach Lance Reynolds

- Graduate Assistant 1979-80
- Assistant Head Coach Snow College 1981
- Assistant Head Coach Ricks College 1982
- BYU Running Backs Coach and later Offensive Line Coach, and Assistant Head Coach 1985-2000

Author's Note: Brian Gunderson

A fellow missionary with me in the North German mission in 1968-69, Brian's story is certainly newsworthy! Brian took his football with him to Germany and would play catch with his companion or with those of us in his district on our preparation days.

He tried out for and made the 1970 BYU team as a sophomore, just, in his words, "hoping for a chance to make the team and contribute."

He was injured on the first day of fall practice. He was holding the ball for a placekicker who missed the ball and kicked Brian's hand, breaking the tendon in the little finger on his throwing hand. An operation failed to fully correct the damage. He couldn't throw for five weeks.

Undeterred, Brian worked hard and moved up steadily until he was the number two quarterback the week before the homecoming game with Utah State. Three days before the game, he practiced with the first team. On the day before the game, coach Tommy Hudspeth told Brian he would start against the Aggies.

So, here he was on homecoming day making his first start against a strong Aggie team with a gimpy finger on his throwing hand and having not played in a competitive game in five years.

Utah State was a good team with a very strong quarterback named Tony Adams. But BYU was fired up with its hungry quarterback at the helm and a future nation's leading rusher "Fleet" Pete Van Valkenburg.

"Coach Hudspeth let me call most of my own plays which made me feel even more a part of things," Brian said. "The team gave me great support. They said, 'Whatever you call, we'll run.'"

For the record, Brian was 6 for 12 passing for 60 yards, with one interception. He was 4-5 in the second half. He also had 21 yards rushing on seven carries. Not flashy, but he engineered two drives for scores. Pete Van Valkenburg was the big star of this game, gaining 178 yards on 36 carries and two touchdowns. He was named WAC back of the week for his stellar performance.

The opportunistic Cougars had other heroes.

Linebacker Ron Tree intercepted a fumble and ran it back 22 yards for a touchdown. Joe Liljenquist kicked two field goals. Chris Farasopoulos had two interceptions and 135 return yards. The win breathed new life into the Cougars.

Aftermath

Brian Gunderson & pinky (BYU photo)

I ran into Brian on campus a few days after the homecoming game. He told me about his mangled pinky finger and then said, "The finger has healed a little crooked. But it actually has helped improve the velocity and accuracy of my passes." I shared this anecdote with Sports Information Director Dave Schulthess, who arranged for a BYU photographer to snap a photo of Brian showing off his crooked pinky finger!

The following week, the Cougars beat Wyoming, 23-3 in Provo for their only WAC win of the year. Brian threw for 197 yards and two touchdowns. Golden Richards had three receptions for 99 yards. Dave Coon rushed for 67 yards. Dan Hansen, Chris Farasopoulos, and Jeff Lyman each had two interceptions to stifle the Cowboys.

And that was the final Cougar victory in the 1970 season.

Brian, I would say guiding the team to two of its three wins that year was certainly a "contribution" to the team!

Coach Hudspeth didn't write off Brian Gunderson in 1970. LaVell Edwards would follow Tommy's example and greatly expand it with many more players and even greater results when he took over.

Author's Final "Thank You!" to LaVell

By Dave Hanna

Author's Note: this piece is drawn from an article originally published by the Provo Daily Herald's *Cougar Nation* on November 22, 2000, two days before LaVell's last game as BYU's head coach.

What do you give a football coach who has everything?

Take LaVell Edwards for instance. He's given us

Cougar fans so much through the years, you'd like to give him something in return. But what?

He's won 20 conference championships. His teams have been to 22 bowl games. He's even won a national championship. He's coached a Heisman Trophy winner and two Outland Trophy winners. He's beaten Miami when the Hurricanes were Number One. He's beaten Notre Dame in South Bend. He's won a New Year's Day bowl game. He's won many more than he's lost with every conference opponent. And he's one of a handful of coaches who has won more than 200 college games.

Now, Coach Who Has Everything, let me be sure you also have my thanks.

On behalf of all of us, thank you for putting together a winning program. Not only have you won, but you've also developed teams that are really fun to watch.

I'm so glad you never caught Wishbone fever like many coaches did in the '70s. And thank you for preserving the integrity of the BYU program along the way. You and your staff have developed a system that allows the players BYU can attract — mostly players of average physical ability — to neutralize the blue-chip players other programs too often have sold their souls to obtain. Innovation and team commitment have made the difference in your program.

Thank you for finding a way to send hundreds of your players on LDS missions, thereby reminding us all that giving of yourself to serve others need not be a handicap to a career in sports — or medicine, or business, or farming, or education, or parenting for that matter. It took great courage and great faith to institutionalize the missionary athlete as a mainstay of your program. Today the practice is common in all BYU sports. But I know what an enormous risk it seemed to be 28 years ago when you decided to make it happen. Today some of your rivals insinuate the practice gives you an "unfair" advantage, but I haven't seen any of them shipping their players off to the Peace Corps to even the odds!

Thank you for showing us what it means to be loyal to those who have sacrificed for you as you stood by Gary Sheide, Marc Wilson, Steve Young, Robbie Bosco, and Steve Sarkisian on those occasions when many of the "experts" in the stands told you to bench them. Thank you for patiently working with players like Jim McMahon and helping them bloom in your system even though they didn't always fit the mold. I can't help but think both the players and the university have gained from such experiences.

Thank you for also staying with a relatively unknown quarterback named Steve Lindsley as your starter in a game in 1986. Only after umpteen callers second guessed you on the post-game radio show, did you divulge that it was a special day for Steve — the anniversary of his father's death — and you

LaVell and Paul James on the post-game broadcast (Mark Philbrick BYU photo)

weren't about to bench him. Few fans will remember the score or even the opponent that day, but I'm sure Steve and his family will never forget your unwavering support.

Thank you for reminding us by your stoic face, your patience with the callers on the KSL post-game shows, and by what you and Patti will accomplish in the coming years that there is more to life than football.

I guess what I'm trying to say, Coach, is thanks

for showing us a great formula for producing winners—not just in football, but in life as well. Through the years I've bumped into many of your former players. They are still winners and are making a difference in their communities by the things they are doing today. I believe that's your real legacy — and a gift no one else could have given you.

Thanks again, Coach. Please know that a little bit of you will remain with each of us even as you step down.

BYU photos

Epilogue:

13 Games for the Ages

- **1974 BYU vs. (No. 16) Arizona State** (the game that earned LaVell Edwards his first WAC championship. The write-up for this game is found in pages 54-70 in the section Fundamental Two: *Instinctively* Follow the Game Plan).
- **1979 BYU vs. @ (No. 14) Texas A&M** (highest ranked opponent up to 1979)
- **1980 BYU vs. SMU** (The Miracle Bowl)
- **1983 BYU vs. Missouri** (win gave the Cougars a No. 7 final ranking)
- **1984 BYU vs. (No. 3) Pittsburgh** (win put BYU on the national radar map)
- **1984 BYU vs. Michigan** ("Underdog" BYU won the national championship)
- **1985 BYU vs. (No. 4) Air Force** (highest ranked team to visit Provo)
- **1990 BYU vs. (No. 1) Miami (FL)** (Miami fell; Ty Detmer won the Heisman)
- **1991 BYU vs. San Diego State** (On the road, the Cougars erased a late third quarter, 45-17, deficit to tie 52-52.)
- **1991 BYU vs. (No. 7) Iowa** (Cougars tied the Hawkeyes in Ty's last game)
- **1994 BYU vs. (No. 17) Notre Dame** (a stunning win over the nationally ranked Fighting Irish on their home field)

- **1997 (No. 5) BYU vs. (No. 14) Kansas State** (New Year's Day Cotton Bowl victory)
- **2000 BYU vs. Utah** ("Divine Intervention" victory in LaVell's last game)

(The Texas Aggies were the highest ranked BYU opponent to date.)

BYU 18, (No. 14) Texas A&M 17

Date: September 8, 1979
Location: Rice Stadium @ Houston
Weather: Temperature 85° with high humidity
Attendance: 40,000

The enthusiastic BYU Cougars faced some major challenges to open the 1979 season:

1. They were facing the nationally ranked (No.14) Texas A&M Aggies. BYU had never faced such a highly ranked team before.
2. They would battle in Houston's heavy humidity with 40,000+ rabid Aggie fans in a sold-out Rice Stadium.
3. Quarterback Marc Wilson was still recovering from surgery for a ruptured appendix and had been out of service for weeks. And, just in case the lanky quarterback wasn't suffering enough, the flu bug hit him the week of the season's opener!

Coach Edwards made a last-minute decision to start Marc.

First Half

Texas A&M struck first with its defense. LeAndrew Brown recovered a BYU fumble on the 50. A Cougars' personal foul moved the ball to the 35. Nine plays later Aggie fullback David Brothers went airborne from the one and dove into the end zone for a touchdown. David Hardy added the PAT. The Aggies were up, **7-0**.

In the second quarter the Aggies were about to score again. With a fourth and goal at the BYU one, quarterback Mike Mosley and freshman running back Johnny Hector fumbled a handoff at the one and BYU's Dave Francis recovered in the end zone.

Just before halftime Clay Brown punted 49 yards to the A&M one. The Aggies could only get to the nine and punted back to the Cougars at the Aggie 43 with 1:20 to go in the half. Wilson hit receiver Dan Plater for 19. But then the drive stalled. In came kicker Brent Johnson, who hit a 26-yard field goal to make the score **7-3.**

That was the **halftime score**: **Texas A&M 7, BYU 3**

The Cougars indeed had started off slowly. In this first half they only had three first downs, 12 yards gained rushing and 40 yards passing. Wilson was only six of 13 passing with two interceptions.

BYU felt fortunate to be trailing only **7-3**.

Second Half

Texas A&M scored on its first possession in the third quarter. The drive used eight plays to move 51 yards. Quarterback Mosley scrambled and dodged his way through the BYU defense for a seven-yard touchdown. Hardy's kick made it, **14-3,** Aggies.

Marc Wilson drops back to pass. (BYU photo)

Then, with 2:47 to go in the third, things started to break BYU's way. Linebacker Glen Redd recovered an Aggie fumble on the BYU 43.

Wilson and the offense seized this windfall! Wilson, now throwing on every down, moved BYU 57 yards in these four pass plays:

- Eight yards to Scott Phillips
- 12 yards again to Phillips
- 17 yards to Bill Davis
- And the grand finale – A 20-yard strike to Dan Plater for the Cougars' first touchdown.

Brent Johnson's kick made it **14-10**. And everyone in the stadium could see that the Cougars were no longer napping!

The fourth quarter saw the two teams making little progress until Hardy's 37-yard field goal upped the Aggies' lead to **17-10** with 6:44 to play.

The BYU defense had more than acquitted itself thus far in the contest. Now with about five minutes left in the game, the Aggies faced a fourth and one on the BYU 47. They decided to go for it.

But quarterback Mosley was hit hard by the defenders and fumbled the ball. Sophomore defensive tackle Pulusila Filiaga recovered for BYU.

Once again, the two teams traded punts. This time, however, BYU's Tim Halverson blocked David Appleby's punt from the end zone. BYU got the ball on the 19. The Cougar offense took the field with 2:43 to play and A&M still up **17-10**.

Here's what the Cougars did with their last-ditch opportunity:

- Wilson connected with fullback Mike Lacey for nine – but the Aggies were called for pass interference as BYU's Bill Davis was tripped by LeAndrew Brown in the end zone. The ball was placed at the two. First and goal with 1:30 to play.

- Lacey lost one yard on his next carry.
- Then, Wilson rolled to his left and threw a short three-yard touchdown pass to tight end Clay Brown. That made it **17-16** for Texas A&M.

Now the Aggie fans sitting in the end zone were screaming – hoping to prompt an error by the visitors. The crowd was so loud, in fact, that they didn't hear Wilson call for a timeout and ask for quiet.

When time was back in, Wilson then took the snap, rolled to the left again, threw low to Mike Lacey, who made a diving catch for the precious two points.

The Cougars had their first lead, **18-17**.

But there were still 52 seconds left to play. A&M's quarterback Mosley moved his team to the BYU 37 with 15 seconds to play. Future NFL star Curtis Dickey picked up five yards to the 32. Then BYU's John Neal nailed David Brothers for a two-yard loss on a pass completion.

Nine seconds left. A&M's last shot at a win was a 51-yard field goal attempt by David Hardy. It was wide to the left.

BYU's offense came back onto the field and

Wilson fell on the ball to end it.

Final score: BYU 18, Texas A&M 17

	1st	2nd	3rd	4th	Final
BYU	0	3	7	8	18
Texas A&M	7	0	7	3	17

Team Statistics	BYU	Texas A&M
First Downs	14	20
Total Offense Yards	217	404
Rushing Yards	52	279
Passing Yards	165	125
Passes (Att.-Comp.1nt.)	35-17-3	15-9-0
TDs Passing	2	0
Punts	9-430	8-325
Fumbles – Lost	2-1	6-4
Penalties – Yards	6-69	8-66

Aggie coach Tom Wilson said, "We played a good team tonight, a very talented team. We made too many mistakes at the wrong time. We lost our poise when we couldn't put the ball in from the one-yard line."

LaVell Edwards said, "If this isn't the biggest win we've ever had, it has to rank in the top two or three. I had a feeling we were definitely capable of a victory, and the players felt the same way. I have to credit our special teams – well, really everybody – for the win.

"We debated the two-point play and we let Marc call the play. This could be a great team before the season is over although we'll miss Danny Frazier (who suffered a broken neck in the first half). We felt he could be the finest player we've had in years."

Mike Lacey said, "I had no idea that the pass would come to me. But I did know we wanted to go for the two-point play. I also had a personal reason for wanting to win this game. My roommate is Danny Frazier and I wanted to do it for him. He is probably the favorite player on the team.

Cougar Offense Leaders

- **Marc Wilson** was 17 of 35 passing for 165 yards with three interceptions and two TDs.
- **Homer Jones** had seven carries for 53 yards.
- **Dan Plater** caught three passes for 49 yards and one TD.

- **Clay Brown** caught two passes for 17 yards and one TD.
- **Mike Lacey** caught two passes for four yards AND also caught the winning two-point conversion pass.

Cougar Defense Leaders

- **Linebacker Gary Kama** had 17 tackles (one for loss) and one pass break up.
- **Defensive back John Neal** had 12 tackles.
- **Linebacker Glen Redd** had 12 tackles and one fumble recovery.
- **Defensive end Rob Buchanan** had seven tackles (one for loss).
- **Cornerback Dave Francis** had seven tackles and one fumble recovery.
- **Defensive tackle Pulusila Filiaga** had one fumble recovery.

(It Took a Miracle to Beat the Bowl Hex)

BYU 46, Southern Methodist University 45

Date: December 19, 1980

Location: Jack Murphy Stadium @ San Diego

Weather: Temperature 64° Overcast with occasional patches of fog

Attendance: 50,214

"I could just see my epitaph. It will read: 'He won a thousand games, but he couldn't win a bowl game.'"

- LaVell Edwards

"I think this game may wind up being like an NBA game, the last team with the ball might just win."

– Ron Meyer, SMU coach

BYU's 1980 season record of 11-1 laid the foundation for the legendary Holiday Bowl III, pitting the Cougars against the Southern Methodist University Mustangs.

Holiday Bowl officials were elated to have two ranked teams playing in their game: No. 19 Southern Methodist University from Dallas, TX and the powerful Southwest Conference, was selected to face No. 14 BYU in Holiday Bowl III.

The SMU Mustangs finished second in the SWC.

They had a record of 8-3, including wins over Texas, Texas A&M, Rice, and Arkansas. They lost a close game to conference champion Baylor, 32-28, in Waco, TX. The 32 points by Baylor were the most points given up by the Mustangs all season. Eric Dickerson and Craig James were two outstanding running backs (and future NFL stars) for SMU's option offense.

LaVell Edwards said SMU would be the strongest opponent BYU had faced in the Holiday Bowl.

The game was actually two very different games: (1) SMU's overpowering running game for the first three-plus quarters and (2) BYU's overpowering passing game in the final fourth quarter.

Here is a detailed report of this incredible game so you can relate/remember the emotional roller coaster it was:

First Quarter

SMU won the coin toss and the Mustangs' Eddie Garcia kicked off into the end zone.

BYU started from its own 20. The Cougars were stuck in the mud at the outset and had a three-and-out before Clay Brown punted to the SMU 48.

The Mustangs took over for their first drive. They covered 52 yards in only four plays:

- Freshman quarterback Lance Mcllhenny ran for 12 yards and a first down at the BYU 40.

- Tailback Craig James gained three yards.
- McIlhenny pitched to James on the option to the right for 22 yards to the BYU 15.
- Tailback Eric Dickerson scored on a 15-yard sweep around the left side. Garcia's kick was good. SMU was up quickly, **7-0**, using only 2:03 off the clock.

BYU started again from its own 20 and suffered another "three-and-out." Brown punted again.

SMU took over on its 46-yard line and scored again in four plays:

- James gained three.
- McIlhenny gained four.
- James gained two, bringing up fourth down-and-one.
- In punt formation, the play was a fake as the snap went to the short man (James), who swept to the right side and went all the way into the end zone for a 45-yard touchdown. Garcia added the PAT. **SMU led, 14-0,** with five minutes to play in the first.

Once again BYU took over on its 20. The Cougars moved the ball one yard and went back to punt again. This time the ball was hiked over Clay Brown's head and went out of the end zone for a safety. SMU 16, BYU 0

At this point after three possessions, the Cougars

Clay Brown traps the ball en route to a 64-yard TD. (Ron Haase photo)

were without a first down and without a pass completion. And they had scored two points for the Mustangs.

Bare-footed kicker Lee Johnson free kicked the ball to the Mustangs from his 20.

SMU took over at its 36 and moved to within field goal range for their kicker Garcia. He nailed a 42-yarder: **SMU 19, BYU 0** with 4:21 to play in the first.

The Cougars finally scored on their fourth possession: McMahon passed to Phillips for 11 yards and a first down at the 31.

McMahon passed again to Phillips for five to the 36.

Then McMahon hit Brown for 64 yards and a touchdown. Brown's catch was remarkable. He first secured the ball between his left hand and his hip without breaking stride.

Then he finished going the distance to score. Kurt Gunther's kick was good. SMU 19, BYU 7 with 2:34 left to play in the first.

SMU took over on its 20. This time the Mustangs had to punt after four plays.

Freshman Vai Sikahema fumbled the punt, then recovered the ball at the BYU 11 with 16 seconds to play.

Second Quarter

After one play, McMahon's long pass was intercepted by Charles Bruton at the SMU 46.

The Mustangs moved 54 yards in seven plays aided by two BYU penalties for unnecessary roughness. McIlhenny connected with James on a three-yard pass for the touchdown. Garcia's PAT was good to make the score **SMU 26, BYU 7.**

The Mustang kick was taken by Sikahema in the end zone and returned to the 16.

- **Six plays later, BYU was only up to its 20-yard line. Clay Brown came on to punt again, and his kick went to the SMU 43.**

The Mustangs moved forward for seven plays but had to settle for another Garcia field goal from 44 yards out with 6:52 to play. The score was now **29-7.**

The Cougars received the SMU kickoff. Sikahema took it to the 22. Now the BYU offense showed a few sparks:

- **McMahon passed to Braga for 21 yards to the 43-yard line.**
- **McMahon hit Bill Davis for 22 yards. The ball was at the SMU 45.**

Then the two teams traded punts.

With 1:23 to play in the half, Sikahema received the punt and described how his mind worked as he caught the ball: "*As a freshman this is how my 18-year-old mind works: 'They could be 100 to nothing…it doesn't matter what I do out there. If I fumble the football, who cares?'*

"And the ball hits and bounces straight up in the air and they (the defenders) surround the ball. In that split second, I decided – 'they're not watching me – I'm going to do a sprint right through them, catch it on the dead run,' – and they're flat footed. I take off, then pick up a block, and I run 83 yards untouched, accompanied only by my teammates."

Once again, the pass for the two-point

conversion failed. That was the last score of the half.

Halftime Score: SMU 29, BYU 13.

At this point McMahon had completed only six of 15 passes for 101 yards (64-yards of that total on the touchdown pass to Brown).

Third Quarter

BYU kicked off to SMU – the Mustangs returned the ball to the 25.

The Mustangs then went 75 yards in 12 plays for another score. James carried five times for 27 yards. Dickerson carried four times for 25 yards. Dickerson's final carry was a dive up and over the defense for the score. The pass for two points failed. The score now was **35-13** for SMU.

Starting from their own 20, the Cougars answered with a long scoring drive of 80 yards in 10 plays. The big gainers were:

- **McMahon connecting with Scott Phillips for 12 yards and a first down at the BYU 38.**
- **McMahon's next two passes to Phillips gave the Cougars a first down at the 50.**
- **McMahon scrambled for 19 yards to the SMU 31.**
- **Then McMahon hit Phillips for 11 yards down to the 18.**

- **Scott Pettis ran around left end for five yards.**
- **Finally, McMahon found Brown open for 13 yards and the touchdown.**
- **The PAT pass for two failed.**

Cougars still down, 35-19.

SMU's Dickie Blaylock returned the kickoff to the 37. The Mustangs ate up the clock going 14 plays to position Garcia to kick a 42-yard field goal with 1:36 to go in the third.
Score: SMU 38, BYU 19

Fourth Quarter (*Do you believe in miracles?)*

Clay Brown punted to the SMU 35.

The Mustangs' short drive was jammed at the BYU 45. Then Eric Kaifee punted to the BYU nine.

BYU took over and McMahon completed five straight passes:

- **First to Danny Plater for four yards. (11 minutes to play)**
- **Next pass to Braga good for 11 yards and a first down at the BYU 24.**
- **Pass #3 to Phillips for 14 yards at the BYU 38 and a first down.**
- **Pass #4 to Lloyd Jones for seven at the 45. Second and three.**

- **Pass # 5 for two yards brought up third and one at the BYU46.**
- **Incomplete pass made it fourth-and-one. (8:39 to play)**

McMahon recalled what happened next: "*We're down 19 points...and there are about nine minutes left in the game. We're fourth and one around midfield. We hadn't really stopped them all night long. Eric Dickerson and Craig James both had big nights. And they (BYU coaches) send the punting team in... I said, 'If we kick now, we've got no shot. I'm not going out just giving up.'*

"I wouldn't get off the field. I told the offense to huddle up. We had to burn a timeout because I wouldn't come off the field.

"And when I did, I remember calmly (?) explaining to the coaching staff what was going on. I said, 'At least give us a shot to do something.' And I remember LaVell and Doug Scovil looking at each other like they didn't know what to do. I said 'OK, we'll take care of this.' It was fourth down-and-one. If you can't make one yard, you don't deserve to win.

I called the play at the line of scrimmage. *And for some reason they're not covering Clay Brown, the best tight end in the country.* He's got a linebacker over him and that's it."

LaVell's report of the conversation to reporters was slightly different than Jim's: "*What Jim said you couldn't print. We talked about it and decided to go for it."*

The offense then moved 54 yards in 11 plays:

- **McMahon *passed to Brown for 12 yards* to the SMU 42. First down!**
- **The next pass was tipped, but Braga (playing with a hyper-extended knee) caught it for 10 at the 32. Another first down.**
- **McMahon scrambled for a loss of two to the 34.**
- **McMahon passed to Jones for 14 to the 20. First down.**
- **Incomplete - McMahon missed Davis all alone in the end zone.**
- **Then McMahon passed to Phillips for five to the 15.**
- **Another pass to Phillips gained four to the 11. Fourth-and-one (again).**
- **McMahon hit Lloyd Jones for 10 to the one. First-and-goal.**
- **Lane carried for no gain.**
- **Lane again for no gain. Third-and-goal with about five minutes to play.**
- **Phillips swept right to score from the one. The pass for two failed.**

SMU 38, BYU 25 with 4:07 to play.

On the first play after the next kickoff, Craig James took a pitch right, then changed direction, and swept left end for 42 yards and a touchdown. Garcia's kick was good. **Now it was 45-25 with 3:57 to play.**

THE FINAL 3:57

"For BYU it proves to be its third fruitless trip to the Holiday Bowl." (TV announcer Ray Scott's comment at this point.)

SMU's kickoff to the **BYU 18 was returned to the 28 by Cougar Bruce Hansen.**

- **McMahon scrambled for 14 to the BYU 42. First down.**
- **An incomplete 60-yard in-the-air-pass intended for Lloyd Jones. Second and 10.**
- **McMahon passed to Lane for eight at the 50. Third and two.**
- **The next pass to Phillips was caught for 10 and a first down at the SMU 40. (2:57 left)**
- **Incomplete pass. Second-and-10.**
- **McMahon passed to "the best tight end in the country" for 25 yards to the 15.**

"Although in a losing effort, Clay Brown has put on quite a show tonight." (Ray Scott commented again.)

- **McMahon then passed to "gimpy" Braga for 15 and the touchdown. BYU's fourth two-point PAT attempt failed.**

Score 45-31 with 2:31 left.

BYU recovered its onside kick at the 50. The Cougars scored a big touchdown using only four plays:

- **Pettis caught a pass at the 41 for second-and-one.**
- **Next was an incomplete pass.**
- **Third-and-one –McMahon passed to Davis for 40 yards to the one-yard line.**
- **Phillips swept right for the touchdown. Delay of game on BYU, then McMahon passed to Phillips for *two*!**

Now it was 45-39 with 1:58 remaining.

Lee Johnson's onside kick was recovered by SMU at the BYU 47.

- SMU rushed for no gain. Second-and-10.
- Mcllhenny ran for two. **Third-and-8** on the BYU 46. **(1:06 showing on the clock.)**
- Dickerson swept left for *one* yard. **Bill Schoepflin tackled him. (50 seconds left.)**
- Fourth down: Delay of game on SMU. The clock stopped with **18 seconds left.**

SMU set up for a punt.

Bill Schoepflin blocked the punt at the SMU 41. (Now 13 seconds left.)

BYU took over on the SMU 41. First-and-10.

- **Incomplete pass at the 25 with nine seconds left.**
- **Incomplete pass in the end zone intended for Jones. (Three seconds left).**

(Then Ray Scott said: "*McMahon drops back to his own 46...Receivers are there; defenders are there.... Who has the ball?*")

(Clay Brown caught the ball between two defenders in the end zone.)

The referee signaled touchdown! The game announcers' last words:

Ray Scott: "*Touchdown!*"

Grady Alderman: "*Unbelievable! Unbelievable!*"

Then, after much bedlam erupted on the field, Ray Scott finally signed off with:

"Join us tomorrow for the Tangerine Bowl... *I don't how you could ever top this one!*"

McMahon's second half totals were 26 completions in 34 attempts for 345 yards and three touchdowns.

	1st	2nd	3rd	4th	Final
BYU	7	6	6	27	46
SMU	19	10	9	7	45

Team Statistics	BYU	SMU
First Downs	23	25
Total Offense Yards	444	446
Rushing Yards	-2	393
Passing Yards	446	53
Passes (Att.-Comp.1nt.)	49-32-1	1-6-0
TDs Passing	4	1
Punts	5-163	4-165
Fumbles – Lost	2-0	2-0
Penalties - Yards	8-80	7-65

LaVell Edwards said, "Obviously, I'm still in kind of a trance. It was just the greatest finish I've ever seen, ever been exposed to. The normal things they say about not giving up definitely apply here."

Later the legendary coach said, ""If I had any sense at all I would quit right now."

SMU coach Ron Meyer was a class act as he said, "This comeback wasn't a miracle. BYU just played solid football. It's tough to take a loss like this. BYU is capable of beating anyone in the country due to their ability to throw the ball. They kept doing what they do well."

One writer asked coach Meyer, "Who do you compare BYU with?"

Meyer replied, "There's no one who compares with BYU. They are unique. They are the only one of their kind. No one compares with them."

Another question: "Is BYU a good team?"

Meyer: "Hey, listen, we are a very good team and they beat us. BYU can play with any team in the country."

Cougar Offense Leaders

- **Jim McMahon** was 32 of 49 passing for 446 yards with one interception and four TDs.
- **Clay Brown** had five catches for 155 yards and three TDs.
- **Scott Phillips** carried eight times for 24 yards and two TDs and also caught 10 passes for 81 yards
- **Vai Sikahema** had two punt returns for 87 yards and one TD.
- **Bill Davis** had four catches for 75 yards.
- **Lloyd Jones** had three catches for 31 yards.

Cougar Defense Leaders (Defensive statistics not available)

Who caught THE ball? There was some confusion over whether Brown caught the ball cleanly or shared the reception with an SMU defender. "It was a dual catch," said Brown, "Me and the defender came down with the ball together. The official waited a long time before he signaled touchdown."

The Salt Lake Tribune's Ray Herbat explained why the referee made the right call. *"Under college rules, if both the receiver and the defender have possession of the ball, it goes to the **offensive** team."*

Where is the ball? **Who** *has it?*
(Mark Philbrick BYU Photo)

Bill Schoepflin's Three Contributions

At the end of the game, amid all the offensive fireworks, it must be pointed out how crucial Bill Schoepflin's three contributions were in those last 50 seconds:

Bill Schoepflin (BYU photo)

1.Bill stopped Eric Dickerson on third and eight after a one-yard gain. This forced SMU to punt the ball to BYU. **(50 seconds left).**

Bill Schoepflin (47)blocked the SMU punt with 18 seconds to play to set up the "miracle." (Lenny Ignelzi AP photo)

2. As BYU huddled to receive the Mustangs' punt,

with **18 seconds left**, Bill said, *"I think I can block this kick."* And block it he did!... setting up the McMahon to Brown "Hail Mary" pass to tie the game at 45-45. **With no time remaining!**

3.Finally, Bill was the holder for Kurt Gunther's successful kick for the extra point – the one that *really* won the game.

Kurt Gunther was asked, "Did you feel the pressure?" Kurt replied, "I don't know. I didn't let myself think about pressure, just what I had to do to kick the ball."

Final Score: BYU 46, SMU 45

LaVell in the post-game locker room to the team: *"What can you say after a game like that?"*

"Hallelujah," shouted Bill Davis.

Jim McMahon summed it up best, *"It was just that, a miracle...Somebody was looking out for us. They wanted LaVell to win that game."*

Ray Scott added later, *"Brigham Young in an absolutely unpredictable, wild finish has defeated SMU in one of the most spectacular college football endings I have ever, ever seen."*

(This win secured a No. 7 national ranking - second highest ever)

BYU 21, Missouri 17

Date: December 23, 1983 – Evening
Location: Jack Murphy Stadium @ San Diego
Weather: Temperature 55° Clear
Attendance: 51,480

Everyone was interested to see what this year's Holiday Bowl would be like. Would it be another contest to go down to the wire before being settled in the final seconds? Or would BYU be overmatched with a team from a "big" conference like Ohio State?

The opponents for this year's bowl game were the Missouri Tigers, the runners up in the Big 8 conference. The Tigers had a very strong defense and had defeated both Oklahoma and Oklahoma State just weeks before this game. Those two schools had a combined total of 10 points in the two games. Missouri's offense was a typical Midwest ground attack that ran the ball down the opposition's throat. The Cougars would have to be at their best to win this one.

Both teams' defenses were in top form in this contest. Missouri caused five BYU turnovers (three pass interceptions and two fumbles) and six quarterback sacks. BYU caused four turnovers (two pass interceptions and two fumbles). One of the

Tiger fumbles led to a big BYU touchdown on the Cougars' first play after the turnover.

First Half

The Missouri defense was the top *offensive* force in the Tigers' first half of play – their 10 points in this half were the product of three BYU turnovers (two Steve Young pass interceptions and one fumble recovery).

Early in the first quarter Young's pass was intercepted by Jerome Caver at the BYU 43-yard line. The highlights of the Tigers' eight-play touchdown drive:

- Running back Jon Redd had two runs of 12 and eight yards.
- Quarterback Marlon Alder's run for seven yards put the ball at the two.
- Fullback Eric Drain scored from two yards out. Brad Burditt kicked the extra point: **Missouri 7, BYU 0**.

In the second quarter the Cougars countered with a four play, 70-yard drive. Highlights were:

- Fullback Casey Tiumalu's impressive 18-yard sweep around right end.
- Missouri's 10-yard penalty, setting up the Cougars at the 10.

- Young's 10-yard draw play up the middle for the touchdown. Lee Johnson's kick was good. **Score tied,** 7-7.

After a Missouri punt, Young's pass intended for Kirk Pendleton was tipped by Terry Matichak and intercepted by Reco Hawkins. The Tigers nudged forward eight yards on three plays, yielding to Burditt on a fourth-and-two to kick a 38-yard field goal just before the half.

Halftime Score: Tigers 10, Cougars 7

Third Quarter

The action picked up when BYU linebacker Todd Shell caused a Redd fumble and David Neff recovered for BYU.

On the first play after taking over, Young hit Stinnett over the middle for a 43-yard touchdown. BYU took the lead for the first time. Lee Johnson's PAT made it **14-10.**

Fourth Quarter

Missouri's Drain scored on a two-yard run. **Tigers on top again, 17-14.**

*Then **four plays** were pivotal in the game's final three minutes and 57 seconds.*

Play No.1: The Tigers rushed for 252 yards in the game but now, with 3:57 to play, on fourth and one at the BYU 7, they were blocked by a wall of Cougars.

BYU took over on downs.

The good news was BYU had the ball. The bad news was they were 93 yards away from the end zone and time was running out. Here's what happened on the 10-play drive in the next 3 minutes and 34 seconds:

- Young connected with Mike Eddo for 17 yards to the 24.
- Young was sacked by Tiger Bobby Bell back to the 11. Second-and-21

Play No. 2: Young, noticing the Tiger weak safety edging up for another blitz, audibled, and hit Eddo in the middle (where the safety had just vacated on the blitz) for 53 yards all the way down to the Missouri 36 with 2:35 to play.

- Steve Harper caught a four-yarder from Young. Second-and-six on the Tiger 32 with 2:10 to go.
- Young found Hamilton for seven and a first down at the 25 (1:42 on the clock).
- Tiumalu on a draw play lost two to the 27 (1:26 to go).
- Second-and-12 on the Missouri 27, Young to Tiumalu for 11 down to the 16. (0:53)
- Third-and-one. Young dropped back, was sacked by Robert Curry, and fumbled – but Craig Garrett outmaneuvered two Tigers

for the loose ball – and recovered for the Cougars. Now it was fourth-and-10 on the 25 with 37 seconds to go.

Play No. 3: Young passed 11 yards to Hamilton on a difficult deep out pattern for the first down at the 14.

- Assistant coach Norm Chow sent down the play from the press box to LaVell with 31 seconds to go.

Play No.4: *(Fake Right 28 Quarterback Screen Left)* Eddie Stinnett took a handoff from Young and raced to the right. Then he stopped, turned, and threw left across the field to Young, who made a fingertip catch, got a crucial block from Adam Haysbert to elude the last defender, and raced into the end zone for the winning score with 23 seconds to spare.

Missouri tried desperately to score, but the Cougar defenders held fast:

- Cary Whittingham knocked down the first pass.
- Kyle Morrell batted down the second.
- Finally, Morrell intercepted a "Hail Mary" pass in the end zone as time expired.

Final Score: BYU 21, Missouri 17.

	1st	2nd	3rd	4th	Final
BYU	0	7	7	7	21
Missouri	7	3	0	7	17

Team Statistics	BYU	Missouri
First Downs	23	19
Total Offense Yards	370	338
Rushing Yards	42	81
Passing Yards	328	86
Passes (Att.-Comp.1nt.)	37-25-3	16-7-2
TDs Passing	2	0
Punts	3-128	5-184
Fumbles – Lost	3-2	2-2
Penalties – Yards	3-25	6-78

Steve Young is the receiver *of Eddie Stinnett's 14-yard winning TD pass!*
(Mark Philbrick BYU photo)

Missouri coach Warren Powers said, "It was a very hard-fought game. We played extremely well and I'm very disappointed in the loss, but I'm proud of the way we played, especially our defensive effort. Nobody likes to play as hard as we did, lead for most of the game, and lose on a trick play in the last minute.

"BYU is an excellent team and deserved to win. I think Steve Young is the best quarterback I've ever seen in college football, and I've seen a few games. He has a great arm, tremendous athletic ability, and speed. He's just a very gifted athlete. That deep out he threw to Hamilton on fourth down was right on the money."

LaVell Edwards said, "Sometimes it seems like those things are meant to happen. The TD was a great call, a great pass, and a great run.

"I don't think we've run that play *(Fake Right 28 Quarterback Screen Left)* all season. We've fiddled with it a bit in practice, and we put it back in the playbook this week. We always run a few plays like that – double passes and reverses, just to liven up the practice. But honestly, when the play came down to me, it was the last thing I expected. My heart sunk, but by that time I was too numb to notice. I never had a thought of vetoing it. I was just hoping it would work. The execution was perfect. Stinnett laid the ball up perfectly and Steve caught the ball on his fingers."

"I certainly know how Missouri feels right now. We missed a chip-shot field goal and lost to Indiana and beat SMU on a big play. The dramatics of this game can't compare to the SMU game. We won that one on a last-second, desperation pass.

"What pleases me the most is that in spite of all the problems, our defense finally played well here."

Steve Young said about the winning play: "If I hadn't gotten into the end zone on that one, my grandmother would have called me and told me how she could have scored…We've run that play in practice a few times and either I drop it, or Eddie overthrows me."

Cougar Offense Leaders

- **Steve Young** was 24 of 36 passing for 314 yards with three interceptions and one TD; he also had 12 carries for minus seven yards (42 gained, 49 lost), AND he caught one pass for 14 yards and the game-winning TD.
- **Eddie Stinnett** had five catches for 60 yards and one TD and also THREW one pass for 14 yards and the winning TD!
- **Casey Tiumalu** carried 11 times for 62 yards, and also had four catches for 33 yards.
- **Mike Eddo** had two catches for 70 yards.
- **Adam Haysbert** had three catches for 53 yards.
- **Waymon Hamilton** had three catches for 24 yards.

(No defensive stats available)

(This win put the Cougars on the national rankings radar screen.)

BYU 20, (No. 3) **Pittsburgh 14**

Date: September 1, 1984

Location: Pitt Stadium @ Pittsburgh

Weather: Temperature 73° Overcast

Attendance: 40,263

BYU, with a lot of new starters, traveled to Pittsburgh to take on the No. 3 ranked Pittsburgh Panthers in the season opener for both teams.

The Cougars were unranked as this new season began. Undoubtedly, the "experts" didn't think last year's No.7 team would do much this time around. Pittsburgh had gone 8-3-1 the year before with wins over Tennessee, Florida State, Louisville, Syracuse, and Notre Dame. The Panthers finished ranked No.15. This year's No.3 ranking indicated "those in the know" believed the Panthers were destined for much greater things in 1984.

The game was the first-ever ESPN broadcast of a live regular-season college football game. In other words, the Cougars were on the big stage right out of the starting gate for this one.

First Half

BYU took the opening kickoff and on its first play from scrimmage took a play from the 1983 Holiday Bowl playbook. Quarterback Robbie Bosco pitched the ball back to the running back, who happened to be reserve quarterback Blaine Fowler. Fowler fired a pass to receiver Glen Kozlowski for a gain of 38 yards.

Thereafter, neither team did much in the first half. Bosco was only one for five with his first passes.

The Pitt Panthers were no better. Twice when the Panthers were in field goal range (including one first down and goal to go at the BYU four), they chose to go for a touchdown, but failed to convert. The potential high-scoring duel failed to materialize.

In the second quarter the Cougar offense finally found some traction, driving 56 yards in nine plays. The highlights were:

- Fullback Lakei Heimuli ran for 15 yards.
- Robbie Bosco gained eight and 14 yards on the ground.
- Bosco connected with Adam Haysbert for 12 and eight yards.
- Lee Johnson cashed in with a 37-yard field goal with 10:15 remaining in the half.

Halftime Score: BYU 3, Pitt 0

Third Quarter

Pittsburgh's best offense in the third quarter was its defense:

- Panther Bill Callahan intercepted a Bosco pass and returned it 78 yards for a touchdown. Mark Brasco kicked the extra point. **Pitt 7, BYU 3**
- Next Keith Tinsley intercepted another Bosco pass at the BYU 30 and returned it 10 yards to the 20.
- Pitt quarterback John Congemi's 14-yard pass to Chuckie Scales set up the score.
- Running back Marc Bailey dove into the end zone from the one. Brasco's kick was good.

Pitt was gathering steam with a 14-3 lead. There was 8:31 remaining in the quarter.

But then it was the Cougar defense's turn to spark its offense. Cornerback Mark Allen intercepted Congemi's pass and returned it 10 yards to the Pitt 21. In only two plays the Cougars scored when Heimuli covered the final 12 yards for the score. The try for two points failed. **Pitt 14, BYU 9** with 4:53 remaining in the third.

Fourth Quarter

The Cougars pitched another shutout in the fourth quarter, 11-0, to stun the highly ranked Panthers on their home field.

BYU started off with a nine-play drive that

gained 77 yards, highlighted by:

- Bosco's pass of 33 yards to Glen Kozlowski, who stretched out full in the air to make the catch.
- Bosco completed passes of 22 yards each to tight end David Mills and wide receiver Richard Orr.
- Lee Johnson's 25-yard field goal with 9:15 remaining in the game. **Pitt 14, BYU 12**

The winning drive began with 3:05 to play in the game.

The Cougars needed only five plays to navigate the 74 yards to paydirt:

- Starting from his own 26, Bosco passed to Kozlowski for nine yards.
- Heimuli went up the middle for nine yards. First-and-10 at the BYU 43.
- Bosco scrambled for a gain of seven.
- Long incomplete pass.

Adam Haysvbert hauls in Bosco's pass and races 50 yards for the winning score. (ESPN screenshot)

- Third down at midfield. The Pitt defense moved up, expecting a short pass. Instead, Bosco went deep to hit Haysbert, who had cut to the middle behind defender Keith Tinsley, caught the ball just after it brushed Tinsley's arm, and sprinted the rest of the way to the end zone.
- Then Bosco slipped into the end zone for a two-point conversion.

Final Score: BYU 20, Pittsburgh 14

	1st	2nd	3rd	4th	Final
BYU	0	3	6	11	20
Pitt	0	0	14	0	14

m Statistics	BYU	Pitt
First Downs	19	19
Total Offense Yards	423	344
Rushing Yards	60	146
Passing Yards	363	198
Passes (Att.-Comp.1nt.)	44-26-2	36-19-2
TDs Passing	1	0
Punts	7-299	7-324
Fumbles – Lost	0-0	0-0
Penalties – Yards	8-77	7-57

One final piece of drama:

As Pitt was desperately driving to salvage the win, BYU defensive back Jeff Sprowls went up with the

Pitt receiver for the ball. But the ball was overthrown – way out of bounds…Then a penalty flag was dropped and the official signaled pass interference.

Didn't that official know there can't be any pass interference on an uncatchable ball?

Those on the BYU sideline vehemently pointed that out to the official! After the argument settled down, the official announced, "Personal foul, not catchable, same penalty."

LaVell said afterwards, "I can't believe they would call it a personal foul."

Pitt coach Foge Fazio said, "We didn't realize Bosco could run as well as he did. In fact, in the first half I think their whole offense was him scrambling. We put pressure on him and did a good job there. But give him a lot of credit. *I've never seen a team get hurt by two big plays like that and go down 14-3, hang in there, and get back in the game.*"

Fazio also had high praise for Cougar defensive lineman Jim Herrmann. "He (Herrmann) is at least an All-American. He stood Bill up (consensus All-American offensive tackle Bill Fralic) several times."

"We didn't make any plays at all. Their offense had a lot more poise than ours. Our offense didn't play with any confidence. I guess we have to go back to square one and see what our offense can do. They produced only seven points and that was on a 20-yard drive.

"We could have got a couple of field goals if the coach would have had them go for it. I thought we had to show some superiority. I thought we had to pound them. We should have been taking the short stuff they were giving us rather than keep throwing those alley-oops. (Pitt converted only seven of 19 third downs and only one of four fourth downs).

"After the game I reminded them, it is a long season. A team (Miami) last year lost its first game and won the national championship."

LaVell Edwards said, "Defense is what wins games. We've always been proud of our defense, but they have been overshadowed by our offense. I don't think I've ever had a stronger defense going into a season. I don't know that we've ever had a better total defensive outing than we did today."

"It always feels good to win, but what I get the most pleasure from is how we hung together as a team.

"When he (Bosco) was going through those rough spots, I told him, 'This is where we find out some things.'"

Cougar Offense Leaders

- **Robbie Bosco** was 25 of 43 passing for 325 yards with one TD and also carried 11 times for 38 yards (19 after -19 yards on sacks).
- **Adam Haysbert** had nine catches for 141 yards and one BIG TD.
- **Glen Kozlowski** had three catches for 82 yards.
- **David Mills** caught five passes for 60 yards.
- **Lakei Heimuli** carried eight times for 44 yards and one TD and also caught one pass for minus three yards.

Cougar Defense Leaders

- **Steve Haymond** had 11 tackles (five solo, one for loss).
- **Marv Allen** had 11 tackles (three solo, one for loss) and one sack.
- **Kurt Gouveia** had 10 tackles (three solo).
- **Kyle Morrell** had nine tackles (four solo) and one pass break up.
- **Mark Allen** had five tackles (two solo), two pass interceptions and one pass break up.
- **Cary Whittingham** had nine tackles (two solo).
- **Jeff Sprowls** had eight tackles (six solo) and two pass break ups

Fact Check: Later in the 1984 season, *Sports*

Illustrated writer Douglas Looney, referred to an article he wrote earlier in the year in which he stated Pitt All-American offensive tackle Bill Fralic "toyed" with BYU's Jim Herrmann during the Cougars' win over Pitt, and that Herrmann's "nose would grow long" from claiming that he had held his own with Fralic.

The source that said Herrmann "held his own" with Fralic was none other than Pitt coach Foge Fazio, who said after the BYU-Pitt game, "He (Herrmann) is at least an All-American. He stood Bill (Fralic) up several times." (Sept. 2, 1984 Daily Herald p.6)

LaVell Edwards agreed, *"I thought he (Herrmann) did a great job. I think he had at least a standoff and if you have that against a guy who's supposed to be the greatest ever to play that position, you've had a pretty good day."* (Ibid.)

(Fulfilling the Impossible Dream)

BYU 24, Michigan 17

Date: December 21, 1984 – Evening

Location: Jack Murphy Stadium @ San Diego

Weather: Temperature 51° High Clouds

Attendance: 61,243

For the first and only time in college football history, the 1984 Holiday Bowl was THE BOWL game to be playing in and to be watching live in the stadium or on television.

The largest crowd in Jack Murphy Stadium history for any event, 61,243, was on hand. Thousands more throughout the United States were watching on the "minor" Mizlou TV Network.

Some of us BYU fans even watched the game live on AFN TV in Brussels, Belgium as did others in their various international links. It took real loyalty to watch a game that started at 2:30 a.m. on Saturday morning in Brussels. But we had a roomful of BYU alumni (including a mission president, a branch presidency, and a high councilor) who shook the walls of the house with our cheering during the ups and downs of the game.

The centerpiece of attention, of course, was the BYU Cougars and their quest for the "impossible dream" of the NCAA football championship. The Cougars were the only undefeated NCAA team (12-0) at the regular season's end. They possibly might be crowned the champion if they could beat a good Michigan team in the Holiday Bowl. But they would have to win enough votes from the Associated Press and United Press International polls to be named No. 1.

Going 13-0 would be easier than getting enough votes.

The difficulty poll members were having could be answered in one word as expressed by father Tevye in the musical "Fiddler on the Roof": "*TRADITION*!"

BYU's situation did not fit with tradition of the times. BYU did not represent any of the "big time" college conferences (such as the Big 10, Big 8, Southeastern Conference, Southwestern Conference, Atlantic Coast Conference, or the PAC 10 Conference). Nor were they an independent powerhouse like Notre Dame or Penn State. All of the previous "modern" football champions had come from these pools (though some conferences had changed their names through the years). Also, these champions always had sealed their position as number one by winning a major bowl game (Rose, Cotton, Sugar, Orange) on New Year's Day.

Everybody knows if you don't fit in with tradition,

there must be something wrong with you.

Critics of BYU's right to the title cited a plethora of reasons to vote for another team rather than this non-traditional candidate:

- BYU was in the Western Athletic Conference – a group of "weaker" football schools in the less-populated western states.
- The specific teams BYU had defeated in 1984 were from these "weaker" schools with two exceptions – Pittsburgh and Baylor.
- Meanwhile, there were truly "strong" teams from the big-time conferences that were also lobbying for the top spot: Oklahoma, Washington, Florida, and Nebraska.

Before we get to the game itself, we need to answer an important question:

Who were the Michigan Wolverines?

One of the criticisms levelled at BYU's claim to Number One was that the team they beat in that "weaker bowl" was only 6-5 heading into the game. As we have seen before, relying on statistics alone can actually distort one's understanding of reality. The 1984 Wolverines were much stronger on the field than their record indicated.

- Even the critics had to admit that Michigan's Bo Schembechler was one of the best coaches in all of college football.

- The Wolverines started the 1984 season by defeating the No. 1-ranked team and defending 1983 national champion: Miami (FL) Hurricanes, 22-14. In that victory the Wolverines intercepted six passes off All-American quarterback Bernie Kosar, sacked him five times, and forced two fumbles.
- Seven Michigan defensive starters returned from the 1983 team that finished 9-3 and ranked No. 8. These were BYU's opponents in the Holiday Bowl.
- Michigan was 3-1, in '84 losing only to No. 16 ranked Washington, before starting quarterback Jim Harbaugh broke his arm and was finished for the season.
- The 1984 Wolverines gave up an average of 13.8 points per game (15th best in the nation).

I believe the public at large (including the pundits) did not understand either of the teams that squared off in the 1984 Holiday Bowl.

Now, let's get on with the game! Once again, we will use the play-by-play summary to give you the best "up-and-down feel" for this emotional roller coaster game.

First Quarter

Michigan received the opening kickoff and started from its own 20. The top two running backs,

Rick Rogers and Bob Perryman were the offensive work horses during this game. On this drive:

- Rogers went up the middle for two.
- Perryman picked up six.
- On third down quarterback Chris Zurbrugg passed to tight end Sim Nelson for seven and a first down at the 35.
- A pitch to Rogers on the left side lost three. **BYU's Steve Haymond was in for the stop.** Second-and-13.
- Zurbrugg's pass was incomplete. Third-and-13.
- Zurbrugg hit receiver Vince Bean for 13 to the Michigan 45. First down.
- Three runs gained eight yards before BYU's defense stiffened.
- There was no gain on third-and-two.
- The Wolverines' Monte Robbins punted the ball to the BYU 10.

BYU took over on the 10 with 10:16 to play in the first.

- **Lakei Heimuli lost three on a draw play.**
- **Heimuli gained three. Third-and-10.**
- **Robbie Bosco passed to Glen Kozlowski for 19 yards up to the BYU 29. First-and-10.**
- **Bosco connected with a wide-open Heimuli for 21 to the 50. First down.**

- **Heimuli lost five yards on a draw. Second-and-15 at the BYU 45.**
- **Bosco's pass was incomplete. Third-and-15.**
- **Bosco's pass was *intercepted by Michigan's Brad Cochran.***

Michigan took over on its 35, first-and-10.

- Perryman gained 10 yards.
- The next three plays gained only four yards.
- Robbins punted on fourth-and-six to the BYU 10 with 6:17 to go in the first.

BYU took over on its own 10-yard line.

- **Bosco passed to Kozlowski for nine to the 19, second-and-one.**
- **Heimuli gained one for the first down at the 20.**
- **Bosco passed to Kelly Smith for eight yards.**
- **On second-and-two Bosco was hit and fell to the ground**. *Bosco was hurt. Michigan's Mike Hammerstein was flagged for unnecessary roughness.*

But BYU also was flagged for illegal motion. The penalties offset each other. The down was repeated. *(Thus, according to the game's official log, Bosco's injury never occurred.)*

- **Blaine Fowler came in to replace Bosco. His first pass was batted down with 4:47 to play. Third-and-two.**

- **Fowler hit tight end David Mills for 14 yards and the first down at the 42.**
- **Fowler scrambled for four to the 46.**
- **Fowler hit Heimuli for eight. First down at the BYU 44.**
- **Fowler passed to Mills for seven. Second-and-three at the Michigan 49.**
- **Penalty on BYU**

Second Quarter

(Bosco returned to the field and tested the bandages supporting his damaged knee, ankle, and ribs.)

BYU's Lee Johnson kicked his only punt of the game to the Michigan 16.

Michigan took over at the 16, first-and-10.

- Rogers gained four to the 20. Second-and-six.
- Rogers ran for 14 to the 34. First-and-10.
- Rogers ran for three to the 37.
- Rogers ran for nine. Third-and-one.
- Perryman ran for no gain. (**BYU's Marv Allen on the stop.**)
- Fourth-and-one. Robbins punted.

BYU took over on its 20; Bosco was back in at quarterback.

- **Bosco hit Kelly Smith for 10 to the 30. First-and-10.**

- **Bosco to Smith again for 15. First down at the 45.**
- **Bosco to Smith once more for 10 yards down to the Michigan 45. Another first down.**
- **Bosco passed to Heimuli to the Michigan 39. Second-and-six.**
- **Illegal procedure by BYU. Michigan declined.**
- **Bosco scrambled for a first down at the Michigan 26 with 9:40 to play.**
- **Bosco passed to Smith to the 16. Second down and a foot to go.**
- **Heimuli ran to the five. Gain of 11 yards. First down.**
- **Smith ran into the end zone from the five for the touchdown. Lee Johnson's kick was good with 8:37 to play in the second.**

BYU 7, Michigan 0
Drive: nine plays, 80 yards 3:56 off the clock

Michigan received the kickoff and started on its 20.

- Rogers gained five to the 25. Second-and-five.
- Rogers for no gain. Third-and-five. **BYU's Leon White on the tackle.**
- BYU blitzed Zurbrugg and **Leon White sacked him** back at the 16.

- Robbins came in for the punt. **A bad snap was recovered by Thor Salanoa at the five with 6:36 to play in the half.**

BYU first-and-goal at the Michigan five.

- **Bosco's short pass was to Mills at the three.**
- **Heimuli gained one to the two. 5:58 to play.**
- **Bosco rolled out to the right – fumbled the ball into the end zone.**

Kevin Brooks recovered for Michigan making it a touchback for Michigan with 5:49 to play in the half.

Michigan started from its 20.

- Zurbrugg passed to Bean for 20. First-and-10 at the 40.
- Rogers ran for three. Second-and-seven at the 43.
- Penalty on Michigan. The ball was spotted on the 33.
- Zurbrugg passed to Bean to the 21 for the first down.
- Perryman ran for three. Second-and-seven.
- Fumble recovered by Michigan …fourth-and-three with 2:00 to play.
- Field goal attempt – penalty on Cary Whittingham for running into the kicker.
- First down. Ball on the 10. Rogers ran for five.

- Rogers up the middle for five and the touchdown with 1:13 to play.

Drive: 11 plays 80 yards 4:36 elapsed.
BYU 7, Michigan 7

BYU started at its 17 with 1:08 to play in the half.

- **Bosco passed to Mills for 17 to the 34. First-and-10.**
- **Incomplete pass. Second-and-10.**
- **Bosco hit Haysbert for 16 at the 50.**
- **Pass interference on Michigan at the Michigan 35.**
- **BYU penalty for a false start. First-and-15 at the Michigan 40.**
- **Bosco passed to Mills for 23 to the 17.**
- **Johnson's 31-yard field goal was good with 0:4 to play.**

Drive: six plays, 83 yards 1:04 off the clock

Halftime Score: BYU 10, Michigan 7

Second Half

Michigan kicked off.
Thor Salanoa returned the ball to the BYU 27.

- **Heimuli ran a draw play for seven. Second-and-three.**
- **Bosco passed to Mills for nine at the 43. First-and-10.**

- ***Bosco's pass was tipped and intercepted by Mike Mallory at the Michigan 49.***

Michigan ball first-and-10 on its own 49.

- Perryman for ran for three. Second-and-seven at the BYU 48.
- Rogers gained two. Third-and-five.
- Zurbrugg lost 19 yards on a **sack by Leon White**. Back to the Michigan 35.
- Monte Robbins punted to the BYU 37.

BYU took over on its 37.

- **Bosco on a QB draw gained four to the BYU 41. Second-and-six.**
- **Michigan offsides. Second-and-one at the BYU 46.**
- **Late hit on Bosco.** ***(What? Another one?)*** **Michigan penalized 15 yards.**
- **Heimuli on a draw for 15 to the Michigan 26.**
- **Bosco fumbled in the backfield. Michigan recovered.**

Michigan Ball at its own 33. First-and-10.

- Rogers gained eight to the Michigan 41. Second-and-two.
- Perryman ran for seven to the Michigan 48. First-and-10.
- Rogers dropped for a loss of one to the 47. Second-and-11.

- Jamie Morris carried for four yards to the BYU 49. Third-and-seven.
- Zurbrugg passed to Paul Jokisch for a gain of 14 yards to the BYU 35. First-and-10.
- Morris gained four to the 31. Second-and-six.
- Holding penalty on Michigan. First -and-19 at BYU 44.
- Incomplete pass Second-and-19.
- Perryman to the 35. Third-and-10.
- Penalty: Zurbrugg passed to an ineligible lineman (loss of down). Fourth down.
- Robbins' 47-yard punt went into the end zone for a touchback.

BYU took over on its own 20-yard line. (5:55 left in the third)

- **Heimuli ran 15 yards to the BYU 35.**
- **Heimuli ran the draw play for eight to the BYU 43. Second-and-two.**

Lakei Heimuli breaks loose against Michigan. (Mark Philbrick BYU photo)

- **Bosco passed to Smith for eight to the Michigan 49. First-and-10.**
- **Bosco hit Salanoa for 14 to the Michigan 35. First down.**
- **Bosco pass incomplete.**
- **Bosco pass incomplete.**
- **Johnson attempted a 53-yard field goal.** It was blocked with 3:20 to play in the quarter.

Michigan ran the ball for 14 yards to the BYU 43.

- Perryman picked up 19 to the BYU 18.
- Morris gained three to the 15.
- Penalty on Michigan. Second-and-five at the 13.
- Gerald White to the 10. Third-and-two.
- Zurbrugg passed to Perryman for 10 and the TD.

Drive: six plays for 47 yards 3:01 off the clock

Michigan 14, BYU 10

Vai Sikahema fumbled the ensuing kickoff at the BYU four-yard-line with :15 to play.

- **Bosco passed nine yards to Kelly Smith at the 14. Second-and-one.**
- **BYU fumble recovered by Kevin Brooks at the BYU nine-yard line with six seconds left.**

Michigan took over first-and-goal at the BYU nine.

Fourth Quarter

- Zurbrugg lost back to the BYU 15.
- Third down pass incomplete. Fourth-and-14.
- Bob Bergeron kicked a 32-yard field goal.

Michigan extended the lead to 17-10 with 14:14 to play in the game.

BYU received the kick in the end zone. Touchback. The Cougars started from their 20.

- **Bosco passed to Kelly Smith for eight to the 28.**
- **Heimuli, on a draw, gained 13 to the 41.**
- **Penalty on BYU. First-and-15 at the 36.**
- **Bosco 12-yard pass to David Mills. Second-and-three at the 48.**
- **Bosco sacked back at the 44-yard line. Third-and-seven.**
- **Bosco hit the wide-open Haysbert at the Michigan 35-yard line. First-and-10 with 11:35 to play.**
- **Bosco to Bellini for 19 yards to the Michigan 16.**
- **Bosco to Mills for nine yards to the seven.**

- **Bosco connected with Kozlowski in the back of the end zone for the seven-yard touchdown.**

Drive: eight plays for 80 yards with 3:23 off the clock.

Glen Kozlowski "climbed the ladder"to catch Robbie Bosco's TD pass in the back of the end zone that tied the game at 17-17. (Deseret News photo)

(Kozlowski's comment about Bosco's touchdown pass, *"Shows you what kind of competitor Robbie Bosco really is. Not many two-legged quarterbacks could have made that pass."*)

Michigan received Lee Johnson's kick and started on its own 20.

- Rogers lost three to the Michigan 17. **(Leon White on the tackle)**
- Pass incomplete.
- Zurbrugg **sacked by Brad Smith** at the nine. Fourth down-and-11.
- Robbins' punt went from the end zone to the BYU 40 with nine minutes to go.

BYU took over on its 40. First-and-10.

- Clipping penalty on BYU moved the Cougars back to 21. First-and-10. 9:30 to play
- Heimuli ran for five to the 26.
- Bosco threaded the needle to Mills for 16 to the 41.

Interception: Bosco's next pass was tipped into Jim Scarcelli's hands.

Michigan started at the BYU 45. 8:23 to play in the game.

- Perryman ran for seven. Second-and-3 at the BYU 38 with 7:52 to play.
- Perryman for first down at the 33.

- Michigan penalty for blocking below the knee. First-and-20 at the BYU 45.
- Morris ran to the 40. Second-and-17.
- Perryman caught the ball at the 34-yard line. Third-and-11.
- **Gouveia sacked** Zurbrugg back at the 45. Fourth down.
- Robbins punted for 36 yards.

BYU took over on its 17 with 4:36 to play.

- **Bosco scrambled for nine+ yards. Second-and-inches for the first down.**
- **Heimuli ran for one and a first down at the 27 with 3:50 to play.**
- **Kelly Smith swept right for one yard. Second-and-nine.**
- **Bosco connected with Bellini plus Michigan face mask penalty moved the ball to the Michigan 30 for a first down.**
- **Heimuli draw play lost two. Second-and-12. with 2:55 to play**
- **Bosco hit Heimuli for seven to the 35.**
- **Bosco hit Smith for 15 to the 20. First down with 1:39 to play**
- **Pass to Haysbert inside the 15. Second down-and-four with 1:35 to play.**
- **Incomplete intended for Smith. Third down-and-4. 1:30 to play.**

- **Bosco passed to Smith for 13 and the touchdown! Johnson's PAT was good.**

Score now was 24-17 for BYU.

Winning drive: 10 plays 83 yards 3:13 off the clock with 1:23 left to play

Michigan's Gilvanni Johnson returned the kick to the 30.

- Zurbrugg scrambled for no gain. Second-and-10.
- **Marv Allen intercepted Zurbrugg's pass at the BYU 49.**
- **Penalty on BYU (for excessive celebration???)**

The clock ran out.

Final Score BYU 24, Michigan 17

	1st	2nd	3rd	4th	Final
BYU	0	10	0	14	24
Michigan	0	7	7	3	17

Team Statistics	BYU	Michigan
First Downs	32	13
Total Offense Yards	483	202

Rushing Yards	**112**	**120**
Passing Yards	**371**	**82**
Passes (Att.-Comp.1nt.)	**49-35-3**	**15-7-1**
TDs Passing	**2**	**1**
Punts	**1-45**	**7-274**
Fumbles - Lost	**4-3**	**2-0**
Penalties - Yards	**9-82**	**11-112**

Michigan coach Bo Schembechler was "surly" when interviewed after the game, but finally admitted, "I think I would have to vote for Brigham Young (No. 1) on the basis of their winning so many games."

LaVell Edwards said, "Just another ho-hum Holiday Bowl. If you had asked me if we could turn the ball over six times against a team like Michigan and win, I'd have said no. But we did. That's the mark of a good team…This is the fifth time this season we've had to drive late in the fourth quarter to win or seal a win. We did it against Pitt, Hawaii, Wyoming, and Air Force.

"Bosco is incredible in those situations. He just comes alive. He's on target and never throws a bad pass. And he was under tremendous pressure from the Michigan defense. (**NOTE:** on BYU's final two touchdown drives, Bosco completed 11 of 12 passes for 141 yards.)

"I'm just pleased, happy, and relieved we won. I don't know when I've ever been more washed out… I'm totally elated. It's finally over. We're not used to the attention and the demands on our time.

"Before the season, Playboy Magazine picked us third or fourth in our conference. But that's OK. They don't have much of a circulation in Provo.

"Are we the national champions? Yes, we are. I said it before, and I believe it now. We are No. 1, and I don't care what anyone else says…Anyone who saw the game, saw the adversity we had to overcome, and saw the win, would have to solidify our position as No. 1."

In the end the two coaches agreed about one thing:

LaVell: *"I've never seen a more courageous performance than Robbie's. At the end of the game, he could hardly walk. He was in pain."*

Bo Schembechler: A few years after the 1984 Holiday Bowl, a television interviewer asked Bo, *"What is the greatest individual performance you have ever seen?"*

Bo replied (after a very brief pause): *"Robbie Bosco, BYU. He had all the pressure in the world on him, and we threw everything we had at him... and he just kept coming back."*

Cougar Offense Leaders

- **Robbie Bosco** was 30 of 42 passing for 343 yards with three interceptions and two TDs and also carried six times for 16 yards.
- **Lakei Heimuli** carried 16 times for 82 yards and also had four catches for 40 yards.
- **David Mills** had 11 catches for 103 yards.
- **Kelly Smith** had 10 catches for 88 yards and one TD and also carried three times for seven yards and one TD.
- **Glen Kozlowski** had three catches for 35 yards and one TD.
- **Mark Bellini** had three catches for 48 yards.
- **Adam Haysbert** had three catches for 42 yards.

Cougar Defense Leaders

- **Kyle Morrell** had 11 tackles (nine solo).
- **Leon White** had nine tackles (seven solo, one for loss) and two sacks.
- **Steve Haymond** had six solo tackles (one for loss).
- **Marv Allen** had six tackles (five solo), one interception and two pass deflections.
- **Brad Smith** had five solo tackles and one sack.

- **Kurt Gouveia** had four solo tackles (one for loss) & two pass break ups.

Lynn R. Johnson, Rick Egan SL Tribune staff photo

Shout Out to James White: Leon's father who was bedridden with bone cancer and who watched the game from a special cart-bed on the sideline. Leon played at Helix High School in San Diego.

The Aftermath

The Associated Press and United Press International (Coaches) polls were the two most credible media polls who ranked the top football teams.

The week of November 13 both polls had Nebraska at No. 1, South Carolina at No. 2 and BYU at No. 3. That was the first AP poll that BYU received any votes (11) for No. 1. The UPI poll also had BYU No. 3 with 12 votes for No. 1.

Then on November 17 when BYU was beating Utah 24-14, South Carolina lost to Navy and Nebraska lost to Oklahoma. The Cougars were voted

No. 1 by both wire services in the next polls. And they stayed there to the end!

After beating Utah State in the regular season finale, LaVell said, *"Everyone has been phoning me…asking me if BYU should be No. 1 or shouldn't be No. 1. I think we deserve it more than anyone else. I'm sure Nebraska would like to have its game with Syracuse to play over. That Oklahoma would like to have Kansas over. That South Carolina would like to play Navy over.*

"We've had our Kansas and Navy and Syracuse and who-have-you and this team has survived every one. This team has what it takes to win when those games came up and have won every week. I think this team deserves to be No. 1 because it is No. 1."

As expected, there was no shortage of others' opinions about who should be No. 1.

NBC anchor Bryant Gumbel proved to be a lightning rod when he said, "Can you believe BYU is No. 1?" (turning his thumbs down and giving a raspberry to the Cougars.) *"Who do they play, anyway? Bo-Diddley-Tech?"*

NBC was flooded with angry calls and letters. KSL radio was requested by NBC to give out a different number to requesters to avoid clogging the normal phone lines.

KEYY radio in Provo called NBC but was told Gumbel had "gone home for the day."

While Gumbel was making his comments on NBC, LaVell Edwards and Robbie Bosco were interviewed on CBS, congratulating them on their new ranking.

Prior to New Year's Day, Oklahoma coach Barry Switzer said if his team won the Orange Bowl game convincingly over Washington, his Sooners should be voted number one.

Washington won the game, 28-17 and Oklahoma finished No. 6 in the polls.

About the Bo Diddleys:

- BYU beat Baylor who beat Texas who beat SMU.
- BYU beat Michigan who beat Miami (Florida) who beat Florida who beat Syracuse who beat Nebraska.
- BYU beat Air Force who beat Notre Dame who beat USC who beat Washington.
- BYU beat Pittsburgh who beat Penn State who beat Boston College who beat North Carolina who beat Kansas who beat Oklahoma.
- BYU didn't beat anybody who beat anybody who beat them.

Michigan football after 1984

From that 1984 team, 14 defenders (10 starters) returned in 1985. With a healthy quarterback Jim

Harbaugh driving the offense, the '85 team went 10-1-1 losing only to No. 2 Iowa, 12-10. The Wolverines finished No. 5 and beat five ranked teams.

The Man in the Arena

(Ode to Robbie Bosco and the Cougars?)

"It is not the critic who counts; not the man who points out how the strong man stumbles, or where the doer of deeds could have done them better.

The credit belongs to the man who is actually in the arena, whose face is marred by dust and sweat and blood; who strives valiantly; who errs, and comes short again and again, because there is no effort without error and shortcoming; but who does actually strive to do the deeds;

Who knows the great enthusiasms, the great devotions;

Who spends himself in a worthy cause;

Who at the best knows in the end the triumph of high achievement, and

Who at the worst, if he fails, at least fails while daring greatly, so that his place shall never be with those cold and timid souls who know neither victory nor defeat."

—Theodore Roosevelt

Former BYU great Robbie Bosco reflects on national championship season

By Dave McCann Deseret News

Lying on a locker room table inside the bowels of Jack Murphy Stadium, BYU's team doctors offer junior quarterback Robbie Bosco a couple of suggestions — "do you want a shot or some pain medication?"

Bosco pondered his options while at the same time wondered how in the world this was happening to him, and of all nights, this night?

The No. 1-ranked Cougars had come to San Diego to face Michigan in the 1984 Holiday Bowl. Hanging in the balance was an unbeaten season and shot at the national championship. Bosco's problem was he couldn't get his balance after taking a hit early in the game.

"I throw a pass to (Glen) Kozlowski to the left side and a guy rolls up on my leg," Bosco recalled. "My foot gets caught up in the turf and he just keeps rolling."

Bosco tried to get up but couldn't.

"I'm thinking, 'You have got to be kidding me?' This is the first quarter!"

The Gladiator

"No, I don't want any painkillers," Bosco told the team medics. "I want to have a clear mind going back out there."

With his leg heavily taped, he got off the table and walked out of the locker room where his dad was waiting.

"I'm going down the tunnel to get to the field, and I met my dad halfway," Bosco said, fighting his emotions. "My dad wasn't the kind of person to do that. He would stay up in his seats or behind the fence at practice until LaVell (Edwards) would say, 'Louie, come out here.' That meant a lot to me."

A few steps later, Bosco appeared under the stadium lights and the predominant BYU portion of the sold-out crowd of 61,243 erupted.

"It was as if all the fans were looking down there and waiting and then I stepped out from the tunnel, and it was awesome," Bosco said. "It was probably one of the most amazing things I've ever experienced."

With backup quarterback Blaine Fowler on the field running the team, Bosco grabbed a football and started to warm up. "I'm thinking, 'Oh man, I'm not sure I can do it?" he said. "I can't plant very good on my leg, and they taped it up super tight."

With a high ankle sprain, ligament problems in his knee and a cracked rib, Bosco walked over to quarterbacks coach Mike Holmgren to try and convince him that he was ready to go back in.

"Uh, no," Holmgren stated while shaking his head in disbelief.

"I said, 'Yes! I'm going in!'" Bosco recalled saying. "So, I ran in and said, 'Blaine, let's go. Sorry.'"

Fowler left the game just as he had in the 1982 Holiday Bowl when an injured Steve Young surprised the team by putting himself back in — also against Holmgren's wishes.

Bosco huddled up his teammates and took a look around.

"I could just feel it," he said. "I could feel the look in all of their eyes that 'Here we go! Let's go!' That was a feeling I had never experienced."

The Cougars, handcuffed by five turnovers, and with Bosco's left leg draped in tape from his foot to his thigh, rallied from a 17-10 fourth-quarter deficit to beat Michigan 24-17 on Kelly Smith's touchdown catch with 1:23 to play.

"The feeling was if we don't win this game, we are going to be just like a dozen other BYU football teams and we aren't going to stand out," Bosco said. "In our minds as players, we had to win this game. It meant that much to us."

(Up to this time (No. 4)AFA was the highest ranked team ever to come into Provo)

BYU 28 (#16), Air Force 21 (#4)

Date: November 16, 1985
Location: Cougar Stadium
Weather: Temperature 36° Cloudy, Overcast
Attendance: 65,393

This BYU-Air Force game had never been so significant for either school:

- They were the top two teams in the WAC standings.
- They were both nationally ranked in the top 20: (Air Force No. 4, BYU No. 16).
- Representatives of 12 bowl games were in the crowd. The winner would most likely land in a New Year's Day bowl.
- Air Force was one of the nation's leading rushing teams; BYU was the leading passing team.

Special Note: because teammate Glen Kozlowski's BYU career was over due to his knee injury, Robbie Bosco asked coach Edwards for permission to wear Koz's number seven jersey for this game as a tribute to him. Permission granted: number seven in this game was worn by Robbie. Said Koz, *"It was one of the most moving things that has* *ever happened to me."*

First Half

"Bizarre!" is the only word that describes this game! The football universe was upside down and Cougar Stadium was the site for this disorder!

For starters, the host Cougars took forever to complete their first pass and were fumbling around while the visiting Falcons scored three times *through the air* for a **21**-7 lead!

Actually, Air Force also fumbled once in the early going…and that ball went out of bounds, so the Falcons maintained possession. On the very next play they scored the game's first touchdown on a 22-yard pass from quarterback Bart Weiss to receiver Randy Jones. The PAT made the score **7-0**.

Exactly 20 seconds later Air Force defender Tom Rotello intercepted a Bosco pass and returned it 25 yards for another AFA touchdown. **Air Force 14, BYU 0** with less than three minutes off the clock.

Then the Cougars drove for their first touchdown: a 22-yard pass from Bosco to Mark Bellini. Gary Webster's PAT made it **14**-7.

Another Bosco pass backfired as Falcon Dwan Wilson picked it off and returned this one 58 yards for a TD. Tom Ruby's extra point made the

Halftime Score Air Force 21, BYU 7.

(Time Out: *Halftime chat between the two number 7s: Koz smiled as he said, "I told Robbie that number 7 had never played so badly. So, he went out in the second half and relaxed, and did the job.")*

Third Quarter

BYU kicked off to Air Force.

The Falcons returned the ball to their 24.

- Weiss was dropped for no gain by **Shawn Knight**. Second down-and-10.
- Pitchout left to Jones. **Rob Ledenko hurdled the blocker to drop Jones for no gain.** Third down-and-10.
- Pitchout right to Jones. **Steve Sanders dropped him for no gain.** Fourth-and-10.
- Mark Simon punted to the BYU 28.

Vai Sikahema was mostly a blur to the Falcons! (Youtube screenshot)

Vai Sikahema caught the ball and darted

untouched right up the middle through the Falcons – 72 yards – for the touchdown!
The extra point was no good.
(The home crowd was hysterical– screaming at full volume and thundering with their stomping feet on some temporary end zone bleachers!)
Air Force 21, BYU 13 with 12:47 to go in the third.

Kickoff to Falcon Tom Rotello; he returned the kick to the Air Force 46. First down-and-10.

- Evans dove for two yards. Second-and-eight.
- Weiss on a keeper option to the left picked up seven. Third-and-one at BYU's 45.
- Evans gained two for the first down at the BYU 44.
- Evans for three. Second-down-and-seven at the BYU 41.
- Weiss nearly fumbled, but recovered. Third-and-seven.
- Incomplete pass.
- Simon punted into the end zone.

BYU started first-and-10 from its 20.

- Tom Tuipulotu gained six. Second down-and-four.
- Tuipulotu ran for three more. Third-and-less-than-one to go.
- Bosco sneaked for the first down to the 31.
- Smith carried for no gain. Second-and-10.

- Bosco to Bellini for eight. Third-and-two at the BYU 39.
- Bosco to David Miles for nine yards to the BYU 48. First down.
- Bosco to Heimuli for 12 yards to the AFA 40. Another first down.
- Heimuli on a draw play lost a yard. Second down-and-11 from the AFA 41.
- Falcons offsides. Second-and-five on the AFA 36.
- Falcons personal foul. BYU first down on the AFA 21. (5:30 to play)
- Bosco scrambled and lost four. Second down-and-14 at the AFA 25.
- Incomplete pass. Third-and-14.
- Bosco passed to Bellini for 25 and a touchdown.
- PAT attempt penalty on BYU for five yards. Two-point conversion from the eight. Bosco pass to tight end Lance Lindley was good.

Score tied, 21-21.

The scoring drive was 80 yards in 14 plays. Time 4:57.

BYU's kickoff to the Falcons went into the end zone.

Air Force first down-and-10 at the AFA 20.

- Evans optioned left for a loss of one. Second down-and-11. **(Marc Sherman tackle)**
- Pitch back to the right for eight. Third down-and-three at the AFA 27. (3:59 to go.)
- Weiss on a keeper to the left for a first down.
- Evans went up the middle for two. Second down-and-eight.
- Incomplete pass. Third-and-eight on AFA 33.
- Weiss to Greg Pshsniak for no gain.
- Simon punted to Sikahema at the BYU 16.

BYU first down at its own 16.

- Bosco to Bellini for seven to the BYU 23. Second down-and-three.
- Heimuli ran for three. First-and-10 at the 26.
- BYU penalized 15 yards (unsportsmanlike conduct). First-and-25 at the 14. (1:39 to go)
- Incomplete pass. Second-and-25.
- Bosco to Sikahema to the 19. Third-and-20.
- Bosco sacked at the BYU 11.
- Towle punted to the Falcon 42.

Fourth Quarter

Air Force first-and-10 at its own 42

- Jones ran for three. Second-and-seven on the AFA 45.
- Johnny Smith dropped for no gain by **Leon White**. Third down-and-seven.

- Pitchout to the left was fumbled out of bounds. Fourth-and-seven.
- Simon punted out of bounds to the BYU 19.

BYU first-and-10 at its 19

- Heimuli on the draw lost four. Second-and-14 from the 15.
- Bosco to Sikahema for eight. Third down-and-six at the 24.
- Bosco connected with a leaping Bellini for 31 yards to the AFA 45. First-and-10.
- Bosco screen to Sikahema for four. Second down-and-six.
- Tuipulotu swept right for six and the first down at the AFA 35.
- Bosco's pass was intercepted by A. J. Scott on the AFA 26. (10:13 to go)

Air Force ball first down-and-10 on its 26.

- Evans up the middle for one. Second-and-nine.
- Weiss kept for four. Third-and-five.
- Weiss for four before **Steve Sanders** stopped him. Fourth down.
- Simon punted to the BYU 24.

BYU first and 10 on its 24 with 8:16 to play in the game.

- Sikahema ran to the right for one. Second-and-nine.

- Bosco passed to Bellini for 12 to the BYU 37. First-and-10.
- Bosco sacked back on the 24. Second down-and-23. (7:25 to play)
- Bosco to Heimuli for seven. Third-and-16 at the BYU 31.
- Bosco dropped back and connected on a long pass with Sikahema (covered by linebacker Terry Maki). Vai raced into the clear, caught Robbie's long pass at the 32, and outran Maki and cornerback Dwan Wilson to the end zone to complete the 69-yard touchdown play.

Robbie Bosco never gave up! (Deseret News photo)

- Webster's kick was good. With 5:41 to play, it was **BYU 28, AFA 21**

(Drive 78 yards in seven plays – 2:36 off the clock)

BYU kicked off to the Falcons. **Cougar freshman Troy Long made a jarring tackle** at the AFA 17 with 5:29 to play.

(Déjà Vu #1?) *This situation was reminiscent of the 1982 Air Force game in Provo – the inaugural game in expanded Cougar Stadium – when BYU was leading by seven with one minute to play. Air Force received the kickoff and drove 99 yards for a touchdown and two-point conversion to nip the Cougars, 39-38.)*

Air Force began on its 17.

- Weiss quick pass to tight end Hugh Brennan for seven. Second down-and-three.
- Evans ran up the middle for nine and the first down at the AFA 33.
- Weiss to Brennan again for nine. Second down-and-one.
- Evans for the first down at the AFA 49. (3:54 to play)
- Weiss ran left for three to the BYU 48. Second down-and-seven. (3:21 to play)
- Evans **stopped hard by Shawn Knight**. Third down-and-six at the BYU 47. (3:00 to play)
- Weiss passed to Jim Bush for a first down at the BYU 38. **Kurt Gouveia on the stop.** (2:30 to play)

- Weiss rolls right. **Leon White dropped him for a loss of three.** Second down and 13 to go.
- Incomplete pass. Third down and 13 at the BYU 41. (1:47 to go)
- **~~Pass intercepted by Rodney Thomas~~** BUT was nullified by:
- Two penalties (1) for roughing the passer on BYU and (2) personal foul on Air Force.

(Déjà Vu #2?) *In 1982 a roughing the passer penalty against BYU gave the Falcons new life for their winning score.)*

Falcons awarded the ball first down-and-25 at the BYU 41 (1:34 to play)

- Weiss rolled left and hit Tyrone Jeffcoat at the BYU 18. Second down-and-two.
- A fumble on the handoff in the backfield was recovered by the Falcons. Third-and-four. (40 seconds to play)
- Long incomplete pass. Fourth down-and-four. (24 seconds to play)
- Pitchout to the right, one missed tackle. **Cary Whittingham made a saving tackle** at the 11. First down-and-10. (16 seconds to play)
- Weiss optioned to the left for four. **Jason Buck on the tackle.** Second-and-goal at the seven. (Falcon timeout stopped the clock with 11 seconds to play)

- Weiss passed left to Marc Munafo, who rolled on the ground and dropped the pass – stopping the clock. (:04 to play)
- Weiss dropped back and, **with Ken Smith in his face,** blindly lobbed a deep left pass into the end zone. **Rob Ledenko picked off the pass.**

(L) Ken Smith (R) Rob Ledenko (BYU photos)

Game Over!! Final Score: BYU 28, Air Force 21

	1st	2nd	3rd	4th	Final
AFA	14	7	0	0	21
BYU	0	7	14	7	28

Team Statistics	BYU	Air Force
First Downs	20	13

Total Offense Yards	308	237
Rushing Yards	-35	136
Passing Yards	343	101
Passes (Att.-Comp.1nt.)	49-29-4	18-9-1
TDs Passing	3	1
Punts	5-245	8-352
Fumbles - Lost	1-0	3-0
Penalties - Yards	5-60	6-49

Post-game hysterics:

- The crowd swarmed the field and congregated in the north end zone where Ledenko's interception had sealed the victory. *(Was there anybody left in the stands?)*
- One of the leaders of the swarm was none other than LaVell Edwards! ("LaVell's never led the crowd like that before!" exclaimed one of his former players.)
- The crowd lifted Leon White and Jason Buck on to their shoulders and carried them to the ramp.

Fisher DeBerry said, "BYU's defense did a great job in defensing our wishbone. BYU is probably the best defensive team we have played all year."

LaVell Edwards said, "This was a classic football game. Air Force is a tremendous team, as good as any we've played this season. I told our players I have never been prouder of a comeback than today's."

(*About the earlier growing chorus of boos aimed at Bosco as his interceptions mounted up*) "A lot of people are spoiled around here. Bosco has only won 22 of 24 games for us in two years. That's the way it goes, I guess. I can remember when nobody got excited enough to boo around here."

Cougar Offense Leaders

- **Robbie Bosco** was 29 of 49 passing for 343 yards with four interceptions and three TDs.
- **Mark Bellini** had nine catches for 143 yards and two TDs.
- **Vai Sikahema** had four catches for 87 yards and THE TD and also five punt returns for 89 yards (including the 72-yard TD that sparked the entire second half comeback).
- **Lakei Heimuli** had six catches for 37 yards.
- **Kelly Smith** had six catches for 32 yards.
- **Trevor Molini** had two catches for 18 yards.
- **Scott Norberg** had one catch for 17 yards.

NCAA Records

Vai Sikahema

- **Most career combined kick returns (punt and kick) – 192** (old record 190 by Devon Ford, Appalachian State (1973-76)

Robbie Bosco:

- **Most pass completions two years – 574** (old record 566 by Jim McMahon (1980-81)
- **Most pass attempts two years – 895** (old record 883 by Todd Dillon, Long Beach State (1982-83)
- **Most plays total offense two years – 1037** (old record 1031 by Todd Dillon, Long Beach State (1982-83)

Cougar Defense Leaders

- **Shawn Knight** had 12 tackles (seven solo, one for loss)
- **Marc Sherman** had nine tackles (five solo) and one forced fumble.
- **Cary Whittingham** had nine tackles (three solo) and one QB hurry.
- **Jason Buck** had eight tackles (two solo, one for loss), one sack, and three QB hurries.
- **Steve Sanders** had seven tackles (five solo)

- **Rodney Thomas** had five solo tackles and that ~~one interception~~ cancelled by a BYU penalty.
- **Ken Smith** had five tackles (two solo) and one BIG QB hurry.
- **Leon White** had five tackles (two solo, one for loss).
- **Jeff Sprowls** had four tackles (two solo, one for loss), one forced fumble, and one pass break up.
- **Rob Ledenko** had three solo tackles and one interception (THE GAME CLINCHER)

Special Shout Outs to the Defense:

- **The powerful Air Force offense scored only seven points in this game!**
- **Between 5:54 in the first period and 5:41 in the final period Air Force gained only 63 yards and had only three first downs**
- **Air Force quarterback Bart Weiss was averaging 95 yards rushing per game. In this game he gained only a net of 27.**

The game ball: In a team meeting prior to the game, the team decided to dedicate this game to coach Edwards. They felt as a team they had something to prove and wanted to give him something. "It was something they did on their own,"

LaVell said. They gave me the ball in the locker room after the game."

The Bowl Game: The Cougars accepted a bid to the Citrus Bowl in Orlando, Florida to play against Ohio State.

No gain without pain: In addition to losing Kozlowski for the season before the game, the following injuries struck these Cougars in the game:

- Kelly Smith reinjured the knee that had sidelined him against Utah State.
- Trevor Molini sprained an ankle and was sidelined briefly before returning.
- Ladd Akeo, who was recovering from a shoulder injury, injured his other shoulder.
- And, it became apparent more than ever, that Robbie Bosco's throwing shoulder was not 100 per cent.

BYU 28, (No. 1) Miami (FL) 21

Location: Cougar Stadium

Date: September 8, 1990

Weather: Temperature 93° Clear

Attendance: 66,235 (new Cougar Stadium record)

There were some subtle connections between the BYU and Miami (FL) football programs:

In 1976 our family was in Orlando, Florida to attend the Tangerine Bowl played by BYU' and Oklahoma State. While we were there, I read in the local newspapers that LaVell Edwards was interviewing for the head coaching position at Miami. I didn't think LaVell would consider leaving BYU, but it was clear Miami wanted to reverse its recent losing history like LaVell was doing in his startup at "Quarterback U." Miami ended up hiring Howard Schnellenberger in 1979.

Schnellenberger was successful and Miami became known as a passing team and was a national power. Miami quarterbacks Bernie Kosar, Vinny Testaverde, and Steve Walsh were named All-Americans. Testaverde also won the Heisman Trophy.

The Hurricanes won national championships in

1983 and 1985, sandwiched around BYU's national title in 1984. While Oklahoma and other schools in the NCAA football "establishment" argued that BYU didn't deserve to be the national champion, Miami was silent.

BYU and Miami first faced off in 1988 in Miami. BYU fell behind 34-3 in the first half of that one as interceptions and other miscues put them in the deep hole. Ty Detmer came into the game in the second half, throwing for 212 yards and two touchdowns but Miami won big, 41-17.

Now in 1990 Miami was the defending national champion and again ranked number one. The Passing Giant of the East was coming to play the Passing Giant of the West. And Ty Detmer was being touted as a candidate for the Heisman Trophy.

Another record crowd at Cougar Stadium (66,235), including an unprecedented number of media representatives, and a nationwide ESPN audience all were watching this gigantic milestone in the LaVell Edwards' Era:

First Half

BYU won the toss and elected to receive. The Cougars in five plays moved into Miami territory before Ty Detmer fumbled at the Miami 42.

Miami recovered the ball and took over. After three plays gave the Hurricanes a first down, the

Cougar defense took over:

- Quarterback Craig Erickson was sacked by Rocky Biegel and Alema Fitisemanu for a loss of 10 to the Miami 47. Third-and-20.
- Then **Dewey Gray and Mark Smith** squeezed Erickson for no gain. Fourth-and-20 and Paul Snyder punted the ball to the BYU 26.

BYU took over on its 26 with 9:26 to go in the first.

Ty Detmer was fired up to get his Cougars moving. He started by completing three passes:

- **to Brent Nyberg for three yards.**
- **to Chris Smith for 11 yards.**
- **to Matt Bellini for another 11 yards; this one moving into Miami territory at the Hurricane 49.**

Then a couple of hiccups: and illegal motion penalty and an incomplete pass brought up a second-and-15.

- **On the next snap there were no open receivers, so Ty scrambled for 16 yards and a first down at the Miami 38.**
- **Then Ty passed to Bellini again for 13 yards and another first down at the Miami 25.**
- **Mike Salido was hit hard and fumbled at the Miami 21.**

Miami recovered at its 21. Then the Hurricanes

started their own drive. They moved in eight plays for the game's first touchdown. The big gainers were:

- Steve McGuire ran nine yards to the Miami 40. First down.
- Alex Johnson ran 40 yards to the BYU 20. First down.
- McGuire on a left sweep for six yards to the BYU 14. Second and four.
- McGuire ran the final 12 yards in two carries for the touchdown. Huerta's kick was good. **Miami 7, BYU 0**

(Drive of 79 yards in eight plays with 3:44 elapsed; 3:07 to go in the first)

BYU received the kickoff and started off very slowly. They committed a personal foul, backing them up ten. First-and-20. Then everything stalled and Earl Kauffman came on and punted the ball away.

Miami took over on its 35. The Cougar defense again lowered the boom on the visitors:

- Kaufusi pressured Erickson to throw an incomplete pass.
- Erickson was sacked back at the 28 by Rick Wilson and Fitisemanu. Third and 17.
- Miami penalized for delay of game. Third and 22 from the Miami 23.

First Quarter ended, 7-0, for Miami

Second Quarter

- Erickson's pass was incomplete. Miami was stymied by BYU's storming defense. Snyder punted.

BYU took over on its 40.

Ty Detmer and the Cougars were now on the hot seat. The Cougars were trailing the Hurricanes again; no doubt reminding Ty of the disastrous 41-17 loss two years before. BYU turnovers fueled that lopsided loss to the Hurricanes; now the Cougars already had two turnovers in this game!

Ty was determined to get a score and not repeat '88's history.

- Ty passed to Brent Nyberg for 12 at the Miami 48. First down.
- Then he connected with Bellini and Bellini dragged players for an extra five yards to the Miami 35. First down.
- Detmer passed to Andy Boyce to the 31. Second and six.

Detmer keeper for no gain. Third and six.

- Detmer to Bellini at the 18 for a first down.
- Bellini ran left for four.

- Detmer scrambled to the left and connected with Bellini from the 14 for the touchdown. Kauffman kicked the PAT. **Game Tied, 7-7**

Matt Belini (BYU photo)

After the touchdown Ty grabbed Matt and slammed his helmet with his fist,

(**Author's Note:** "I remember thinking to myself, 'Careful, Ty! Don't injure your hand!'")

The Cougar defense forced a Miami punt. The offense moved the ball inside the 10 in five plays before the Hurricane defense stiffened.

So, Kauffman came on and kicked a 32-yard field goal. to put the Cougars in the lead again. **BYU 10, Miami 7 (Drive 59 yards in nine plays with 1:50 elapsed)**

The two teams both bogged down and traded punts and turnovers. Detmer threw an interception, but the Hurricanes blew this opportunity as they fumbled their first snap and BYU recovered the ball. The Cougars didn't fare any better. After five plays Andy Kauffman came in and missed a field goal.

A few minutes later the Hurricanes got the ball back and finally regained the lead:

- First, Erickson connected with Lamar

Thomas for eight to the BYU 34.

- Then Johnson ran for eight to the 26. First down.
- Erickson went long to Thomas down to the BYU 4.
- McGuire plunged twice to score the TD. Huerta kick was good.

Miami 14, BYU 10 (1:43 to play in the second.)

BYU received the Miami's kick at its 26.

In less than two minutes the Cougars moved 74 yards for a touchdown:

- Detmer passed to Smith for five to the 31.
- Detmer passed to Salido for six to the 37 (1:12 to go)
- Detmer connected with Bellini for eight to the 45. Second-and-two. (43 seconds to go in the half))
- Detmer was sacked for a loss of eight back to the 37.
- Detmer connected with Nyberg for 19 to the Miami 44. First down. (31 seconds to play).
- Detmer passed to Bellini for 19 to the 25. (23 seconds left)
- Detmer hit Salido for 23 to the two. (14 seconds to go)

- Detmer found Boyce in the back of the end zone for the touchdown. Kauffman's extra point was good (:10 to go)
  (Drive 74 yards in eight plays in 1:08)

Halftime Score: BYU 17, Miami 14

Miami received the second half kickoff and started on its 20.

- Erickson passed to Hill for 10 at the Miami 30. First down.
- McGuire slanted to the left for one yard.
- Johnson rushed for 16 yards to his own 47. First down.
- Incomplete pass. Second-and-10.
- Erickson's pass to Carrol gained seven at the BYU 46. Third-and-three.
- Erickson to Lamar Thomas at the BYU 41. First down.
  - Incomplete pass. (Josh Arnold deflected the ball.)
  - Incomplete pass (broken up by Fitisemanu).
  - Erickson to Carroll at the BYU 31. First down.
  - Incomplete pass. Second-and-10.
  - McGuire up the middle for 10 at the 19. First down.

- Erickson pass to Hill at the five. First-and-goal. (11:52 to go in the third)
  - Leonard Conley ran for the touchdown. Huerta kick good.

Miami 21, BYU 17 (Drive 80 yards in 13 plays in 3:12)

BYU received the ball at its 26.

- Detmer tossed to Bellini who shook off a tackle and got to the 33-yard line. Second-down and three.
- Tuipulotu ran for seven to the 39. First down.
- Detmer passed to Boyce for eight at the BYU 47.
- Detmer hit Smith for eight at the Miami 38. First down.
- Tuipulotu ran to the right for eight at the 30.
- Detmer passed to Matt Zundel for 19 to the 11.
- Two incomplete passes meant it was Kauffman time. He came on and booted a 28-yard field goal with 9:26 to go in the third.
Miami 21, BYU 20

After the kickoff Miami started on its 20.

- Erickson, pressured by Kaufusi, threw incomplete.

- Erickson connected with Thomas for 15 yards to the 35. First down.
    - Incomplete pass. Second and 10.
    - Erickson passed to Carroll for nine. Third and one.

Rich Kaufusi (BYU photo)

- **Fourth and a short yard to go. Rich *Kaufusi slipped in between two offensive linemen to tackle McGuire behind the line.***

BYU took over on the Miami 43

- Detmer passed to Bellini at the 35. Second-and-two.
- Tuipulotu rushed into the line for three at the 33. First down.
- Detmer hit Smith at the 26. Second-and-four.
- Detmer to Nyberg at the 24. Third-and-one.
- Tuipulotu into the line for no gain.

- On fourth-and-one at the 24, Detmer ran wide left, then sidestepped the defender for a first down at the 19.

Ty Detmer slips by a Hurricane. (Tom Smart Deseret News Photo)

- Detmer passed 11 yards to Boyce at the eight for a first-and-goal.
- Corley slanted right for two. Second-and-goal.
- Detmer rolled right and hit Salido cutting across from the left for a six-yard touchdown. **BYU now led, 26-21**.

Andy Boyce (BYU photo)

- The Cougars went for the two-point conversion: Detmer rolled to the right and hit Boyce going left for two. **BYU 28, Miami 21 (Drive 43 yards in nine plays in 4:11)**

Miami started on its 20 after the kickoff.

The Hurricanes used nine plays to get to their 49-yard line. Then the Cougar defense rose up and forced a punt.

BYU started at its 13-yard line with 1:39 to play in the quarter.

Then it was BYU's turn to struggle. Three incomplete passes in a row forced Kauffman's punt from the end zone

Kauffman punted to the Miami 30. The Miami returner lost six yards to the 23

Miami started on its own 23.

- Erickson first pass incomplete. Second-and-10. (1:09 in third)
- Erickson hit Johnson for five to the 30. Third-and-five.
    - Pass to Lamar Thomas to the 40. First down.
    - Johnson ran to the 43. Second-and-seven.

Fourth Quarter

Miami second-and-seven from its 43.

- Erickson passed short for five yards. Third-and-three at the Miami 48.
- Fourth down-and-one at the 50. Maguire got one yard for the first down.

- Erikson on a keeper gained six to the BYU 44. Second-and-four.
- Leavitt dropped Johnson for a loss. Third-and-seven from the BYU 47.
- Erickson passed to Thomas to the BYU 27. First down.
- Erickson connected with Spencer at the 16. First down.
- **Miami fumble recovered by Fitisemanu at the BYU 15.**

BYU took over on its 15.

- Salido on a draw for seven yards to the BYU 22.
- Detmer sacked back at the 17.
- Incomplete pass. Fourth down.
- Kauffman punted to the Miami 35.

Miami started at its own 35.

- **Sack by Mark Smith at the Miami 25. (Second-and-20)**
- Erickson passed from beyond the line of scrimmage. Loss of down and five-yard penalty.
- Third down from the 25.
- Incomplete pass. (9:00 to play)
- Snyder punted to the BYU 48.

BYU took over on its 48.

- Detmer passed to Nyberg – 15-yard penalty for offensive pass interference.
- Second-and-25. Detmer passed to Smith who fumbled to Miami.

Miami took over on the BYU 35-yard line.

- Leonard Conley ran for two. Second-and-eight.
- Incomplete pass – (**Leavitt on the break-up**) Third-and-eight.
- Erickson passed to Carroll for five at the BYU 29. Fourth-and-three.
- Erickson passed to Rob Chudzinski for 16 yards and a first down at the 13.
- Incomplete pass. Second-and-10.
- Incomplete pass. Third-and-10 from the 13.
- Erickson's pass intercepted by BYU's **Ervin Lee** in the end zone.

BYU took over on its 20.

- Salido ran for four. Second-and-six. (6:00 to play)

Ervin Lee (BYU photo)

- Detmer hit Boyce for three. Third-and-three.
- Pass incomplete. Fourth-and-three.

- Kauffman launched another punt (54 yards!) down to the Miami 28. (5:00 to play)

Miami took over at its 28.

- Erickson passed to Lamar Thomas for 17 yards to the Miami 45. First down.
- Erickson pass deflected by Norm Dixon. Second-and-10.
- Pass to Carroll tackled by Josh Arnold after a gain of three. Third-and-seven (3:48 left)
- Incomplete pass. Fourth-and-seven from the BYU 42.
- Erickson passed 11 yards to Thomas at the 31. First down. (2:42 to play)
- Incomplete pass.
- Erickson passed to Thomas at the 22. Third-and-two.
- Alex Johnson was dropped by **Rich Kaufusi** for a loss of three at the BYU 25. Fourth-and-five (2:17 to go)
- Erickson's deep pass was knocked away by **Ervin Lee**.

BYU took over on its 25.

- Tuipulotu plunged into the line for no gain. Second down.
- Incomplete pass Third-and-10. (1:04 to go)
- Detmer passed 12 yards to Boyce at the BYU 37.
- Detmer took a knee (twice). **Final Score: BYU 28, Miami 21**

	1st	2nd	3rd	4th	Final
Miami (FL)	7	7	7	0	21
BYU	0	17	11	0	28

Team Statistics	BYU	Miami (FL)
First Downs	27	21
Total Offense Yards	474	395
Rushing Yards	68	96
Passing Yards	406	299
Passes (Att.-Comp.1nt.)	49-29-4	52-28-1
TDs Passing	3	0
Punts	4-215	7-250
Fumbles – Lost	5-4	2-2
Penalties – Yards	5-50	8-53

Miami coach Dennis Erickson said, "They just came out and outplayed us. They played better than we did and deserved to win the football game…"

Ty Detmer, to me, is unbelievable. Obviously, he's a great, great quarterback and he showed it tonight."

LaVell Edwards said (in answer to the question**,** "Was this the biggest victory for you?") "Tonight, it certainly seems like it. I was very pleased with our defense, and I thought our offensive game plan put in by Roger French and Norm Chow was excellent."

Ty Detmer aims high! (BYU photo)

Cougar Offense Leaders

- **Ty Detmer** was 38 of 54 passing for 406 yards with one interception & three TDs.
- **Matt Bellini** caught 10 passes for 111 yards and one TD.
- **Andy Boyce** caught nine passes for 96 yards and one TD.

- **Chris Smith** caught seven passes for 90 yards.
- **Mike Salido** caught four passes for 33 yards and one TD and also carried four times for 18 yards.
- **Brent Nyberg** caught six passes for 51 yards.

Cougar Defense Leaders

- **Rich Kaufusi** had nine tackles (two solo, two for loss), one pass break up and four QB hurries.
- **Norm Dixon** had 10 tackles (four solo) and one pass break up.
- **Josh Arnold** had eight tackles (five solo) and one pass break up.
- **Shad Hansen** had eight tackles (two solo).
- **Jared Leavitt** had six tackles (five solo, two for loss) and one pass break up.
- **Alema Fitisemanu** had four tackles (two solo), one pass break up, and one QB hurry.
- **Ervin Lee** had two tackles (one solo), plus one pass break up, and one interception to shut down two deep last-minute Miami drives.

Postgame: Accolades

ESPN Analyst (and former BYU opponent in Holiday Bowl II) Lee Corso: "I have never seen a game plan as perfect as BYU had for this game.

Tonight, it is BYU who is playing like the No. 1 team in the country."

Miami quarterback Craig Erickson: "Ty played an excellent game and ignited the crowd. He never did anything to get the crowd out of it and that caused us problems because we wanted to go on quick calls and we couldn't hear each other. The crowd was a factor."

"(Their defense played) above and beyond the call of duty and just flat-out dominated our offensive line on the front. They played extremely well and handled us. They had an excellent game plan and executed it with emotion."

Miami All-American defensive tackle Russell Maryland said, "It's plain and simple. We got our butts kicked. We came out flat and they came out ready."

BYU 52, San Diego State 52

Location: Jack Murphy Stadium @ San Diego
Date: November 16, 1991
Weather: Temperature 57° Clear
Attendance: 56,737

Who could ask for any more drama than this contest between the top two teams in the WAC standings? BYU, perennial conference champion, with an unblemished 6-0 record in conference play. San Diego State's Aztecs, one game behind at 6-1. The winner would be the likely champion this time around.

Then consider the contest between superstars on the two teams: All-American quarterback and former Heisman Trophy winner Ty Detmer against the Aztecs' sensational freshman running back Marshall Faulk, a record setter in his first year and bound for NCAA and NFL Halls of Fame in the future.

Before the night was over, the two teams would combine for 104 total points and 1,462 yards of total offense. But those impressive numbers paled in comparison to the dynamics which saw a 14-14 tie in the second quarter balloon into a 45-17 Aztec lead by the middle of the third period. And then to see a full house of frenzied Aztec fans watch helplessly as Ty Detmer & Co. scored five touchdowns to finally draw even in the last 36 seconds of play.

All of that action. All of those points. And in the end no winners or losers. A 52-52 draw.

Let's fill in the blanks:

First Quarter

BYU would reveal its own freshman-wonder running back from Las Vegas in this game, Jamal Willis, (who would gain 66 yards and score one TD on the ground and then lead all Cougars with eight catches for 163 yards and two TDs). Jamal caught the first of Detmer's six touchdown passes from 31-yards out. Earl Kauffman's PAT was wide. **BYU 6, SDS 0.**

Jamal Willis (BYU photo)

Then the Aztecs revealed their "mad bomber," quarterback, David Lowery, who hit Darnay Scott with a 75-yard touchdown pass. Andy Trakas added the extra point. **SDS 7, BYU 6.**

Faulk boosted the Aztecs with his two-yard scoring run to end the first quarter. Trakas kicked the PAT. **Aztecs 14, Cougars 6.**

Second Quarter

The Cougars scored next to tie the score. Ty Detmer hit receiver Nati Valdez for a 20-yard score. Unfortunately, Nati broke his collar bone on the touchdown. Mark Atuaia took his place and caught Detmer's pass for the two extra points to tie the score, **14-14.**

Then it was "Mad Bomber" Lowery again, this time launching an 80-yard bomb to Faulk for the touchdown. Trakas added the extra point. **Aztecs 21, Cougars 14.**

Earl Kauffman returned on the next BYU possession and kicked a 37-yard field goal. **Aztec 21, Cougars 17**.

The Aztecs then alternated their scoring stars on the final two drives of the first half:

- Marshall Faulk topped off one scoring drive with a four-yard dash. Trakas booted the extra point. **Aztecs 28, Cougars 17**.
- Then it was Lowery's turn. Dave caught the Cougar secondary crowding up a little too closely – and went downtown again to Darnay Scott for a 79-yard touchdown strike. Trakas still had enough leg strength to add the extra point.

Halftime Score: Aztecs 35, Cougars 17

Third Quarter

The few BYU fans in the stadium just *knew* that Detmer could reverse things. And he did – but not right away.

The Aztecs drove down the field and Lowery went through the air to Faulk for a 15-yard score. Trakas was on point again. **Aztecs 42, Cougars 17** –

and still counting…

Trakas closed out the Aztecs scoring in the third quarter with a 41-yard field goal to make it: **Aztecs 45, Cougars 17**.

NOW! The Cougars began opening *their* flood gates:

- Willis scored first on a 49-yard touchdown pass from Detmer. New kicker Keith Lever added the PAT. **Aztecs 45, Cougars 24**.
- The Cats stopped the Aztecs on the next drive and rode Detmer's arm to move down to the Aztecs' 10. From there Ty found tight end Byron Rex open in the end zone for another score. Lever's kick was good again. **Aztecs 45, Cougars 31**.

  That ended the third quarter.

Fourth Quarter

The momentum had already shifted in the Cougars' favor, but San Diego State wasn't going to roll over and play dead. Still, the Cougars kept whittling away at the Aztecs' lead.

- Peter Tuipulotu was on the receiving end of Detmer's 20-yard scoring pass. Lever's kick cut the lead to seven: **Aztecs 45, Cougars 38**.

Now the few Cougar fans in the stadium were in a frenzy! The stadium on the whole, however, was stunned and silent. The locals had seen before what

BYU had done elsewhere to SMU, Missouri, Air Force, Miami – and to the Aztecs in this very stadium!

When the Aztecs received the following kickoff, the crowd gathered its strength once again. And their leader on the field was, once again, David Lowery.

This time the "Mad Bomber" connected with receiver Keith Williams for a 47-yard touchdown. Trakas' kick was true again. The Aztecs extended their lead to **52-38**. Would this be enough?

Detmer and the Cougars didn't think so. They drove for a pair of desperate touchdowns. First, Ty and Mark Atuaia repeated their magic from the earlier two-point conversion and connected on a four-yard touchdown lob. Lever's extra point made it, **Aztecs 52, Cougars 45**.

The worn and frazzled BYU defense bent, but didn't break to the Aztecs on their final drive. Andy Trakas' 41-yard field goal attempt was wide with just over two minutes to play.

Now the ball was in Ty's hands yet again, and he knew just what to do. The Cougars drove down to the five

Finishing one last drive. (AP photo)

in the red zone. The Aztec defense was on high alert for another short touchdown pass. So, Ty slipped the ball to freshman sensation Willis for a five-yard TD run! Lever's kick was good and with 36 seconds to spare, the Cougars got their tie.

Final Score: BYU 52, SDS 52

The tie meant the Cougars again were WAC champions and bound for the Holiday Bowl!

	1st	2nd	3rd	4th	Final
BYU	6	11	14	21	52
SDS	14	21	10	7	52

Team Statistics	BYU	SDS
First Downs	37	30
Total Offense Yards	767	695
Rushing Yards	168	127
Passing Yards	599	568
Passes (Att.-Comp.1nt.)	54-31-3	39-26-1
TDs Passing	6	5
Punts	4-145	4-154

Fumbles – Lost	**0-0**	**2-1**
Penalties – Yards	**11-79**	**6-79**

San Diego coach Al Luginbill called it the lowest moment of his athletic career.

LaVell Edwards said, "(Ty) is absolutely unbelievable. Just unbelievable."
(About playing for the tie): "We decided if it came down to a tie, we'd go for that because it would put us in a position to win the title. There was never any question of not kicking that PAT for the tie.

Cougar Offense Leaders

- **Ty Detmer** was 31 of 54 passing for 599 yards with three interceptions and six TDs.
- **Jamal Willis** caught eight passes for 163 yards and two TDs and also carried 11 times for 66 yards and one TD.
- **Eric Drage** caught four passes for 117 yards.
- **Peter Tuipulotu** carried 15 times for 85 yards and also caught three passes for 33 yards and one TD.
- **Byron Rex** caught five passes for 51 yards and one TD.

- **Nati Valdez** caught two passes for 27 yards and one TD – which sidelined him with a broken collar bone. (*Talk about sacrificing your body for a score!*)
- **Mark Atuaia** caught one pass for four yards and one TD and also caught a two-point conversion pass.

Special Shout Out: Ty Detmer's 599 yards passing were his career best for one game. He passed to 10 different receivers. In addition to the six listed above, he also connected with:

- **Tyler Anderson** (three catches – 67 yds)
- **Micah Matsuzaki** (two catches – 77 yds)
- **Tom Nowatzke** (two catches – 38 yds)
- **Eric Mortensen** (one catch – 22 yds)

Cougar Defense Leaders

- **Josh Arnold** had 10 tackles (seven solo) and one interception.
- **Scott Giles** had nine tackles (six solo, one for loss), and two sacks.
- **Tony Crutchfield** (just off the injured list) had eight tackles (five solo).
- **Rocky Biegel** had seven tackles (four solo, one for loss).

- **Patrick Mitchell** (redshirt freshman inserted as a starter just before game time) had seven tackles (four solo).
- **Randy Brock** had five solo tackles and two sacks.
- **Dewey Gray** had five tackles (four solo).

1991 Ty Detmer's Last Comeback

BYU 13, (No. 7) Iowa 13

Location: Jack Murphy Stadium @ San Diego
Date: December 30, 1991
Weather: Temperature 59° Partly Cloudy
Attendance: 60,646

WAC champion BYU vs. Big 10 runner-up Iowa in a scenario that had not favored BYU in past years. The Cougars had lost both previous Holiday Bowl encounters to the Big 10's Indiana (38-37) and Ohio State (47-17). This year's Iowa opponents were ranked No. 7 and boasted a record of 10-1 with victories over three nationally ranked Big 10 teams, including Ohio State on its home field in Columbus, OH. Iowa had the Big 10's stingiest defense.

The Cougars, on the other hand, appeared to be severely mismatched. The Cats had opened the season with three straight road losses to powerhouses

Florida State, UCLA, and Penn State. They went on to win eight games and again finished as WAC conference champions. They had a landmark tie against WAC rival San Diego State, falling behind 45-17 in the third quarter, only to come storming back to finish at the final gun with a tie, 52-52.

The main cause for concern among the Iowa Hawkeyes was the fact that BYU had a quarterback by the name of Ty Detmer. The 1990 Heisman Trophy winner and holder of 59 NCAA passing records (and tied for three others), Ty had one tendency that worried the Hawkeyes the most: *Ty Detmer did whatever it took (even the "impossible") to avoid a loss!*

The most recent example was the November 16 road game against San Diego State. Ty threw six touchdown passes, including four in the second half as the Cougars scored their tying points with 36 seconds left on the game clock.

The two coaches in this Holiday Bowl game were two of the all-time greats in the history of NCAA football:

- LaVell Edwards would end his career with 257 wins – No. 8 on the all-time list.
- Hayden Fry earned 232 wins to finish No. 13 among all college coaches.

A record crowd of 60,646 was on hand at the Cougars' "second home," San Diego's Jack Murphy

Stadium, for this duel between two giants.

First Half

The Hawkeyes started off like they would uphold the Big 10's tradition of beating BYU in a bowl game. Iowa's All-Big 10 quarterback Matt Rogers was a solid performer and completed 19 of 28 passes for 221 yards in this game. Running back Mike Saunders would gain 103 yards at 5.4 per carry and would score both touchdowns for the Hawkeyes.

The Hawkeyes received the opening kickoff and proceeded to move 74 yards in 5:16 for the game's first score. Rodgers completed all four passes on the drive for 31 yards. And Saunders carried seven times for 40 yards and scored from 13 yards out. Kicker Jeff Skillett missed the extra point, setting the tone for both sides the rest of the night. **Iowa 6, BYU 0.**

In the second quarter Iowa started a 13-play, 89-yard drive that ended with Saunders' five-yard touchdown dash with 12:12 to go in the half. Skillett's PAT was good this time and the Hawkeyes were up, **13- 0.**

And that was the Hawkeyes' final score for the night.

The Cougar offense finally kicked into gear with 4:43 left in the half. Detmer led the Cougar charge that went 78 yards in nine plays. The big gainer was a 43-yard Detmer-to-freshman Tim Nowatzke pass that moved the Cougars down to the Iowa 35. Detmer even overcame a sack by Iowa defender John Hartlieb and kept the drive alive by evading Iowa's players and finding open receivers. He hit fullback Tom Tuipulotu coming out of the backfield for a nine-yard touchdown. Earl Kauffman's PAT kick was no good.

Halftime Score: Iowa 13, BYU 6.

Second Half

The two defenses were even stronger in the second half.

Iowa was shut out in the second half:

- Zero points
- 130 yards total offense
- Only 11:31 of clock time

The Cougars fared somewhat better:

- Seven points
- 243 yards total offense
- 18:29 of clock time

BYU got its second touchdown and tying score in the fourth quarter from an 87-yard drive in 13 plays.

- Detmer drove the Cougs down to the Hawkeye 35.
- Then Ty was sacked by Iowa's Teddy Joe Faley and Hartlieb for a loss of 12 back to the 47.

- Facing third and 22, Ty scrambled and flicked a pass to Jamal Willis, who dodged several defenders to the Hawkeye 29. Fourth down and four. Time for some Detmer magic.
- Ty spotted sophomore receiver Tyler Anderson streaking into the end zone, lofted the ball to him over the outstretched arms of defender Scott Plate, and the Cougars had their touchdown! Kauffman's extra point was good. **BYU 13, Iowa 13 with 11:36 to play.**

Ty escaped the Iowa pressure. (Mark Philbrick BYU photo)

BYU finally got the ball again with 4:19 on the clock and 77 yards to go:

- Detmer opened with an 11-yard pass to Eric Drage.
- Then a long pass was incomplete.

- Another pass was good for eight yards to running back Jamal Willis. Third and two at the BYU 42.
- Detmer hit Drage again for 11 yards and another first down at the Hawkeyes' 47.
- Against a heavy blitz, Detmer dumped off a pass to Peter Tuipulotu for 13 yards.
- On third and one, Detmer ran a keeper around the right end for a first down to the 16.
- Then Detmer rolled left, looked for a receiver, and passed across the middle to tight end Byron Rex. The pass was a little high and Rex tipped it into the hands of Carlos James for the game-saving interception.

Final Score: BYU 13, Iowa 13

	1st	2nd	3rd	4th	Final
BYU	0	6	0	7	13
IOWA	6	7	0	0	13

Team Statistics	BYU	IOWA
First Downs	26	20
Total Offense Yards	430	346

Rushing Yards	**80**	**125**
Passing Yards	**350**	**221**
Passes (Att.-Comp.1nt.)	**44-29-1**	**28-19-1**
TDs Passing	**2**	**0**
Punts	**2-88**	**4-139**
Fumbles – Lost	**0-0**	**0-0**
Penalties – Yards	**7-60**	**7-61**

Iowa coach Hayden Fry said, "I thought BYU did a magnificent job. Time after time they moved the ball and ate up a lot of grass, and our defense was about as good as we've ever had inside the 20-yard line, taking into consideration how many points BYU normally scores.

"We really played a chess game to keep (Detmer) off balance – any time you hold Brigham Young to 13, you should win the game. Everybody's real sad and heartbroken in our locker room."

LaVell Edwards said, "It didn't entirely surprise me we played well defensively. It surprised me we didn't take advantage of our scoring opportunities. Ty said it best – 'after thinking about it a while – we'll feel good about tying a great team like Iowa.'"

Why not kick for the winning points?

Ty Detmer said, "It shouldn't have been thrown. I know better than to throw a pass like that at that time in the game. Get the team in the middle of the field, kick a field goal and the game is over. I just tried to make something happen that I shouldn't have done. It was a bad decision…I'm not gonna lose sleep over a tie. But I will lose some sleep over that last pass."

But LaVell said, "The long layoff had affected the kickers more than other players on the team. Both kickers were uneasy during the entire game."

Kauffman and Lever both missed earlier field goals. Kauffman also missed an extra point. In other words, out of eight possible kicking points, BYU only put one of them on the scoreboard.

Iowa's kicker Jeff Skillett also missed one field goal and one extra point.

This was one of the rare times when "settling for a field goal" was not the obvious, safer choice.

Iowa Players Praised Detmer:

Linebacker John Derby: "Ty is an unbelievable quarterback."

Defensive Back Brian Wise: "Detmer is every bit as good as they say, if not better. We had pressure on him, we thought we had him. He'd find a way to get out of it."

Cougar Offense Leaders

- **Ty Detmer** was 29 of 44 passing for 350 yards with one interception and two TDs.
- **Peter Tuipulotu** caught eight passes for 85 yards and one TD carried 12 times for 44 yards.
- **Byron Rex** caught six passes for 71 yards.
- **Jamal Willis** carried 13 times for 61 yards and also caught five passes for 39 yards and two TDs.
- **Eric Drage** caught five passes for 62 yards.
- **Tyler Anderson** caught two passes for 33 yards and one TD.
- **Tim Nowatzke** caught three passes for 60 yards.

Cougar Defense Leaders

- **Patrick Mitchell** had nine solo tackles and two pass break ups.
- **Shad Hansen** had nine tackles (seven solo, one for loss), two sacks. and one interception.
- **Josh Arnold** had eight solo tackles (three for loss) and one pass break up.
- **Rocky Biegel** had six tackles (five solo).
- **Tony Crutchfield** had five solo tackles, one pass break up, and one interception.
- **Dewey Gray** had four solo tackles.

1994 BYU 21, Notre Dame 14
Location: Notre Dame Stadium @ South Bend
Date: October 15, 1994
Weather: Temperature 60° Partly Cloudy
Attendance: 59,075

This was the third year in a row that these two teams met on the football field. Notre Dame had won the first two games handily, 43-16, in '92 in South Bend and 45-20 in '93 in Provo. Now the two teams were at it again, this time in the Irish's backyard.

This year's story actually began before any of the action in South Bend. Provo Herald's Dick Harmon described the opening volleys this way:

"South Bend, Ind. – When Evan Pilgrim read the words in the Notre Dame student newspaper "*The Observer," he shook his head. "Bad mistake. Not good at all."*

Pilgrim knows. You don't tick off a Tongan and Samoan.

The comments Pilgrim referred to were observations by associate sports editor Mike Norbut Friday which read: "BYU's interior linemen John Raass and Mike Ulufale are a rug (that) running backs wipe their feet on while running into BYU's secondary."

Raass and Ulufale took offense. BYU's entire defense took exception."

First Half

Notre Dame started the game as if to fulfill the *Observer's* prediction. The Irish struck like lightning on their first offensive series when running back Randy Kinder broke through the BYU defense for a 41-yard touchdown. Steffan Schroffner's PAT was good. **Notre Dame 7, BYU 0.**

The Cougars' kicker David Lauder put BYU on the scoreboard with a pair of field goals from 49 and 48 yards. **Notre Dame 7, BYU 6.**

Then the Cats went airborne for their first touchdown – 19-yard touchdown pass from John Walsh to Jamal Willis. Lauder's PAT put them ahead **13-7**.

Then it was Notre Dame's turn to score again.

The Irish covered 74 yards in only seven plays and 2:25 minutes to regain the lead with only 39 seconds until halftime. Quarterback Ron Powlus connected twice with wide receiver Derrick Mayes to lead the comeback. First, he hit the speedy Mayes with a 55-yard bomb to the BYU 20, then the two connected from seven yards out for the score. Schroffner's extra point kick was good.

Halftime Score Notre Dame 14, BYU 13

There was no scoring in the third quarter, though the Cougars did dodge a big bullet on the Irish first drive of the second half. The Irish moved into the red zone and had a first-and-goal at the BYU three. But BYU's John Pollock sacked Powlus for a loss of 18 on third-and-three. Then Chad Lewis blocked a field goal attempt to slam the door shut for good. (This was Chad's third blocked field goal of the season!)

In the fourth quarter the Cougars moved 77 yards in 13 plays taking 5:20 off the clock. Jamal Willis and Hema Heimuli did the heavy lifting on the scoring drive:

- Willis gained 22 yards on one sweep.
- Heimuli snagged a 14-yard screen pass from Walsh.
- Willis scored the touchdown from the two.
- Heimuli caught the two-point conversion pass.

Hema Heimuli (BYU photo)

Final Score: BYU 21, Notre Dame 14

	1st	2nd	3rd	4th	Final
BYU	3	10	0	8	21
Notre Dame	7	7	0	0	14

m Statistics	BYU	Notre Dame
First Downs	20	18
Total Offense Yards	430	695
Rushing Yards	104	115
Passing Yards	216	242
Passes (Att.-Comp.1nt.)	31-17-1	28-14-1
TDs Passing	1	1
Punts	3-123	4-170
Fumbles – Lost	5-3	3-1
Penalties – Yards	4-25	6-51

The Ups and Downs of the Game

This was a hard-fought battle, but the Cougars served up more punishment than they received.

- The Irish were shut out in the second half.
- Irish quarterback Ron Powlus was sacked four times for a loss of 55 yards and finally had to leave the game late in the fourth quarter with a concussion.

- After the game linebacker Stan Raass turned a cartwheel on the turf. Guard Evan Pilgrim lifted receiver Tim Nowatzke up in the air.
- After Randy Kinder's early 41-yard TD run, the Irish gained only 74 additional rushing yards in the game.
- One Notre Dame coed yelled in a weak voice: "I'd rather lose than be a Mormon."

Notre Dame Coach Lou Holtz said, "We got beat by a football team that controlled the line of scrimmage and protected the passer better than we did...Please don't ask me for any answers. I don't have any, I wish I did... But let us congratulate BYU. BYU is a fine, fine operation.

"I think our football team is really trying. It is trying in practice and it's trying in a game. It's just not very productive."

LaVell Edwards said, "This was a very big victory for us. We've had a few of them over the years and this one ranks right up there.

"I was particularly pleased with our defense and making the plays when we had to.

"We have better linemen (than last year). Of course, we struggled a bit when they first came out… All their guys that played on the line today played last year... Four of them are seniors. Two or three are very good players."

Cougar Offense Leaders

- **John Walsh** was 17 of 30 passing for 216 yards and one TD.
- **Jamal Willis** caught five passes for 83 yards and one TD and also carried 18 times for 75 yards and one TD.
- **Hema Heimuli** caught one pass for 14 yards, carried 10 times for 21 yards and also caught a two-point conversion pass.
- **David Lauder** kicked two field goals and one extra point for seven points.
- **Bryce Doman** caught two passes for 44 yards.
- **Itula Mili** caught three passes for 26 yards.
- **Tim Nowatzke** caught three passes for 25 yards.

Cougar Defense Leaders

- **Jon Pollock** had eight tackles, (seven solo) one sack.
- **Shay Muirbrook** had six solo tackles (three for loss), one sack and one interception.
- **Stan Raass** had four tackles (three solo).
- **Scott Albrecht** had four tackles (three solo).
- **Travis Hall** had four tackles (two solo) and one sack.
- **Randy Brock** had three tackles (two solo, three for loss) and one sack.

- **Chad Lewis** had one solo tackle & one blocked field g(**No. 5) BYU 19, (No. 14) Kansas State 15)**

1997 Cotton Bowl

Date: January 1, 1997

Location: Cotton Bowl @ Dallas

Weather: Temperature 71° Clear

Attendance: 71,928

Two ranked teams meeting in a New Year' Day Bowl. What could be better than this? Both teams were excited to play this game. But BYU players were a bit confused by the "cold shoulder" the KSU Wildcats were giving them: refusing to shake hands with the Cougars at the pre-game social events, as well as "trash talk" side comments and quips about the pitiful WAC conference and BYU's team.

Then it was game time. Time to put up or shut up!

First Half

That both teams were very skilled and evenly matched was obvious from the outset of this game.

BYU won the toss and kicked off to the Wildcats.

KSU's Mike Lawrence gained 12 yards in five

carries and quarterback Brian Kavanagh completed one of three passes for 17 yards to move the Wildcats to their own 49-yard line. Then they stalled, suffering a penalty for delay of game and two incomplete passes to bring up fourth down. Then they punted into the end zone.

BYU started from its own 20. The Cougars started off very well:

- **Steve Sarkisian completed two passes (to James Dye for 19 yards and a 10-yarder to Kaipo McGuire).**
- **K. O. Kealaluhi ran a reverse for 15 yards and a first down.**
- **Brian McKenzie ran for four off the right side. Second-and-six at the 31.**
- **Sarkisian passed to McGuire for two to the 29.**
- **Then an incomplete pass. Fourth down.**

Ethan Pochman's field goal kick missed from 47.

KSU took over on its 29 and moved to its 48-yard line aided primarily by BYU's pass interference.

BYU's Tim McTyer intercepted a pass and returned it to the KSU 36.

BYU took over first-and-10. Then the Cougars skidded badly with an incomplete pass and Sarkisian being sacked twice to bring up fourth

down.

Alan Boardman's quick punt was downed at the KSU two-yard line.

Then the Wildcats were pushed back again. Kavanagh was **sacked by Shay Muirbrook in the end zone for a safety. This gave the Cougars their first lead: BYU 2, KSU 0** with 3:34 to play in the first quarter.

KSU's free kick was shanked by James Garcia for 25 yards.

BYU took over first-and-10 on the KSU 45.

- **Dustin Johnson ran 16 yards to the KSU 29. First-and-10.**
- **Johnson again for five to the KSU 24. Second-and-five.**
- **Ronny Jenkins gained three down to the 21. Third-and-two.**
- **Pass incomplete. Fourth down.**
- **Pochman came on and kicked a 39-yard field goal. BYU 5, KSU 0.**

KSU took over on the 20. But the Wildcats had no luck with this possession. Garcia punted for 50 yards to the BYU 35.

The Cougars started to move the ball again until Sarkisian was sacked at the KSU 42. Boardman punted from the 47 into the end zone.

KSU took over on the 20 and moved to its 48 with Lawrence gaining 15 on the ground and

Kavanagh passing for 10 and running for six before Tim McTyer broke up the pass that would have extended the drive. Garcia was called on again to punt from his 48. And he hit a beauty that pinned back the Cougars to their three-yard line.

BYU started from its three and faced a third-and-11 after two short McKenzie runs and a false-start penalty.

Sarkisian connected with Chad Lewis at the 15 for the first down. Three plays later Sarkisian scrambled for nine and a first down at the BYU 26.

The next pass was incomplete and then Sarkisian-to-Chad Lewis worked again for 15 yards and another first down at the 41. But Sarkisian was sacked again to bring up fourth down and Alan Boardman's punt.

KSU's Chris Canty took the punt at his 37 and returned it to the BYU 44 with 29 seconds to go to the half.

On came Kavanagh to try something great with the last few seconds. First, he completed a short pass of three yards to his tight end Jarett Grosdidier. Then an incomplete pass followed. Third down. Then Kavanagh passed to Kevin Lockett for a first down at the BYU 41 with five seconds to go in the half.

Time for a quarterback bomb. Kavanagh delivered by heaving a pass into the end zone intended for Kevin Lockett. The pass was deflected by BYU's Eddie Sampson into the hands of KSU's Andre Anderson for a touchdown. Jamie Rheem booted the extra point, and everyone headed to their locker rooms.

BUT the officials ruled that BYU was off-side on the PAT and KSU coach Bill Snyder wanted to try for a two-point conversion. Everyone came back onto the field and Mike Lawrence ran for KSU's two points.

Halftime Score: KSU 8, BYU 5

Second Half

BYU received the kickoff took over on its 20. After eight plays and moving to the KSU 43, things bogged down. Sarkisian was sacked for the third time. Then Boardman's punt traveled only 21 yards.

KSU took over on its own 22. First down. After two plays gained very little, it looked like the defensive stalemate would continue. Then KSU struck like a LaVell Edwards-inspired tornado! Kavanaugh connected with wide receiver Kevin Lockett on a slant pass – Lockett zipped through the BYU defenders for 72 yards and a TD. Rheem's PAT was good. Out of nowhere the scoreboard read: **KSU**

15, BYU 5

In a game in which points had been hard to come by, the 10-point spread looked like a big gulf.

But Sarkisian brought the Cougars back. He passed to McGuire for 10 and a first down at the BYU 30. Then he found Atuaia open for 20 to the 50. First down.

KSU offsides. **BYU first-and-five at the KSU 45. Then Johnson was stopped for no gain.**

Sarkisian passed to Johnson to the KSU 23. Gain of 17. First down. Sarkisian's next pass was incomplete. Then Sarkisian was sacked back to the KSU 34. (This was KSU's seventh sack – for a loss of 41 BYU yards)

Then came a *series* of third down passes:

- **(See no evil number 1):** KSU pushed the BYU receiver out of bounds while the ball was in the air. The officials merely called it an incomplete pass) –Fourth down.
- **(See no evil number 2):** On another drive Kealaluhi was held with the ball in air and then pulled down before the ball hit the ground – right in front of the official.) Incomplete pass – the ball went over to KSU. **(BYU coaches were livid!!!)**

KSU took over on the BYU 33.

- Lawrence for four. Second down and six.
- Lawrence no gain.

- Pass incomplete. Fourth and six.
- Garcia punted.

Dye returned the punt 14 yards to the BYU 25. BUT…

Holding Penalty on BYU -10 yards. Ball on the 15. First & 20.

- **Jenkins lost two to the 13.**
- **Sarkisian passed to McGuire for 19 yards. Third-and-three.**
- **Defensive holding call on KSU. First down for BYU at the 50.**
- **Johnson ran right to the 42. Second-and-two.**
- **McKenzie ran for six to the 47. First down.**
- **Pass incomplete.**
- **Sarkisian ran to the KSU 40 for a first down.**

Fourth quarter

- **Sarkisian pass incomplete. Second-and-10.**
- Mario Smith intercepted Sarkisian's pass at the KSU 24.

KSU took over.

- Lawrence lost two to the 22. Second-and-12
- Penalty on KSU delay of game third-and-17.
- Kavanagh to Anderson for a short gain. Fourth down.
- Garcia's 49-yard punt to the BYU 43.

BYU took over at its 43-yard line.

- **Sarkisian to Dye for 20 at the KSU 43. First down.**
- **Jenkins ran right for seven.**
- **Sarkisian to Lewis at the KSU 32. First down.**
- **Sarkisian completed a 32-yard bomb to Dye for the TD. PAT by Pochman was good.**

Score: KSU 15, BYU 12

KSU started at its 20.

- Kavanagh pass to Grosdidier at the 26. Second-and-four.
- Lawrence bulled to the KSU 35. First down.
- Pass incomplete. Second-and-10.
- Kavanagh sacked by Muirbrook at the KSU 26. Third-and-19.
- Kavanagh passed to Dean at the KSU 30. Fourth-and-15 with 9:14 to play.
- Punt to the BYU 26. **Dye returned it to the BYU 38.**

BYU first-and-10 at its 38.

- **Sarkisian passed to Chad Lewis for 18 to the KSU 44.**
- **Johnson ran for four. Second-and-six at the 40.**
- **BYU five-yard penalty back to the KSU 45. Second-and-11.**
- **Pass incomplete. Third-and-11.**

- **Sarkisian sacked (KSU sack #8).**
- **Boardman punted 49 yards into the end zone.**

KSU took over at its 20.

- Lawrence lost back to the 17. Second-and-13.
- Pass incomplete.
- Kavanagh sacked by Bloomfield back at the KSU seven-yard line. Fourth-and-23.
- Punt to BYU.

BYU took over at the KSU 40 after a KSU penalty for holding. (4:59 to play)

- **Sarkisian connected with a pass to Lewis for seven at the KSU 33.**
- **Sarkisian to Kapo McGuire at the 31. First down.**
- **Sarkisian scrambled to the 28. Gain of three. Second-and-seven.**
- **Pass incomplete. *McGuire lost his helmet from Mario Smith's tackle and fell unconscious onto the field. Smith started celebrating.***

(KSU players continued the trash talk they had bombarded the Cougars with the entire week of the game: *"They don't hit like that in the WAC!"* hollered All-American cornerback Chris Canty, who, ironically, was sidelined by severe leg cramps). Other KSU players laughed at and mocked McGuire lying silent on the field. KSU coaches did nothing and said nothing to their players.)

Kaipo was Steve Sarkisian's roommate and Steve was really furious!

"That was uncalled for," K.O. Kealaluhi said. *"McGuire is the smallest man on the field and playing as hard as anyone. The hit was good, making fun of him wasn't."*

"It was classless and made us sick." linebacker Brad Martin added.

The Cougars had their fill of their opponents' "put downs." Sarkisian & Co. immediately quieted the Wildcats!

LaMar Chapman, a freshman replacement for the sidelined Canty, was assigned to cover K.O. Kealaluhi.

- **On the very next play from the KSU 28, Sarkisian threw a long dart to a streaking Kealaluhi, who had faked Chapman out of position, and was wide open for the TD pass. Pochman's PAT was good.**

With 3:39 to play, it was BYU 19, KSU 15

After the PAT, Steve Sarkisian ran over to the KSU sideline. He had listened long enough to the Wildcats' constant taunting. Now they were going to hear from him! He yelled at the Wildcats and fired his "guns-a-blazing" gesture at them. He was flagged for "unsportsmanlike conduct."

The penalty was marked off on the kickoff. KSU started at its own 28.

- Kavanagh passed to Grosdidier to the 44 for a gain of 16. First down.
- Kavanagh scrambled for one to the 45.
- Lawrence ran for five.
- Pass incomplete. Fourth-and-four.
- Kavanagh passed to Lockett at the 39. First down. (1:58 to play)
- Pass incomplete.
- Kavanagh to Lockett slant pass for 13 to the 26. First down. (1:44 to play)
- Kavanagh keeper to the 17. Second-and-one.
- Pass incomplete. Lockett caught the ball in the air but was pushed out of the end zone.
- KSU delay of game penalty pushed the ball back to the 22.
- **Kavanagh sacked by Muirbro**ok at the 28. Fourth-and-12. (1:23 to go)
- Kavanagh hit Lockett at the 12. First-and-10. (1:17 to go)
- *Kavanagh's next pass was* ***intercepted by Omarr Morgan who stepped in front of Jimmy Dean at the four-yard line.*** (50 seconds to go).

BYU took over on its four. Sarkisian twice took a knee.

Sarkisian's final words: "How sweet it is!"

Final Score: BYU 19, KSU 15

Kansas State coach Bill Snyder said, "They're the No. 5 team in the nation and they deserve to be. I thought our defense was on the field way too long in the second half, and they did wear down."

LaVell Edwards said, "These guys hung together through 15 games and played hard every week. This is a marvelous tribute to the kids. We hung in there and kept playing. It's been a special feeling all year long. This is the best defense we have ever had at BYU. The big thing was who could persevere the longest. I told the guys (at halftime) if we were in it in the fourth quarter we'd have a shot. "Obviously, it was a great victory for us to beat a great football team."

	1st	2nd	3rd	4th	Final
BYU	**5**	**0**	**0**	**14**	**19**
KSU	**0**	**8**	7	**0**	**15**

Team Statistics	BYU	KSU
First Downs	**24**	**14**
Total Offense Yards	**350**	**274**
Rushing Yards	**59**	**41**
Passing Yards	**291**	**233**
Passes (Att.-Comp.1nt.)	**36-21-1**	**28-14-2**
TDs Passing	**2**	**2**
Punts	**5-194**	**7-322**

Fumbles – Lost	**1-0**	**1-0**
Penalties – Yards	**8-59**	**7-55**

Cougar Offense Leaders

- **Steve Sarkisian** was 21 of 36 passing for 291 yards with one interception and two TDs.
- **James Dye** had four catches for 70 yards and one TD.
- **Chad Lewis** had five catches for 79 yards.
- **K.O. Kealaluhi** had two catches for 37 yards and one game-winning TD and also had one carry for 15 yards.
- **Kapo McGuire** had five catches for 51 yards.

Cougar Defense Leaders

- **Shay Muirbrook** had 12 tackles (11 solo, five for loss), six sacks, and one safety!
- **Henry Bloomfield** had 11 tackles (nine solo, two for loss) and two sacks.
- **Brad Martin** had nine tackles (eight solo).
- **Omarr Morgan** had six solo tackles, and two pass break ups and one big interception that preserved the win.
- **Tim McTyer** had six tackles (five solo, one for loss), one pass break up and one interception.

("Divine Intervention" – LaVell's final game)
BYU 34, Utah 27
Date: November 24, 2000
Location: Rice-Eccles Stadium @ Salt Lake City
Weather: Temperature 36° Partly Cloudy
Attendance: 45,064 (Utah home game record)

This was the last time the Utes would face a LaVell Edwards team – "that team in the south" to coin Urban Meyer's famous nickname for the BYU Cougars. And after losing 21 of 28 games played against LaVell, the Utes were ready to start a new win streak beginning with this one on their home field. But both the Cougars (5-6) and Utes (4-6) were just shadows of their former selves.

The Cougars weren't in a particularly charitable mood for LaVell's last game in the series. They really wanted to win this one!

Typical of the strong emotions on both sides, the lead in this contest would be hard to hold. The 45,064 mostly red-clad Utah fans were giving their all to encourage their Utes.

First Half

Imagine the scene when Utah's Andre Dyson intercepted Brandon Doman's first pass in the game at the BYU 24 and returned it all the way for a touchdown with only 52 seconds off the clock! How could one describe the Utes fans' unbridled pandemonium?

Ryan Kaneshiro added the extra point and with some poor Utah fans still flowing into the stadium from the parking lot (and missing this golden moment), it was **Utah 7, BYU 0.**

Then, as fate would have it, Dyson played a part in BYU's first score later in the quarter. The Cougars were facing a third-and-six when Andre was called for pass interference. The ball moved 15 yards to the Utah 48. Then after a couple more plays Doman ran for 17 yards to the Utah 35. The drive stalled, forcing the Cougars to settle for Owen Pochman's 45-yard field goal. **Utah 7, BYU 3**.

For the rest of the half, the Cougars struck for 10 straight points, while holding the Utes scoreless.

- First, Jared Lee intercepted Ute quarterback Lance Rice's pass at the Utah 31. The Cougars needed only five plays to cash in for six points. Luke Staley carried for nine yards down to the 12. Then Brian McDonald finished it off from the three. Pochman's PAT was good. **BYU 10, Utah 7**.
- Next, the Cougars capitalized on Pochman's 38-yard field goal to close out the first quarter: **BYU 13, Utah 7**.

In the second quarter there were only three field goals scored. BYU got two of them from Pochman from 35 and 22 yards out. **BYU 19, Utah 7**.

Utah's Kaneshiro closed the first half scoring with his 40-yard field goal.

Halftime Score: BYU 19, Utah 10

Second Half

The defenses ruled the third quarter. The only score came on Brandon Doman's 36-yard touchdown pass to receiver Mike Rigell. Pochman booted the extra point. **BYU 26, Utah 10.**

At this point there wasn't much for the Ute fans to cheer about. LaVell's team was riding high and ready to celebrate their coach's historic career. The few BYU fans in Rice-Eccles Stadium were celebrating "to excess" in the minds of the rest of the crowd.

Then, in the fourth quarter, those ornery Utes deviated from the script! Utah inserted quarterback Darnell Arceneaux into the lineup and he came on like a gangbuster:

- On his first play, he hit receiver Cliff Russell for a 42-yard gain.
- He led the rejuvenated Utes to finish a 54-yard drive that ended with Ryan Kaneshiro's 33-yard field goal. **BYU 26, Utah 13.**
- The Utes' next drive covered 64 yards capped by running back Thomas Fortune's first

career touchdown from two yards out. Kaneshiro's kick was good. **BYU 26, Utah 20.**

- And finally, a five-play 29-yard drive that ended with Arceneaux's 20-yard TD pass to tight end Matt Nickel. Kaneshiro's PAT put the Utes ahead: **Utah 27, BYU 26,** with only 2:16 left in the game.

You can imagine the scene at this point in Rice-Eccles Stadium…a total eruption of exhilaration from the large crowd.

In this delirious scenario, Brandon Doman stepped onto the field to finish only the third start in his career…against the best pass defense in the country! He had not managed to get even one first down on the Cougars' four previous possessions.

On third down, Doman was still trying to find an open receiver when he was sacked by the Utes' Kautai Olevao.

Then it was fourth-and-13 with the ball on his own 17 and only 1:04 remaining – and BYU still trailing the Utes, 27-26.

Watching from up in the stands, Brandon's older brother Cliff and his father Verl both were in agony. "I told Cliff I'd been praying and if it was meant to be, it would be," Verl said.

It appeared to all that LaVell would finish his career with this losing season…the first one since his second year in 1973.

Offensive coordinator Lance Reynolds told Robbie Bosco, "I hate for it to end like this, not here, this way for LaVell."

Then lightning struck for LaVell's Cougars. In typical BYU fashion, the picture was transformed in 35 seconds:

- Brandon took the snap, dropped back, and found an open Jonathan Pittman for a *34-yard gain* at the Ute 49.

Jonathan Pittman (BYU photo)

- *Then lightning struck for the second time in the same place:* Doman and Pittman connected again on the next play – this time for 36 yards and another first down to the Utah 13.
- From there Luke Staley ran for nine yards down to the four with 30 seconds left.
- Then Doman rolled out to the right on a quarterback keeper and cut back left through the defense for the touchdown with 23 seconds to spare. He added the *coup de grâce* with a pass to receiver Soren Halladay for two points.

Doman runs to Daylight (BYU photo)

Final Score: BYU 34, Utah 27

	1st	2nd	3rd	4th	Final
BYU	13	6	7	8	34
UTAH	7	3	0	17	27

Team Statistics	BYU	UTAH
First Downs	21	14
Total Offense Yards	384	322
Rushing Yards	100	70

Passig Yards	**284**	**252**
Passes (Att.-Comp.1nt.)	**29-16-1**	**34-16-1**
TDs Passing	**1**	**1**
Punts	**5-217**	**6-231**
Fumbles - Lost	**3-0**	**2-1**
Penalties- Yards	**7-69**	**7-84**

Utah coach Ron McBride said, "BYU deserves the credit. We had the momentum and had them pinned on fourth and 13, and they made a play."

LaVell Edwards said, "Like I said all along, I really, really love this team. It has been so frustrating to see them come out and work as hard as they did and not reap anything from it. But tonight, they did. It all paid off. What an ending, huh?...Brandon Doman made a heckuva throw and Pittman made a nice catch. When they completed that one, I thought we were going to win…There couldn't be a better way to go out."

Salt Lake Tribune sportswriter Phil Miller wrote *"Cold, impersonal science says God doesn't attend football games. But Brigham Young Cougars couldn't come up with any other explanation. They were left for dead under the tires of a furious Utah comeback, their graves dug in a fourth-down-and-13 hole and facing the nation's top-ranked pass defense and the roar of a delirious Rice-Eccles Stadium crowd Friday night. Yet through what everybody was calling "divine intervention" the Cougars somehow staged a 34-27 victory as improbable and miraculous as any in LaVell Edwards' historic career.*

Final Record for LaVell's 29-year career: 257 wins, 101 losses and three ties.

Ron McBride and LaVell Edwards: friendly rivals to the end. (KSL Photo)

Utah linebacker Kautai Olevao said, "When I sacked Doman, I really thought it was over. A miracle like that was bound to happen seeing that it was LaVell's last game."

BYU cornerback Michael Lafitte said, "I

thought the game was over at that point. But I said a little prayer, and it came true."

Utah quarterback Darnell Arceneaux said, "LaVell Edwards must have had the football gods with him. I thought we had won."

Utah receiver Steve Smith added, "God wasn't going to let LaVell lose."

Receiver Jonathan Pittman, who caught the two long passes to set up the final touchdown, said, "This almost was like a miracle. Someone was looking down on us. In LaVell's last game, someone was looking down on us."

Quarterback Brandon Doman said, "I can't believe what just happened. I can't believe it…I can't tell you how great it is to end LaVell's last game with a win like this. This is BYU football; we always come back like this."

Defensive tackle Hans Olsen said, "That right there was a fantastic finish to a crappy season. Finally, we put something together, and showed some heart. We let those guys back in it, but what a war. Any time you have the Cougars and the Utes, it's going to be like that. It's going to be crazy…What an awesome feeling. What a sendoff for LaVell."

Cougar Offense Leaders

- **Brandon Doman** was 16 of 29 passing for 284 yards with one interception and one TD and also had 18 carries for 64 yards (net of 39 after sacks) and one TD.

- **Jonathan Pittman** had four catches for 117 yards.
- **Kalani Sitake** had four catches for 54 yards and also had four carries for 16 yards.
- **Luke Staley** had 17 carries for 30 yards and also had two catches for 14 yards.
- **Margin Hooks** had three catches for 25 yards and also had one carry for 15 yards.
- **Mike Rigell** had one TD catch for 36 yards.
- **Tevita Ofahengaue** had two catches for 38 yards.
- **Brian McDonald** had three carries for 15 yards and one TD.

Cougar Defense Leaders

- **Paul Walkenhorst** had 10 tackles (four solo).
- **Justin Ena** had nine tackles (three solo, one for loss).
- **Isaac Kelley** had seven tackles (four solo, three for loss) and one sack.
- **Hans Olsen** had seven tackles (two solo, two for loss), and one sack.
- **Jared Lee** had six tackles (two solo), two pass break ups, and one interception.
- **Michael Lafitte** had five tackles (three solo, one for loss), and one pass break up.

- **Tyson Smith** had five tackles (one for loss) and one pass break up.

More "Divine Intervention": *"Yes, it was in 2000, I went to the game with my family and promised them that I won't get into any fights.*

"We were on the southwest side and there were eight guys, Utes fans sitting around us, and they were drunk, swearing right from the beginning of the game. I was trying to control myself, and my son and daughters kept looking at me while my wife got hold of my hands. At the beginning of the third quarter, I jumped up and told them, 'I am here with my family to enjoy the game, and I would appreciate if you guys stop swearing and throwing things around.' I was ready to fight as I have in the past in Utah, Wyoming, and everywhere BYU played.

"We were surprised that the swearing and throwing stopped even at the last drive by Doman for the winning TD. At the end of the game all eight of the guys came over and shook my hands and expressed how sorry they were for the way they had acted. We talked for few minutes before my family joined the celebration."

www.ingramcontent.com/pod-product-compliance
Lightning Source LLC
La Vergne TN
LVHW020648110826
845149LV00012B/1949

* 9 7 9 8 9 9 9 7 3 9 0 1 8 *